Script and Seal Use on Cyprus
in the Bronze and Iron Ages

Script and Seal Use on Cyprus in the Bronze and Iron Ages

Edited by

JOANNA S. SMITH

ARCHAEOLOGICAL INSTITUTE OF AMERICA
BOSTON, MASSACHUSETTS

Colloquia and Conference Papers 4

Cover illustration: Clay tablet with Cypro-Minoan text, ca. 1200 B.C. (Enkomi [Dikaios] 1687, Cyprus Museum, Nicosia). (Photo by J.S. Smith)

∞The paper in this book meets the guidelines for permanence and durability of the Committee on Production Guidelines for Book Longevity of the Council on Library Resources.

Cover and text designed by Peter Holm, Sterling Hill Productions
Printed in the United States of America by Sheridan Books

05 04 03 02   5 4 3 2 1

Library of Congress Cataloging-in-Publication Data

Script and seal use on Cyprus in the Bronze and Iron Ages / edited by Joanna S. Smith.
p. cm. — (Colloquia and conference papers ; no. 4)
Papers presented at a conference held in 1997 and sponsored by the Institute. Includes bibliographical references.
Contents: Problems and prospects in the study of script and seal use on Cyprus in the Bronze and Iron Ages / Joanna S. Smith — Marks on pots : patterns of use in the archaeological record at Enkomi / Nicolle E. Hirschfeld — Device, image, and coercion: the role of glyptic in the political economy of Late Bronze Age Cyprus / Jennifer M. Webb — The display and viewing of the syllabic inscriptions of Rantidi Sanctuary / Georgia Bonny Bazemore — The stamp seals of Cyprus in the Late Bronze Age and the Iron Age / Andres T. Reyes — Seals and writing in the ancient Near East and Cyprus : observations from context / Barry B. Powell.
ISBN 0-9609042-7-1 (alk. paper)
1. Cylinder seals—Cyprus—Congresses. 2. Inscriptions, Cypro-Minoan—Congresses. 3. Inscriptions—Cyprus—Congresses. 4. Cyprus—Antiquities—Congresses. I. Smith, Joanna S., 1965–. II. Archaeological Institute of America. III. Series.
CD5391 .S35 2002
939'.37—dc21 2002018944

CONTENTS

## CHAPTER 6

Seals and Writing in the Ancient Near East
and Cyprus: Observations from Context
Barry B. Powell

227

CONTRIBUTORS

GEORGIA BONNY BAZEMORE
Rantidi Forest Excavations

NICOLLE E. HIRSCHFELD
Program in Aegean Scripts and Prehistory
University of Texas at Austin

BARRY B. POWELL
Department of Classics
University of Wisconsin-Madison

ANDRES T. REYES
Groton School

JOANNA S. SMITH
Department of Art History and Archaeology
Columbia University

JENNIFER M. WEBB
Department of Archaeology
La Trobe University

Preface

◆

Joanna S. Smith

Epigraphical studies of ancient scripts and iconographical studies of seals have long been part of scholarship on Cyprus and elsewhere in the Mediterranean basin.[1] Over the course of the last decades, however, research has begun to focus not only on traditional epigraphical and iconographical approaches to this material on Cyprus, but also on what can be termed a contextual approach to scripts and seals, an approach that attempts to view these tools of recording within their wider cultural context.[2]

Many of these contextual studies specifically concern the archaeological contexts of inscribed objects, seals, and seal impressions and the significance of patterns observed for the social, economic, political, and religious aspects of life on Cyprus during the second and first millennia B.C. On the island they range from island-wide and regional,[3] to site-specific studies.[4] Also of importance for all of these island-specific studies are those that concern Cyprus's international connections.[5]

At this time, research into the function and importance of Cypriot writing and seals continues. However, while now more integrated with a wide range of archaeological information, these studies are frequently related to either the Bronze Age or the Iron Age, seals or scripts, or on-island or international contacts. The purpose of the 1997 Archaeological Institute of America colloquium, "The Archaeology of Script and Seal Use on Cyprus in the Second and First Millennia B.C.," that led to the series of papers for this volume, was to explore different approaches to the contextual study of Cypriot scripts and seals and, beyond that goal, to achieve a more integrated

view of cultural continuities and discontinuities through time, in space, and
among different methods of recording on Cyprus.

In this effort, the colloquium gathered together those scholars who have
made concerted recent attempts at placing Cypriot seals and scripts into the
cultural context of ancient Cyprus (fig. 1) as well as the Mediterranean and
Near East (fig. 2). As a respondent, Barry Powell was chosen because he
was interested in Mediterranean scripts and seals but had not worked inten-
sively with material from the island. His task was to comment on the papers
and to place them into the larger picture of writing traditions in the
Mediterranean and Near East, particularly the traditions that led to the
development and spread of the alphabet.[6]

Organized as a series of five papers preceded by an introduction and followed by a commentary, the format used for the colloquium closely resem-
bles the contents of this volume. Four of the papers are specific to either the
Bronze or the Iron Age, script or seals. The two Bronze Age papers
(Hirschfeld, Webb) precede the Iron Age papers (Bazemore, Reyes). In each
pair, the paper concerning script (Hirschfeld, Bazemore) comes first. The
first paper (Smith) addresses both periods and both scripts and seals, pulling
them together within the context of a discussion of the definition of a contextual approach and the problems and prospects for research. Both the
preface (Smith) and the commentary (Powell) address the purpose and

Fig. 1. Map of Cyprus showing sites mentioned in this volume

Fig. 2. Map of the Mediterranean and Near East showing sites mentioned in this volume

results of the five papers in the volume, commenting on the overall success of the papers to reach the goal set out for the colloquium.

The first paper (Smith) draws the papers in the volume together in two ways. First, it sets out a brief history of writing and seal use on the island during the Late Bronze Age (LBA, 1650–1050 B.C.) and the Iron Age through the Classical period (1050–312 B.C.). Second, it defines and discusses the contextual approach used by all the contributors. After addressing the overall material and methodological concerns of the volume as a whole, the paper covers seven different problem areas in the study of writing and seal use on Cyprus, giving both examples and solutions, or approaches to possible solutions that can be achieved by using the approach as defined earlier in the paper.

The seven topics range from artifactual issues to context- and publication-related problems: the lack of provenance for many artifacts, the perishable nature of many materials, the lack of clay sealings on Cyprus, our inability to read the contents of some inscriptions such as those in Cypro-Minoan, biases inherent in the archaeological record, incomplete or inaccurate publication, and lack of incorporation of specialist studies into synthetic works.

Solutions to these problems range from suggestions for further work to specific reinterpretations of bodies of information using the contextual approach. For instance, the example used to illustrate possible solutions to the fourth problem, undeciphered inscriptions, shows how the probable content of Cypro-Minoan texts from Kalavasos-*Ayios Dhimitrios* can be deduced by analyzing the forms of the signs, the structure of the inscriptions, and the archaeological contexts of the inscribed objects. The texts appear to be a series of economic lists used by people in Building X, an elite building that housed vast quantities of olive oil.

The first of the two Bronze Age papers (Hirschfeld) is a case study of the use of writing at the site of Enkomi. Using a sample of ca. 250 marked vases, the paper shows that no changes in marking systems took place during the period often noted to be one of cultural shift, from the Late Cypriot (LC) IIC to the LC IIIA and IIIB periods (13th and 12th centuries B.C.), and that marking instead varied by vessel type, most particularly by the origin of the vessel rather than its specific shape. The potmarks that can be assigned definitely to the Cypro-Minoan script appear only on vases of local and Mycenaean manufacture. Signs on other vase types, notably amphorae, commonly known as Canaanite jars, may perhaps belong to another system of marking entirely. The continuity and regionality of potmarking systems at Enkomi may eventually help scholars better detect directed trade between one region and another ca. 1200 B.C.

The second of the Bronze Age papers (Webb) deals with mechanisms of seal production and distribution. Again the author focuses on the site of Enkomi, although patterns island-wide are also addressed. Iconographical patterns and details about the materials and methods used to make different groups of LBA seals at Enkomi suggest that they were produced by specialists attached to centralized authorities, rather than by part-time or itinerant seal cutters working to meet individual demand. This hypothesis allows the author to suggest that seals may have been important within a system of wealth finance.[7] Cylinders of the Elaborate Style might, for example, have served as payment to state personnel, allocating to the seal owner explicit rights to staple goods and other services controlled by the state. This implies a high degree of centralized control over the ownership and use of seals within a tithe- or tribute-based system of regional interaction on Cyprus.

Of the Iron Age papers, the first (Bazemore) discusses the display of Cypriot Syllabic inscriptions at the sanctuary site of Rantidi-*Lingrin tou Dhiyeni*. In this work the author considers the context of the sanctuary in its region, particularly its connection with the main sanctuary of the goddess at Palaepaphos, the history of work at the site, and the significance of the finds there for Iron Age Cypriot literacy. However, the main purpose of the paper is to investigate the context of inscriptions, on basins and slabs of limestone, in the sanctuary with respect to the structures, other inscriptions, and potential viewers, some of whom were literate. Evidence for the use and reuse of the sanctuary area from the Cypro-Geometric period through the Early Roman period can be found not only among the inscriptions, many of which are almost illegible because of erasure and reinscription over time, but also in the reuse of inscribed stones in building construction, the cutting and infilling of votive pits and probable oracular chambers, the use of tombs nearby, and finds of terracottas and ceramics.

The second Iron Age paper is a study of stamp seals on the island (Reyes). It covers the range of stamp seals from the end of the second millennium B.C. into the Cypro-Geometric (ca. 1050–750 B.C.) and Cypro-Archaic (ca. 750–475 B.C.) periods. Both the origins of the stamp-seal tradition and different groups of seals are considered. The author draws together iconographical, material, chronological, and contextual evidence in order to comment on the function and importance of stamp seals on the island for on- and off-island interaction. The reemergence of the stamp seal during the Iron Age may be related to increased economic relations between Cyprus and the Near East. Phoenician and Greek artistic styles are present, giving clues to specific areas of interaction between different regions of Cyprus and the wider Mediterranean world.

In the concluding paper Powell sets out to draw all of Cypriot seal and script use into the wider context of Near Eastern and Mediterranean sealing and writing systems. Along the way he points out patterns in terms of iconography, materials, and writing tools. Although the approach taken is a general one, the conclusion is acute. He notes that the presence on Cyprus of multiple seal forms and scripts throughout its history finds many parallels among multilingual societies of the Near East, in which several scribal traditions coexisted. This observation sets Cyprus apart from the Greek and Roman worlds, in which only a single scribal tradition was prominent in a culture at any one time through the Classical period.

Although not the focus of specific papers in the colloquium, or in this volume, nonindigenous script and seal traditions on Cyprus receive mention in several papers. Egyptian, cuneiform, Luwian hieroglyphic, Phoenician, and Greek alphabetic inscriptions form part of the Cypriot inscriptional repertoire during the Bronze and Iron Ages. Some inscriptions in these scripts appear on imported artifacts and several were made and used on Cyprus.[8] Imported seals from Mesopotamia, Syria, Anatolia, Egypt, the Levant, and Greece also occur throughout the periods covered in this volume.[9] Further contextual exploration of the indigenous scripts of Cyprus, namely Cypro-Minoan and Cypriot Syllabic, the cylinder and stamp seals of the island, as well as the full range of other scripts and seals used on the island would be fruitful topics of future papers and colloquia.

Ellen Herscher's help with the organization of the original colloquium held at the 1997 Annual Meeting of the Archaeological Institute of America was integral to its success. Generous funding by the Kress Foundation made travel to and attendance at the colloquium possible for Joanna S. Smith and Jennifer M. Webb. Graduate student funding from the Archaeological Institute of America made Nicolle E. Hirschfeld's attendance and participation possible. We all thank them for making it possible for us to meet together at the meetings in Chicago. My original call for papers to the participants in the colloquium was met with enthusiasm by all contributors, a spirit that has survived through to the final form of this volume. Naomi Norman, Daniel Pullen, and Marni Walter of the Archaeological Institute of America have been helpful as I prepared the papers for publication. I thank one and all for their support and wish each one success in their future endeavors.

NOTES

[1] Seminal studies on Bronze and Iron Age Cypriot scripts and seals by scholars most noted for their research in this area are, for example, E. Porada, "The Cylinder Seals of the Late Cypriote Bronze Age," *AJA* 52 (1948) 178–98; J. Boardman, *Archaic Greek Gems* (London 1968); E. Masson, *Cyprominoica: Répertoires, documents de Ras Shamra, essais d'interpretation* (*SIMA* 31:2) (Göteborg 1974); O. Masson, *Les inscriptions chypriotes syllabiques: Recueil critique et commenté*[2] (Paris 1983).

[2] The earliest study of this kind, however, appeared in 1941, see J.F. Daniel, "Prolegomena to the Cypro-Minoan Script," *AJA* 45 (1941) 249–82. T.G. Palaima, "Cypro-Minoan Scripts: Problems of Historical Context," in Y. Duhoux, T.G. Palaima, and J. Bennet eds., *Problems in Decipherment (Bibliothèque des Cahiers de l'Institut de Linguistique de Louvain* 49, Louvain-la-Neuve 1989) 161 called for contextual study of Cypriot scripts. Although E. Porada made frequent references to context in her numerous studies of Cypriot seals (see papers of this volume infra, especially see with P. Dikaios in *Enkomi, Excavations 1948–1958: Chronology, Summary and Conclusions, Catalogue, Appendices,* volume II [Mainz am Rhein 1971] 783–817), J.-C. Courtois and J.M. Webb, *Les cylindres-sceaux d'Enkomi (Fouilles Françaises 1957–1970)* (Nicosia 1987) was the first study of Cypriot glyptic that made determination of function and find context a primary consideration.

[3] See G.B. Bazemore, "The Geographic Distribution of the Cypriote Syllabic Inscriptions,"

in P. Åström ed., *Acta Cypria: Acts of an International Congress on Cypriote Archaeology Held in Göteborg on 22–24 August 1991,* pt. 2 (*SIMA-PB* 119, Jonsered 1992) 63–96; J.M. Webb, "Cypriote Bronze Age Glyptic: Style, Function and Social Context," in R. Laffineur and J.L. Crowley eds., *EIKΩN: Aegean Bronze Age Iconography: Shaping a Methodology* (Liège 1992) 113–21; A.T. Reyes, *Archaic Cyprus: A Study of the Textual and Archaeological Evidence* (Oxford 1994); A.T. Reyes, *The Stamp Seals of Ancient Cyprus* (Oxford 2001); J.S. Smith, *Seals for Sealing in the Late Cypriot Period* (Diss. Bryn Mawr College 1994); J.M. Webb and D. Frankel, "Making an Impression: Storage and Surplus Finance in Late Bronze Age Cyprus," *JMA* 7 (1994) 5–26; G.B. Bazemore, *The Role of Writing in Ancient Society: The Cypriote Syllabic Inscriptions, A Study in Grammatology* (Diss. Univ. of Chicago 1998).

[4] Courtois and Webb (supra n. 2); J.S. Smith, "Cypro-Minoan Inscriptions," in A. South ed., *Kalavasos*-Ayios Dhimitrios *IV: The North-East Area* (*SIMA* 71:5) (Jonsered forthcoming).

[5] N.E. Hirschfeld, "Cypriot Marks on Mycenaean Pottery," in *Mykenaïka (BCH Suppl.* 24, Paris 1992) 315–19; N.E. Hirschfeld, "Incised Marks (Post-Firing) on Aegean Wares," in C. Zerner ed., *Wace and Blegen: Pottery as Evidence for Trade in the Late Bronze Age Aegean* (Amsterdam 1993) 311–18; N.E. Hirschfeld, *Potmarks of the Late Bronze Age Eastern Mediterranean* (Diss. Univ. of Texas at Austin 1999).

[6] B.B. Powell, *Homer and the Origin of the Greek Alphabet* (Cambridge 1991).

[7] T.N. D'Altroy and T.K. Earle, "Staple Finance, Wealth Finance and Storage in the Inka Political Economy," *CurrAnthr* 25 (1985) 187–206.

[8] For example, an archive of Phoenician documents has been found at Idalion, see M. Hadjicosti, "The Kingdom of Idalion in the Light of New Evidence," *BASOR* 308 (1997) 58, fig. 24. On texts in other scripts see papers of this volume, infra.

[9] Some Mesopotamian seals appear in R.S. Merrillees, "A 16th Century B.C. Tomb Group from Central Cyprus with Links Both East and West," in V. Karageorghis ed., *Acts of the International Archaeological Symposium, "Cyprus Between the Orient and the Occident,"* Nicosia, 8–14 September 1985 (Nicosia 1986) 114–48. On other imported seals and the merging of seal carving traditions on Cyprus see papers in this volume, infra.

Script and Seal Use on Cyprus
in the Bronze and Iron Ages

Problems and Prospects in the Study of Script and Seal Use on Cyprus in the Bronze and Iron Ages*

Joanna S. Smith

Scripts and Seals of Cyprus

Scripts and seals formed integral parts of recording and communication systems in antiquity. They were significant both directly and indirectly for the active user and the passive viewer. Literate and illiterate alike lived in societies where inscriptions and seals were symbols of authority, tools of control, votive objects, items of prestige, and personal markers.

Script and seal use on Cyprus is a complex topic, incorporating a wide range of languages, scripts, symbols, images, materials, forms, and functions. In the Bronze Age, mostly the Late Bronze Age (LBA), there are a handful of short inscriptions in well-understood writing forms such as Egyptian hieroglyphic,[1] cuneiform,[2] and Luwian hieroglyphic.[3] More plentiful are inscriptions in the as-yet undeciphered script of the island, Cypro-Minoan.[4] Seals from the period are mostly cylindrical in shape, recalling cylinder seals used throughout the Near Eastern world. Scarabs and a handful of other shapes also draw on outside sources for their form and, sometimes, their decoration. Conical stamp seals of the period and most cylinders bear decoration that is definably Cypriot, though almost always with elements that derive from Syrian, Aegean, or other contemporary iconographic sources.

In the Iron Age and the Classical period, script on the island is a pastiche partly of the Phoenician[5] and Greek alphabets[6] in combination with inscriptions in the linear script of the island, Cypriot Syllabic. Several syllabic texts read as Greek, but many are as yet unreadable and may conform to one or more other language traditions on the island. Some stamp seals continue to be conical in shape, but the scarab and scaraboid, of Phoenician derivation, are the dominant seal forms of the period. In iconography, again there are both Near Eastern and Aegean elements, but most scenes are definably Cypriot.

Fortunately, much of our inscriptional and glyptic information comes from well-documented archaeological investigations. The archaeological record, in combination with epigraphical and iconographical information, provides us with important chronological and functional details. With this information we are able to form and test hypotheses about the social, economic, religious, and political significance of the material.

An Archaeological Approach

An archaeological approach is contextual. It makes it possible to place the evidence for script and seal use within its total environment. That environment exists at many scales, from the smallest detail of an individual sign or glyptic image to the point of view of the scholars who study them. These spatial scales form the elements of our study: signs and images, objects and deposits, structures, sites, regions, and, in the case of Cyprus, the island and its culture as well as neighboring mainland and island cultures.

After carefully evaluating the sources of our evidence and the elements of our study, using the contextual approach we can then consider *relationships*—functional, social, ideological—among different elements and what they then mean. This meaning also exists at varying scales, from the detail of the object to the overall picture of ancient Cyprus and the wider world of the ancient Mediterranean.[7]

This approach is not a rejection of epigraphical and iconographical studies. Rather it takes these studies as they have developed so far in Cypriot studies a step beyond individual inscriptions or glyptic representations. A contextual study could begin with a study of a glyptic image or epigraphical subject before moving on to details of its find context and other related discoveries. The method of application and location of an inscription or glyptic image on an object and the material from which that object was made influence the form and the function of the associated inscription or glyptic image. The object's immediate archaeological context is of prime importance, even if it is not a primary deposit. Associated materials, evidence for the discard of the object—when, where, how, with what, and perhaps by whom—are all important signals to us when we seek to learn about the life of a single piece. Patterns in a single building or area, or within a single site, are important for what they indicate about the use of scripts and seals in a single part of Cyprus. Perhaps these patterns are consistent within a single region. Similarities and differences within regions or within Cyprus as a whole at a single point in time, or through time, are indicative of a tradition or traditions of communication on the island in the Bronze and Iron Ages. As an island, the geographical boundaries of Cyprus help to define the study of communication there in connection with or in opposition to its neighbors.

Any study of writing and seal practices on the island from the Bronze Age through the Classical period, whether of their existence, continuity, or change, is reliant upon and complicated by patterns in the archaeological record. We are dependent on the discovery of the material and its retrieval from archaeological context in order to have data to study. We are equally dependent on information about the archaeological context in order to make sense of the material. On the other hand, the archaeological record complicates our understanding. Not all materials are preserved in archaeological context, and those contexts are not necessarily an accurate record of the breadth and variety of a past society. Our work is also complicated by the accuracy of our own record of those contexts and whether we are able to usefully interpret any meaning associated with the material.

Problems and Prospects

Here I list some of the problematic areas for the archaeological study of scripts and seals on Cyprus, some of the solutions there may be, and some abbreviated examples to illustrate my argument. My discussion divides into seven sections: objects and provenance, archaeological context and preservation, seals and sealings, decipherment and readability of inscriptions, sites and biases of discovery, publication accuracy and accessibility, and specialist vs. generalist scholarship. Papers in this volume by Hirschfeld, Webb, Bazemore, Reyes, and Powell also address certain of these issues, making significant contributions to our understanding of seal and script use within

(Hirschfeld, Webb, Bazemore) and among (Webb, Reyes) sites on the island, as well as within the Mediterranean and Near East as a whole (Powell).

My comments address issues related to understanding the votive and sphragistic functions of seals through study of the seals themselves, the absence of perishable sealing and writing materials in the archaeological record, evidence for both LBA and Archaic-Classical sealing systems through time across the island, the significance and probable contents of a group of undeciphered Cypro-Minoan inscriptions from the single site of Kalavasos-*Ayios Dhimitrios*, imbalances in our interpretations due to patterns of discovery in the archaeological record of the island, issues in the publication of information and how that affects interpretation of seal and script use, and the increased need to integrate the work of specialists and generalists.

The Object: Provenance

Some seals and inscriptions have no provenance. Seals in particular often form parts of unprovenanced private collections or museum collections of gems. Even when seals and inscriptions come from well-recorded excavations, the meaning of their archaeological contexts may be ambiguous. The small size of seals can make them hard to detect, and their place of discovery may not accurately represent their location of use. Many inscriptions are fragmentary and found disassociated from other finds and features. Because information about the find locations of inscribed and glyptic objects can be sparse, it is all the more important that archaeologists record these artifacts carefully to build on the information that is available.[8]

In cases of the absence or ambiguous nature of a record of an object's provenance, the analysis of the object itself is the only way to learn about its significance. Inscriptions and glyptic artifacts are particularly well suited for the analysis of relationships among different details on a material surface.[9] The interrelationship of details of a single seal or inscription can sometimes reveal a surprisingly precise picture of the object's past history. In this way we can view the artifact as a palimpsest of many activities, or a "collapsed act."[10] Traces of manufacture, use-wear, reuse, and breakage can help the archaeologist to decipher some of the history of an artifact's past significance.[11] The reading of these details requires the same careful observation one needs at other levels of archaeological analysis. Further, viewing even an unprovenanced glyptic or inscribed artifact in the context of like materials can clarify its meaning.[12]

Studies of inscriptions in this volume by Bazemore, Hirschfeld, and Smith all illustrate the importance of studying the spatial relationships between an inscription or inscriptions and the object inscribed. Palimpsest inscriptions suggest the reuse through reinscription of inscribed artifacts.[13] Deliberate defacement and reinscription also indicate the probable value and significance of an inscription for the past culture.[14] Pre- and postfiring inscriptions on clay vessels suggest by whom and where a vessel was inscribed.[15] The range in scale of inscriptions is also suggestive of function, from small-scale inscriptions on portable objects such as seals, to inscriptions on portable and nonportable clay vessels, to immovable inscriptions on large and heavy stones.[16] Depending on the function of an inscribed object, it might have been long- or short-lived, influencing its survival and eventual deposition in the archaeological record.

Stylistic features of seals in relationship to their shapes, materials, and other features, as noted by Reyes, Smith, and Webb in this volume, are important pieces of the arguments for seal function and significance. Seals are generally small, portable, and multifunctional (amulets and sphragistic tools). Their detailed carving suggests that they were intrinsically valuable and meant to be kept rather than used once and thrown away. In general, seals may have had long use-lives, ending up in the archaeological record long after their manufacture and in a variety of contexts, some reflecting their variety of functions. Abrasion of a seal's design and recarving can suggest that a seal had more than one owner. Purposeful breakage of a seal suggests deliberate damage of the object to prevent its future use. Seal impressions carry information about the sealer, the sealed object, and the seal itself.

One cylinder seal found in a sixth century B.C. *bothros*, or votive pit, at Kition-*Kathari*, was originally a LBA seal, recarved to suit its Iron Age owner.[17] Its original design compares to Egyptianizing seals at Enkomi. Parts of that design were reworked to create an image that finds its closest parallels among Archaic period cubical stamp seals in the Pyrga style. How this seal came to be used over more than 700 years is unknown, but its use and reuse attests to the complex nature of seal production and the equal importance of seal style and seal context.

An example of a seal that preserves evidence for its use as a votive object, even apart from its discovery in a votive pit of the Late Cypriot (LC) IIC period (13th century B.C.) at Athienou, is a cylinder that was cut in half.[18] Personal examination of this seal revealed that the cylinder was scored around its circumference and deliberately cut in half, not accidentally broken. Possibly this deliberate destruction was intended to make the seal a fit votive offering by preventing its use for sealing. The carved decoration on the seal contains the apotropaic feature of a monster facing frontally.[19] It also preserves a single sign in the Cypro-Minoan script added sometime after the original carving of the seal.[20] The sign is cut more deeply than the rest of the seal decoration, and it crowds and partly cuts into the head of a bull-headed figure. The sign reads properly on the seal, not as it would read in impression, a feature typical of seals intended as votive objects.[21]

Another example of a seal that preserves information about its probable use, this time as a sphragistic tool, even apart from its known archaeological context, is a 14th-century B.C. hematite cylinder seal discovered at Kalavasos-*Ayios Dhimitrios* (fig. 1).[22] Study of the seal alone as well as within the context of iconographically similar LBA seals suggests that it belonged to an elite member of Cypriot society who may well have used it for administrative purposes. Its well-recorded context in an elite burial at Kalavasos supports the hypothesis that it was owned by an individual of high status.[23]

Fig. 1. Cylinder seal with string preserved inside found in tomb 13 at Kalavasos-*Ayios Dhimitrios*. Cyprus Museum, K-AD 1738. Scale 2:1. (Drawing by J.S. Smith)

The Kalavasos seal is somewhat unusual in the specifics of its scene of fowling and the hunt, but it falls into the general category of Cypriot Elaborate Style seals that depicts a Master of the Animals. Cypriot Elaborate Style seals are generally associated with elite burials,[24] suggesting their ownership by those who were in positions of power in society. Elaborate Style

Master and Mistress of the Animals seals are also the most likely to bear inscriptions in the undeciphered Cypro-Minoan script.[25] That these inscriptions suggest some form of administrative authority finds support in the pattern among Near Eastern seals that carry inscriptions, which normally were used more often for sealing than uninscribed seals.[26]

The Kalavasos cylinder was fitted with metal caps, and the string threaded through its stringhole is preserved. At the end flush with the lower end of the engraved scene, the string appears tied in a knot and fills the hole, spilling out over part of the lower edge of the cylinder. The owner probably wore the seal hanging from a string attached by a pin to a garment, as in the Near East. This fashion left the seal free for easy use as a sphragistic tool.[27] The wear on the Kalavasos seal may have resulted from its use as an administrative tool. Continued work on seals of all iconographic groups, their use wear, and other details preserved will continue to provide valuable information about seal use.

The Archaeological Context: Preservation

Many materials associated with writing and seal use do not survive well. Often inscriptions and seals were made of durable media such as clay (which survives well when fired), stone, metal, and bone. However, items such as wood, papyrus, leather, textiles, and wax do not often survive in archaeological context, except under extreme conditions. Any study of scripts and seals relies heavily on the objects that have survived. Sometimes, however, surviving evidence contains clues about other objects that once existed. A brief discussion here of evidence for wooden and other perishable media serves to suggest at least some of the inscriptional and glyptic materials from Cyprus that have not survived for us to study in detail.

Most impressions of seals that date to the LBA were made by seals larger than the standard small stone cylinder and stamp seals. The majority of impressions appear on pithoi, although there are a handful on smaller vessels such as basins.[28] We have, however, none of the large seals that made these impressions. Traces of wood grain in the impressions and the depth and flat method of carving suggest that the original seals were of wood.[29] The carving style, especially of some of the bulls portrayed, parallels that found on LC ivories[30] and contemporary 13th- and 12th-century B.C. small stone seals,[31] indicating that they were created within the larger context of minor arts of that period.[32]

Recognizing that these seals were made of wood cautions us to remember that other materials important for the study of seals and writing, such as tablets and other writing surfaces, may also have been of wood.[33] The only artifacts of similar size and shape to the wooden cylinders rolled on the pithoi from Cyprus are contemporary clay cylinders bearing Cypro-Minoan inscriptions, one from Enkomi[34] and five from Kalavasos-*Ayios Dhimitrios*.[35] It is possible that other inscribed cylinders were made of wood. Manufacturing small wooden cylinders is simple. It requires that a wooden branch be chopped into segments. Then each segment must be smoothed down to the desired cylindrical shape. If inscribed for record keeping, their small size would have been useful, for they would have been easily portable, lightweight, and easily stored. It would have been difficult to tamper with their contents without authorization; changes to texts would be visible easily because they would require that portions of the texts be shaved away. Their cylindrical shape would have maximized surface area relative to the size of the inscribed object, making them an efficient medium for inscription.[36] While it is not possible to prove that Cypro-Minoan records were kept on wooden cylinders similar in size to those used for impressing pithoi, it is possible to show that wooden and ivory writing surfaces existed.

In the Cypriot Iron Age, tablets, probably representing those in wood, appear singly and held by the hand of a statue.[37] The Idalion bronze tablet also may reflect the shape of a wooden tablet.[38] Earlier in the LBA, there may be evidence for waxed writing boards like those known in the Near East from textual references and archaeological contexts.[39] In written sources, wooden writing boards, possibly filled with wax, are best known in Hittite Anatolia.[40] Unlike the flat Classical period writing boards,[41] writing boards from the Near Eastern LBA and Iron Age consisted of at least two rectangular halves, made of wood or ivory. Each board was hollowed out, leaving a raised border. The interior of the hollowed section was scored to receive a fill of wax, often colored with a substance such as orpiment. Hinges connected the boards. One could close the writing tablet to protect the waxed writing surface and any inscriptions impressed into this surface. Unfortunately the wax upon which texts were written does not usually survive in archaeological contexts, although it was used for a variety of purposes in antiquity.[42] Rare examples of inscribed wax survive on bronze bowls at Iron Age Gordion.[43]

A triangular fragment of ivory found at Kition may be a fragment of an ivory writing board.[44] One side is flat; the other preserves a raised edge and a hollowed, scored interior. Ivory hinges similar to those used on the board found in the Ulu Burun shipwreck[45] have been found at Hala Sultan Tekke in a LC IIIA tomb context.[46] However, although it is clear that this hinge mechanism was known in Cyprus, the contextual information from the tomb suggests this hinge belonged to an ivory gaming board and not an ivory or wooden writing board.[47]

Evidence that Cypriots wrote on papyrus, parchment, and leather also exists. Papyrus paper is made from pith in the stems of papyrus plants.[48] First used in Egypt,[49] writing on papyrus outside Egypt was not widespread until the Iron Age.[50] Archaeologically, the earliest evidence for the use of papyrus in the Levant, for example, is found among clay bullae bearing impressions of papyrus dated to the eighth century B.C.[51] Evidence for papyrus use on Cyprus was found at Kition, where a clay sealing with the impression of papyrus on the back was found in an Archaic context (ca. 600–450 B.C.).[52] The sealing bears the impression of a Phoenician seal; however, whether sealed on or off the island, it is unlikely that the sealing existed on Cyprus without its attached document, indicating that papyrus documents were deployed on the island, whether by Phoenicians, or Cypriots, or both. Future publication of sealings from Amathus may confirm the use of papyrus and/or parchment in the Classical period.[53] Ptolemaic period sealings from the *nomophylakeion* in Paphos may also have secured papyrus documents.[54] Earlier, the single clay sealing from a LC IIIA context at Enkomi may also have secured a papyrus document, although wood has also been suggested as the material sealed.[55]

On the basis of sealings from Zakros on Crete, Weingarten suggested that leather rolls, possibly containing writing, were used for record keeping as early as the Bronze Age in the Aegean.[56] Erik Hallager has now shown that flat-based nodule sealings from Crete were once attached to folded parchment documents.[57] Evidence for parchment also exists in the Iron Age, when Babylonians and Assyrians are known to have used it.[58] In the Iron Age of Cyprus, the term διφθεραλοιφός, a writer or painter on skins, appears on the Cypriot Syllabic inscribed bronze tablet from Idalion.[59] The use of ink for writing in the Iron Age of Cyprus is preserved in the form of painted inscriptions on sherds in the Cypriot Syllabary and Phoenician script.[60] There is some evidence for writing in ink during the LBA. A possible stone palette was found at Enkomi.[61] Painted Cypro-Minoan signs appear on vessels, mostly of Aegean origin.[62] One lengthy Cypro-Minoan text is painted on an offering stand from Enkomi.[63] No painted texts appear on LC ostraka, although there is one incised ostrakon from Enkomi,[64] suggesting that others might have existed. Mineral pigments used for ink are natural to Cyprus[65] and are found in several LC[66] and later contexts.[67] Furthermore, the ductus of the linear scripts, Cypro-Minoan and Cypriot Syllabic, is often similar to the linear drawn writing of the Aegean, probably written in ink on parchment documents. [68] However, Cypro-Minoan, particularly at Enkomi, was also written in a punched fashion similar to cuneiform, a script perfectly suited to writing on clay.[69]

The Seal: Sealings

Related to the problem of survival in the archaeological record is that, unlike in the Near East and Aegean, clay sealings have not been found in quantity on Cyprus before the Classical period.[70] These are small lumps of clay on which seals were rolled or stamped in order to assert accountability or control over the contents of the sealed item. Object sealings in particular are useful for the archaeologist because they bear an impression of the seal on one side and the object sealed on the other, making it possible to study the process of seal use in relationship to commodities and storage areas.[71] As already noted, during the LC period, seals were more frequently rolled or stamped directly on pithoi and other clay vessels. Due to the lack of traditional clay sealings made by small stone stamp and cylinder seals of the type that we find in the archaeological record, in Cypriot archaeology we must depend on contextual study of the seals and their archaeological contexts to show that they were once used for sealing in a more traditional sense and functioned in administrative contexts.

Seals that bear inscriptions that read only in impression are the most certain evidence for Cypriot sealing practices apart from the few sealings that do exist. Inscribed seals that read in impression existed in the LBA and the Archaic–Classical periods. There are also seals on which inscriptions read directly on the seal surfaces. From the seals that read in impression we can hypothesize that they were once impressed on clay or wax and in that way used for sealing. What they sealed has not survived. In the LBA seals occur in votive, industrial, mercantile, and funerary contexts. These contexts suggest that they were votive offerings, personal items, and administrative tools.[72] Iron Age contexts, as discussed further on in this text, are not as useful for understanding the overall function of seals during that period.

What follows are comments on the clues to seal function that lie in inscriptions carved on several cylinder and stamp seals of the Late Bronze and Iron Ages. Although the Cypro-Minoan script remains undeciphered, our knowledge of the signs and direction of the script helps us to determine which inscriptions were written to be read on seals and which ones were meant to be read in impression. Frequently both Cypro-Minoan and Cypriot Syllabic signs are symmetrical, making it difficult to determine the orientation of signs. This is true even for readable Cypriot Syllabic inscriptions, some of which can read as one word from right to left, but as another from left to right! Inscriptions that read on the seal surfaces during the LC period are most likely votive and were discussed above. After a discussion of LC inscribed seals and their implications for sealing practices, I discuss Iron Age seals with inscriptions.

In spite of the problems involved in reading the inscriptions, some patterns emerge for the likely use of inscribed LC seals. Inscribed seals found in sanctuaries bear inscriptions written to be read on seal surfaces, while seals from settlements and tombs bear inscriptions that can be read in impression. The inscriptions on seals from sanctuaries accord well with their votive functions, which would obviate a sealing use. Votive seals were inscribed sometime after they were originally decorated in intaglio. It is probable that these seals were inscribed specifically to increase their votive significance.

Among the corpus of LC seals, most of the seals from settlement contexts contain only symmetrical characters that can be read both on the seal and in impression. Only one of these seals was inscribed with an asymmetrical sign; it demonstrates that its inscription was meant to be read only in impression. The cylinder was found in Schaeffer's excavations at Enkomi in a nonfunerary, non-sanctuary context, disassociated from other objects (fig. 2).[73] Roughly carved, the inscription appears as

Fig. 2. Cylinder seal from Enkomi inscribed with Cypro-Minoan characters that read in impression, as seen in impression. Figures filled in with black to emphasize signs. Cyprus Museum, Enkomi (Schaeffer) no. 1958/69. Scale 2:1. (Drawing by J.S. Smith)

four signs at the top of the seal decoration. They read from left to right in impression, the third sign from the left being asymmetrical and assuring the way in which the signs were meant to be read.[74]

Another seal, unfortunately with no context, bears an inscription that reads only in impression. It is preserved only in a plaster impression now in the Walters Art Gallery. The signs appear in a horizontal row across the top of the seal. They were carved as part of the original decoration of the cylinder. Seven signs appear in the inscription, two of which are not well preserved. It is the same asymmetrical sign that is carved on the seal from Enkomi discussed above that indicates that the Walters Art Gallery inscription reads only in impression.[75]

LC seals found in tombs are carved not only with inscriptions that read on their surfaces, but also with inscriptions that read in impression. Those specifically to be read on the seals were sometimes added after the seals were decorated in intaglio. Perhaps, like seals used as votives in sanctuaries, some seals were specifically inscribed prior to their placement in burials.[76] Some of the seals with inscriptions meant to be read in impression were inscribed as part of the original seal decoration. These seals and others meant to be read in impression may have been seals used in life as administrative tools and buried with their owners in death.

One cylinder, found in LC II Tomb 2 at Hala Sultan Tekke, excavated by the Department of Antiquities, bears three separate inscriptions (fig. 3).[77] The tomb may have included horse burials, suggesting that it contained individuals of high rank. The cylinder is decorated with a scene of a kneeling man, a sacred tree, a seated griffin, and infill ornaments. Four Cypro-Minoan signs carved near the top edge of the cylinder appear to be part of the original decoration of the cylinder, because none crowds the rest of the cylinder's decoration. Two additional Cypro-Minoan signs were probably added sometime after the decoration of the cylinder, for they are more deeply carved than the other signs. One free-field sign appears between the head of the man and his arm. The other appears between the backs of the man and the seated griffin. The two signs inscribed after the original decoration of the seal are each symmetrical. One sign carved along the top edge of the scene reads only in impression and is separated from the remaining signs by a guilloche.[78] The remaining signs inscribed along the top edge of the seal constitute a three-sign inscription, probably a single word. These signs read only on the seal surface, not in impression.[79]

Fig. 3. Cylinder seal from Hala Sultan Tekke with three separate Cypro-Minoan inscriptions, as seen in impression. Figures filled in with black to emphasize signs. Cyprus Museum, Department of Antiquities 1968, Tomb 2/230. Scale 2:1. (Drawing by J.S. Smith)

The two original inscriptions on this cylinder read differently: one reads in impression, the other on the seal. Analogy with Near Eastern seal inscriptions suggests that many inscriptions on seals were personal names of seal owners.[80] Perhaps the inscription that reads on the surface of the Hala Sultan Tekke cylinder is the name of the seal owner, and the inscription that reads in impression was a mark used by the seal owner in administrative contexts when (s)he needed the seal for sealing. The signs added later could even have been carved just prior to the placement of the seal in the tomb, possibly as votive inscriptions. A similar practice of inscribing seals for dedicatory purposes is found among the seals deposited in sanctuaries noted above.

Support for the idea that only a single mark was needed for sealing is found in the form of a cylinder seal with a well-preserved context and the single sealing from Enkomi. A cylinder seal with a single symmetrical sign was found at Kalavasos in Building III, in a well-defined LC IIC mercantile or administrative context.[81] Building III was constructed with rubble foundations and mudbrick walls.[82] The rooms of the building were variously associated with storage and the processing of foodstuffs. It contained grape pips, olive fragments, fig seeds, and oat grains.[83] The floor of one room sloped down toward a sunken pithos and may have been used for preparing liquid commodities such as olive oil and wine (A 217, see also A 203). Grinding stones suggest that the grinding of grains took place in the building.[84] Other rooms were full of pithoi, illustrating that the building was outfitted for storing the foodstuffs prepared in the structure (A 205, A 206, A 204, A 201).

One room, A 219, had a hard-packed thick lime floor of higher quality than most floors at the site. The only more carefully constructed lime floors were found in Building X, the large building of ashlar construction found at the site (see below). A 219 was also significantly larger than most other rooms in Building III. Although only half of the room was excavated, the plan suggests that the room was square and outfitted with a central post that stood on a base. Refuse on the floor included a stone mortar (no. 415), a large stone with a squared hole, a sunken pithos, a fragmentary Mycenaean piriform jar (no. 535), a Base Ring II cup transformed into a funnel by means of a hole pierced in its base after firing (no. 591), and a White Painted Wheelmade III bowl fragment (no. 1051). The funnel suggests that an activity concerning the transfer of liquid from one container to another took place here.

Near the central post base and the large stone with a squared hole there was a small hole in the floor. Found in the hole was a group of 14 bronze and stone weights (nos. 441–454) that were adaptable to the weight systems of Mesopotamia, Syria, Egypt, Anatolia, and the Levant.[85] One weight preserves the remains of a cloth sack in which the weights were kept. Among the weights was found an hematite cylinder depicting the Master of the Animals.[86] It is inscribed near the top edge with a single symmetrical Cypro-Minoan sign carved as part of the original design of the cylinder.

The large stone with a square hole may have supported a scale with which the weights found in the hole were used.[87] While the hole in which the weights and seal were found may have been cut in order to hide the deposit, making it a merchant's hoard,[88] the contextual information does not indicate that the deposit was covered over to make the deposit truly hidden. The hole is located near to the central features of the room, the likely use location of the objects. As a storage location for the merchant's weights and seal, placement of the merchant's tools in the hole would prevent their being scattered or lost when they were not in use.

The context of the cylinder from Kalavasos Building III places it firmly in a mercantile context, where it was probably used in the process of administering the weighing and transfer of commodities. However, no sealings exist to prove its administrative use. The extant sealing from Enkomi impressed with a Cypriot cylinder seal (fig. 4) lends support to the idea that a single Cypro-Minoan sign on a seal was significant for sealing practice.[89]

The single clay sealing from Enkomi was mentioned above in the context of perishable writing materials. It was found discarded and reused as part of

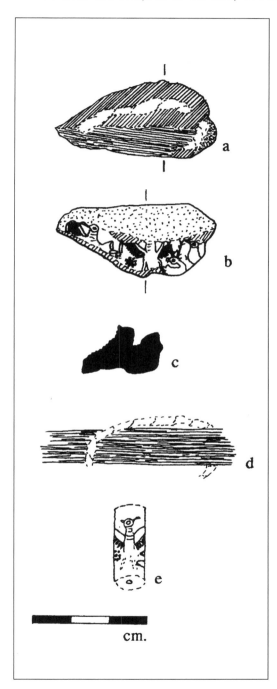

the composition of LC IIC Floor III in Room 24 of Dikaios's ashlar building.[90] The cylinder rolled on the exterior surface of the sealing was small, ca. 2.5 cm in height and 1 cm in diameter. Its size compares well with known cylinder seals from Cyprus. The engraved design includes a heraldic bird whose head faces left in impression. A rectilinear u-shaped mark to the left of the bird is a Cypro-Minoan sign carved deeply, obscuring part of the left wing of the heraldic bird, after the original carving of the seal.[91]

The method of impression shows that the heraldic bird and the Cypro-Minoan sign were the most significant parts of the design for the person who made the impression. The cylinder was rolled,[92] but not in a single consistent rolling. Instead, it was rolled partly

Fig. 4. Clay sealing from Enkomi. (a) impression of object sealed, (b) impression of seal, (c) cross-section, (d) reconstruction of object sealed, (e) reconstruction of seal. Cyprus Museum, Enkomi (Dikaios) 1905/9. Scale 1:1. (Drawing by J.S. Smith)

three times, each time rolling the section of the decoration representing a
heraldic bird. In the impression the bird is visible to the extreme right, in the
middle, and again to the left. Each time the bird is rolled at a slightly different
angle. All three rollings run into one another, but each is distinguishable. This
practice is analogous to Near Eastern seal use, where frequently only the
inscription, or the main figure in the design, was rolled in impression.[93]

Porada identified this seal as Mitannian in style and suggested that the
impression was not made on Cyprus. However, similar seals have been found
at Enkomi. A broken seal carved with a similar design and a single Cypro-
Minoan sign was found in Schaeffer's excavations at Enkomi.[94] Another
cylinder seal from Dikaios's excavations at Enkomi is also carved with a
heraldic bird like that found impressed in clay on the sealing.[95] The presence
of seals at Enkomi that are stylistically similar to the seal rolled on the clay
sealing from the same site suggests strongly that the impression was made on
Cyprus, if not at Enkomi itself. Further, the presence of the Cypro-Minoan
sign on the seal used to make the impression suggests a Cypriot connection
for the use of the seal.[96]

Evidence for the use of inscribed seals to make impressions during the LBA
also appears on two loom weights.[97] Whether these marks are related to the
formal Cypro-Minoan script that appears on longer documents is uncertain,
although in shape the marks compare to known signs.[98] Uninscribed seal-
impressed weights also exist in Cypro-Classical contexts.[99] Other impressions
of Cypriot seals include Elaborate Style seals impressed on clay tablets and
labels or tags found at Ugarit.[100] These seals could have been owned and used
by non-Cypriots; certainly they were used within Ugaritic contexts of seal use.

Frequent seal use on Cyprus was revived with stamp seals in the Archaic
period when the scarab form used by the Phoenicians was adopted and used
for Cypriot designs.[101] The earliest seals of this type date to the seventh century B.C. Production of these seals was prolific into the fifth century B.C.,
after which seal manufacture decreased. Seals inscribed with Cypriot Syllabic
signs in retrograde from this period are particularly important for what they
reveal about Archaic sealing practices as early as the seventh century B.C., a
system only hinted at by a few finds of sealings at sites such as Kition and
Amathus.[102] Inscribed seals in Phoenicia and Greece appear at approximately
the same time.[103] From Cyprus there are not only Cypriot Syllabic inscribed
seals, but also Phoenician and Greek alphabetic inscribed seals with inscriptions in retrograde that were meant to be read in impression. As in the LBA,

Table 1. Scarabs and scaraboids with Cypriot Syllabic inscriptions written retrograde.

Seal	Signs	Inscription	Date	Decoration	Provenance
scarab[a]	ti-we-i-te-mi-wo-se	man's name in genitive	seventh or sixth century B.C.	Theseus, the Minotaur, and Ariadne	near Khrysochou
green stone scarab[b]	te-mi-si-/ti-o a-pa-/te-ki-se	patronymic in genitive and man's name in nominative	possibly sixth or fifth century B.C.	text only, on three lines	Cyprus
green mottled black serpentine scarab[c]	pa-si-ti-mo-se	man's name in nominative	possibly sixth or fifth century B.C	two-line text, schematic animal at end	bought in Nicosia
blue chalcedony scaraboid[d]	pi-ki-re-wo	man's name in genitive	possibly sixth or fifth century B.C	single foot	no provenance
onyx scaraboid[e]	a-ri-si-to-wa-/na-to	man's name in genitive	ca. 500 B.C. or fifth century B.C.	animal contest scene[f]	Ohnefalsch-Richter find, in tomb at Marion
carnelian scarab[g]	pu-nu-to-ni-ko e-mi	man's name in genitive	ca. 500 B.C. or fifth century B.C.	animal contest scene	Salamis
black jasper scaraboid[h]	a-ri-si-to-/ke-le-o	man's name in genitive	ca. 500 B.C. or fifth century B.C.	animal contest scene	no provenance
rock crystal scaraboid[i]	la-wa-ti-ri-so	man's name in nominative	ca. 500 B.C. or fifth century B.C.	youth leaning on staff, holding a hare, with a dog next to him	British Museum excavations at Kourion, Ayios Ermogenis
chalcedony scarab[j]	no-to-sa-to-i	uncertain meaning	ca. 500 B.C. or fifth century B.C.	collapsing warrior	Cyprus
mottled red-brown limestone scaraboid[k]	o-na-sa-to-se	man's name in genitive, written twice	ca. 500 B.C. or fifth century B.C.	satyr carrying an amphora	in a Greek collection
serpentine scarab[l]	pu-ru-ti-to-zo; ?–su-ne-ko(?)	uncertain meaning	ca. 500 B.C. or fifth century B.C.	Mistress of the Animals	from Cyrenaica
carnelian scarab[m]	ta-ma	may be part of a male name	ca. 500 B.C. or fifth century B.C.	head of a bearded man	from Syria
chalcedony scarab[n]	ta-u-o/se-ma	the seal of Thaos	sixth century B.C.	centaur	no provenance

a Cyprus, Collection of G.G. Pierides, no. 974; D.G. Hogarth, *Devia Cypria* (London 1899) 9; *ICS* no. 173; *Catling* no. 11; *AGGems* no. 71.

b Nicosia, Cyprus Museum, no. D6; *ICS* no. 358; *Catling* no. 2; *AGGems* 22, n. 13.

c Oxford, Ashmolean Museum, inv. no. 1970.519; *ICS* no. 367c; *Catling* no. 1; J. Boardman and M.-L. Vollenweider, *Catalogue of the Engraved Gems and Finger Rings I: Greek and Etruscan* (Oxford 1978) no. 72, has shown convincingly that the last sign is not a script character.

d Oxford, Ashmolean Museum, inv. no. 1896-1908/0.14; *ICS* no. 360; *Catling* no. 22; *GrGems* pl. 344.

e Paris, collection de Clerq, inv. no. 2793; *ICS* no. 121; *Catling* no. 19; *AGGems* no. 422.

f *AGGems* labels this group the "Group of the Cyprus Lions."

there are also seals with Cypriot Syllabic characters that read on the seal surfaces, some of which may have been votive dedications.

Thirteen seals with names in Cypriot Syllabic from the seventh through
fifth centuries B.C. read in impression (table 1).[104] None was found in a
well-recorded archaeological context. From this small collection of seals
with retrograde inscriptions that could have been read in impression, it is
clear that they are all of hard stone and are from a variety of stylistic groups.
Striking is the appearance of inscriptions three times on seals depicting an
animal contest and that the names are exclusively male. There are no titles
or placenames. Only once is there a patronymic. Most are in the genitive,
but the nominative is also used. These scarabs and scaraboids with Cypriot
Syllabic inscriptions in retrograde came from Cyprus, but also points east
and west, suggesting that Cypriots may have used their seals widely
throughout the Mediterranean. However, the lack of well-excavated find
contexts makes it difficult to postulate firmly about the breadth and specific
context of the possible administrative use of these seals.

Not only is it possible that Cypriots were active in administrative activities with their neighbors outside of Cyprus, but persons who wrote in scripts
other than the syllabary were probably active seal users on the island as
well. Two scaraboids from ca. 500 B.C. or the fifth century B.C. and said to
be from Cyprus have names written retrograde in the Greek Alphabet.
ΠΥΘΟΝΑΞ appears next to the head of Athena on an agate scaraboid.[105]
ΣΤΑΣΙΚΡΑΤΗΣ appears above the back of a horse on a chalcedony
scaraboid.[106] In addition, a fifth-century B.C. gold ring from a tomb at
Marion bears the name ΑΝΑΞΙΑΗΣ.[107] Two Phoenician seals with personal
names also probably read in impression. One, from the seventh century

---

g Paris, Cabinet des medailles, originally in the Southesk collection, no. A 35; W. Deecke, *Die griechisch-kyprischen
   Inschriften in epichorischer Schrift* (Göttingen 1883) no. 128; O. Hoffmann, *Die Griechischen Dialekte I: Der
   Sudarchaïsche Dialekt* (Göttingen 1891) no. 131; *ICS* no. 356; *Catling* no. 18; *AGGems* no. 421.

h The final sigma is missing. London, British Museum, inv. no. 1909.6-15.1; *ICS* no. 359; *Catling* no. 20; *AGGems*
   no. 423; *GrGems,* pl. 384.

i London, British Museum, inv. no. 96.2-1.157; H.B. Walters, *Catalogue of the Engraved Gems and Cameos* (London
   1926) 15, no. 502; *ICS* no. 183; *Catling* no. 16; *AGGems* no. 287; T.B. Mitford, *The Inscriptions of Kourion*
   (Philadelphia 1971) no. 27.

j Once Tyszkiewicz, Warren, Evans Collections (an impression in Oxford); *Catling* no. 14; *AGGems* no. 265.

k Rhoussopoulos Collection, Athens, 1884, now in Athens, Numismatic Museum; *ICS* no. 362; *Catling* no. 17;
   AGGems no. 292; *GrGems* pl. 340.

l Paris, Bibliothèque Nationale, Cabinet des medailles, Collection de Luynes, inv. no. 250; *ICS* no. 456; *Catling* no. 28.

m Part of the seal is broken away and may have contained one or two more signs. Paris, Bibliothèque Nationale,
   Cabinet des medailles; *ICS* no. 367b; *Catling* no. 12; *AGGems* no. 226.

n Karlsruhe, inv. no. 63/57; *Catling* no. 5.

B.C., is said to be from Cyprus, and depicts a god or king holding a spear and seated on a sphinx throne. The name reads *lgdsr*.[108] The other is said to be from Kition and belongs to the eighth to sixth centuries B.C. It depicts a bird with a cobra in front of it. The name is possibly preceded by a patronymic, *lbnjh bn ihr*.[109]

Nine seals and rings bear names or other words that read on their surfaces. None comes from a sanctuary context, and most have no context information at all. However, by analogy with seals from the Near East and earlier periods on Cyprus, it is likely that these objects were votive, or at least were not meant primarily for sealing. There is no obvious difference between these seals and those with inscriptions in retrograde. They are from a variety of styles. Three are finger rings of silver or glass.[110] Several are scaraboids: one of gray marble has two lines of inscription and no figural decoration,[111] one of carnelian depicts a youth bent over his shield,[112] and one of brown agate shows a goat nursing a kid.[113] A green jasper scarab shows a schematic male in combat with a griffin.[114] A chalcedony Persian pyramidal stamp seal depicts a griffin attacking a deer.[115] Later than the others is an amethyst ringstone, possibly Seleucid in date,[116] with animal decoration. Apart from the possible Seleucid example, they range in date from the seventh through the fifth centuries B.C. They were found on Cyprus, at Marion, Kourion, and Salamis, as well as in Syria. With one exception, a female name in the nominative on a silver ring, the readable names are male and written in either the genitive or the nominative.

Obviously the Archaic and Classical inscribed seals have an advantage over the LBA Cypro-Minoan inscribed examples: we can read their contents. The Cypro-Minoan examples, however, have to a certain extent the advantage of context. Examination of the available information for inscribed seals, the inscriptions, the seal decorations, and their loci of discovery does present a strong case for seals used for sealing during both the LBA and the Archaic to Classical periods, in spite of the paucity of actual sealings. Contemporary with their function as administrative tools, seals of similar types were personal items and votive dedications, placed in tombs and dedicated in sanctuaries.

The Inscription: Decipherment and Readability
Not only can determination of find context be a problem for inscriptions, but also the reading of many inscriptions still eludes scholars. The LBA script of the island, Cypro-Minoan, is still undeciphered.[117] Several Iron Age

syllabic inscriptions are unreadable, although many inscriptions in the Cypriot syllabary read as Greek.[118] Sometimes the only information available for learning about inscribed material comes from contextual study. In these cases, in a way similar to the study of seals, the function of the inscribed object may give us a clue to the meaning of the inscription. However, often the archaeological context is the most important indicator of the meaning and significance of unreadable epigraphic material.

In this volume Hirschfeld makes use of what information there is for the archaeological context of potmarks from Enkomi. However, because of the ambiguous nature of much of this information, she relies more heavily on the relationship of the marks to the vessels inscribed in order to find clues as to their meaning. Bazemore, in her study of Rantidi, is able to make use of archaeological context to underscore her interpretation of inscriptions, the contents of which provide little specific information, as being part of a sanctuary complex.

Another case study in the use of archaeological context to determine function concerns enigmatic clay cylinders found at Kalavasos-*Ayios Dhimitrios*,

Fig. 5. Five Cypro-Minoan inscribed clay cylinders from Kalavasos-*Ayios Dhimitrios*. Top left to right: K-AD 389, K-AD 545. Bottom left to right: K-AD 404 (upside down), K-AD 388, K-AD 405. All in Cyprus Museum. (Photo by A.K. South)

which carry some of the longest inscriptions currently known in Cypro-Minoan. From the shape of the inscribed objects alone we do not know for what they were used. We cannot read their specific contents. Two of the inscriptions appear to be palimpsests, or texts that bear traces of earlier inscriptions that were erased in antiquity. Also among these inscriptions are signs that may be numbers.

The five clay cylindrical Cypro-Minoan inscriptions were found in LC IIC, 13th-century B.C., contexts in Building X at Kalavasos-*Ayios Dhimitrios* on Cyprus (fig. 5).[119] Another Cypriot clay cylindrical text was discovered by Claude Schaeffer in 1967 in his excavations at Enkomi, unfortunately not in an informative context.[120] Published in 1983 and 1989, Emilia Masson interpreted the Kalavasos documents as foundation deposits, based on (1) a morphological comparison to cylindrical Mesopotamian building deposits and (2) the formulaic content of the texts, each observed to begin with the same word.[121] While these inscriptions are indeed cylindrical, in my work with these same inscriptions, among other discoveries, I have found that (1) none come from deposits associated with the foundations of Building X or indeed any other deposit that predates the completed construction of the building and (2) the first word of the inscriptions is not the same.[122]

The cylinder was a common shape used by administrators throughout the Near East. However, normally the cylindrical shape defined the seal used and not the written record. Seals were normally made of stone; however, cylinder seals made of clay are known both in the Near East and on Cyprus.[123] Written records on cylinders made of clay are also rare; when found they are often inscribed with incantations and worn as amulets or buried in foundation deposits.[124]

There are, however, also nonritual small clay cylindrical texts. The three known to me date to the 14th and 13th centuries B.C. One was found at Amarna and is now in the Ashmolean Museum in Oxford.[125] It contains 12 lines of a scribal exercise. Another, also from the Amarna period, was found at Beth Shean.[126] It is pierced for suspension. It contains part of a letter, probably worn around the neck, such that its secret contents would not be intercepted and would be sure to arrive at its destination. A third is a label from Ugarit that refers to a document about the daughter of a Hittite king.[127] It is one of several document labels from Ugarit that bear similarity to tablet labels from Boghazköy.[128]

The cylindrical shape of text, while it may seem unexpected or unknown to us, may have been familiar to the ancient Cypriot, who also used cylindrical seals, both large and small. The largest seals were of wood and were used by administrators to mark large storage vessels, perhaps as a sign of quality or ownership.[129]

The discovery of the cylindrical texts at Kalavasos is important for several reasons. First, they add to the repertoire of long inscriptions in Cypro-Minoan, increasing the body of material we have to work with in trying to better understand this enigmatic script. More than that, however, they were found in well-recorded primary use-related and primary discard-related find locations. Further, all five come from a single building at what appears to be a single point in time. When studying a script it is useful to have not only the inscription and its find location, but also a series of similar inscriptions from one place so that patterns in one text can be compared to other texts that are arguably written in the same script and used within a similar context.

Building X, where they were discovered, was a storage center of large quantities of olive oil.[130] To the west of Building X is Building XI, where olives were crushed to make the oil.[131] Other activities known to have taken place in Building X are eating and drinking, probably elite feasting, to judge by the quantities of imported tablewares.[132] The monumental construction of the building with ashlar masonry has added to the interpretation of this structure as one of importance at the site of Kalavasos, probably a center of administrative activity, involving centralized storage and control by an elite.[133]

All five cylinders were found in secure contexts in Building X. One (K-AD 545) was found amid collapsed building material above the floor and may have fallen from an upper floor or an installation located above floor level.[134] It is burnt and most likely fell to the ground in the conflagration caused by the burning of the oil in the pithos hall that occurred after the abandonment of the building. Two more found nearby (K-AD 405 and K-AD 388) were above a steplike ashlar feature and probably fell from above.[135] Although they were found in a patch of soft soil, and possibly disturbed when the edge of the ashlar was broken in antiquity, what is important is that they were not located underneath or within part of the building structure. Both of these are broken but unfired and unburnt. The remaining two cylinders (K-AD 389 and K-AD 404) were found in a pit cut through part of the floor of Building X near the north side.[136] The find location of these pieces indicates that they were discards. Both are unfired, and the surface of each piece was smudged and mutilated by hand before disposal. One text had been written on twice, the other at least three times.

From the find locations of the pieces, it is clear that all come from the use-life of the building and related discard deposits. However, simply showing that they were not foundation deposits does not remove the possibility that they may have been sacred objects, containing incantations or other texts connected with cult. Masson posited that all five texts began in a formulaic manner, each containing the same first word, and were thus ritual in content. Yet it should be remembered that a formula, although sometimes used for ritual texts, can also be used by scribes when writing lists with purely administrative intent.[137]

We know the first word, or grouped series of signs, of each text because we know where the texts begin and end. As on the Enkomi cylinder, a horizontal line appears across the length of the cylinders above the first lines of text. Problematic is that one of the five texts does not preserve the first line, another is missing the first sign or signs, and another preserves only the first two signs. Of the remaining two inscriptions, one preserves the entire first line of text and the other preserves the first three signs, only the second of which matches the other text. In order to make all texts begin with the same word, Masson had to rely on reconstructions and normalizations of signs that do not represent what actually exists.

Furthermore, what we do have shows that the texts vary in content by means of length and overall sign patterns. Three preserve the full length of text. All are of similar width. One text with particularly small signs and more signs per line

has 15 lines of text. The other two have larger characters yet have only 8 and 4 lines of text respectively. Among the five texts, while there are repeated signs, sign patterns do not suggest that the texts follow any kind of formula.

Fig. 6. Cypro-Minoan inscribed clay cylinder K-AD 404 showing mutilation of artifact in antiquity. Width: 2.60 cm. (Photo by A.K. South)

Fig. 7. Cypro-Minoan inscribed clay cylinder
K-AD 404 showing palimpsest inscription.
Scale 2:1. (Drawing by J.S. Smith)

What then are these inscribed objects? Two main clues suggest that these five clay cylindrical texts are administrative records concerning activities associated with Building X. The first clue is that two cylinders are palimpsests, for they preserve traces of more than one text. K-AD 404 was badly mutilated before it was thrown away (fig. 6).[138] What survives clearly shows part of the earlier text underneath two lines of the later text (fig. 7). Similarly, K-AD 389 preserves three different inscriptions. The final inscription is 15 lines long, its beginning marked by a horizontal line. Two other parts of horizontal lines, however, are also preserved, one in the middle of the seventh line of text and the other at the end of the last inscription. Parts of both earlier inscriptions survive.

The inscription, erasure, and reinscription of a clay text was a scribal practice used particularly on Linear B administrative tablets in the Mycenaean world. Near Eastern examples also exist.[139] Erasure is also a feature of practice inscriptions, when someone is learning how to write. Palimpsests also exist, however, among inscriptions on other materials such as stone, and can be ritual in content, such as at the Iron Age sanctuary of Rantidi on Cyprus.[140] To my knowledge, however, no palimpsest texts in clay from the Bronze Age contain ritual texts. A palimpsest appears to be a marker of records, usually economic in content.

The second clue is that one, probably two, and possibly three texts contain numbers. K-AD 388 ends with seven dots, which are probably numerical notations (fig. 8). These notations also find parallels among Aegean scripts, specifically Linear A, where a dot refers to 10. Similarly, K-AD 545

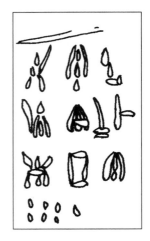

Fig. 8. Cypro-Minoan inscribed clay cylinder K-AD 388 showing possible signs for numbers. Scale 2:1. (Drawing by J.S. Smith)

has what may be a set of four and a set of three dots. The longest text, K-AD 389, has several groups of vertical strokes, often the representations of ones in both Linear A and Linear B. The probable numbers appear both at the end of a text, possibly as totals, and within texts, possibly as ongoing tallies.

Both the presence of palimpsests and the presence of numbers indicate that the cylinders from Kalavasos are unlikely to contain ritual texts but probably contain administrative records, possibly counts of a commodity, possibly something related to the production and storage of olive oil in Building X. These counts were recorded and adjusted by people during the use-life of Building X before the texts were discarded in pits or otherwise abandoned. That the Kalavasos cylinders are probably administrative records does not indicate the contents or meaning of other Cypro-Minoan texts. It does demonstrate, however, how detailed epigraphical and archaeological examination can help us begin to make sense of this material.

The Site: Biases of Discovery

Patterns in the archaeological record often do not lead to a balanced view of ancient society. Our evidence is always only a partial view of what once existed in a past society. On Cyprus, although our record of both the Bronze and the Iron Age reflects only what has so far been discovered, it is certain that there are two major biases in the record now available. First, the record for the Iron Age is distorted in favor of sanctuary and funerary contexts. Second, for both periods, certain areas have been excavated or surveyed more extensively than others, which leads to imbalances in the data available, and it is important to take those biases into account. This second problem is most severe for the LBA, where the site of Enkomi dominates the landscape in terms of excavated volume.

Across the island for the Bronze Age, we have contexts that are religious, funerary, domestic, industrial, and probably administrative. They provide us with a variety of functional contexts and preserve a broad cross section of LBA Cyprus. However, for the Iron Age, with only a few exceptions, the remains are all sanctuary and funerary-related. Based on context, a funerary or votive interpretation of most Iron Age material is the inevitable result. Where people lived, areas of production and centers of authority are still restricted to a few scattered finds.[141] Careful evaluation of the full range and function of inscriptions and seals from this period, however, may lead to clues about less well understood parts of Iron Age Cypriot society.

Above I discussed the probable administrative function of Archaic and Classical period seals from Cyprus. Possible evidence also exists for nonritual and nonfunerary-related functions of nonsphragistic inscribed objects. At the site of Polis-*Peristeries*, a sanctuary of Cypro-Geometric to Cypro-Classical date was found in association with a large votive pit or *bothros*. The *bothros* contained debris from the sanctuary as well as industrial areas to the east and possibly south of the sanctuary area.[142] Although study of this material continues, all pottery from the *bothros* and the sanctuary has been studied in a preliminary fashion.

Among inscriptions from the site are an inscribed scapula bone, a marked loom weight, 10 marked storage vessels, two marked red slip vessels, a coarseware basin, and two closed shapes of uncertain type. Only the marked weight was found inside the sanctuary proper. All remaining inscriptions were found discarded in the *bothros* pit. Preliminary study of all of the material from the sanctuary and the *bothros* suggests that, although a few fragments of pithoi were found within the sanctuary, most were discarded in the pit along with large pithoid amphorae with distinctive large rolled lug handles.[143] Because part of the debris in the pit appears to come from industrial

Fig. 9. Cypriot Syllabic inscribed pithoid amphora handle from Polis-*Peristeries*. Princeton Cyprus Expedition no. R25410/IN64. Length of inscription: 8.0 cm; thickness of handle: 4.11 cm. (Photo by J.S. Smith)

activities located outside the sanctuary, including ceramic manufacture, purple dye production, metallurgy, and bone working, it is possible that the large number of storage vessels in the *bothros* derive from storage areas also outside the sanctuary.

Inscriptions on the storage vessels from Polis-*Peristeries* are enigmatic at best. Five pithoid amphorae, one strap-handled amphora, and four pithoi bear inscriptions. Only two of these, both on pithoid amphora handles, consist of two or more sign inscriptions, in what appears to be the Cypriot syllabary, that plausibly can be taken to represent actual words. One, a two-sign inscription that reads *pi-lo-*(broken), may be *Filo-*, the first element of a compound name. The other, a three-sign inscription, (broken)-*o-u-su*, is not understandable at present (fig. 9).[144] In spite of the difficulty in reading these marks on storage vessels, two points of significance emerge. First, none is identifiable as clearly votive in content. Second, marked storage vessels can be plausibly connected with areas outside the sanctuary and may refer to a system of Iron Age (administered?) storage that is not related to votive or funerary activity.[145]

Another example of bias stemming from the pattern of sites excavated is the emphasis placed on sites that have been more extensively excavated. Certainly it is often necessary to focus on one site to the exclusion or underestimation of others, but it also a useful exercise to calculate the percentage of difference between sites in terms of excavated volume before making conclusions about overall cultural patterns and the possible dominance of one site over others.

The most prominent example of this problem is the site of Enkomi. In this volume two papers focus on that site (Hirschfeld and Webb) because of the sheer volume of available data over other contemporary sites. Webb proposes that Enkomi used and produced a greater number of seals than any other site during the LBA. Rightly she refers to the more than 200 seals that come from different forms of excavation at Enkomi,[146] approximately onequarter of which were discovered in the 175 documented and many more undocumented tombs there.[147] Also rightly she points to Enkomi's continuity in seal use and possibly production over a long period of time, when other sites were occupied for shorter time periods during the whole of the LBA period.

When, however, Enkomi is compared by volume of area excavated and numbers of seals discovered to the prominent and similarly-sized site of

Kalavasos-*Ayios Dhimitrios* at a single, or at least shorter, time period, the two sites appear to have produced and used approximately the same number of seals. Seals at both sites were found scattered in many contexts rather than concentrated in small areas. Kalavasos, however, was only occupied during LC IIC and earlier, thus to compare the two, the LC IIIA and IIIB material at Enkomi should be omitted.[148] Comparison of these two sites is merited in view of not only glyptic material but also inscriptions, Kalavasos being the only site on Cyprus other than Enkomi to produce lengthy inscriptions in the Cypro-Minoan script.

Of the number of seals found at Enkomi, three-quarters of the total number were found in LC IIIA and IIIB levels,[149] showing that only a fraction definitely can be associated with the LC IIC period, even fewer with earlier levels at the site.[150] This fraction accounts for approximately 50 seals. Approximately 25% of all seals from the site were found in tombs. Taking the size of Enkomi as estimated at 15 ha[151] and approximating its excavated area as one-quarter of that, the total area uncovered at the site is 3.75 ha.

Kalavasos, by comparison, has so far unearthed 11 seals,[152] 3 of which come from the fewer than 20 tombs so far excavated, accounting for 27% of the total, a number that compares well with the figure for seals in tombs at Enkomi. Kalavasos-*Ayios Dhimitrios* is estimated to be 12 ha in size,[153] only about 6% of which has been excavated, leaving an uncovered area of approximately 0.75 ha. When seen in comparison with the area uncovered at Enkomi, the area from which evidence was uncovered at Enkomi is five times larger than that so far excavated at Kalavasos. Taking the total number of seals so far found at Kalavasos, 11, and multiplying by 5, we come out with a total of 55 potential seals, a number that compares favorably with the proposed total from Enkomi for the same time period.

The Publication: Accuracy and Accessibility

Incomplete or inaccurate publication makes study of some Cypriot seal and script information difficult. Although many inscriptions and seals have been published in full, with clear photographs, drawings that reflect the observations of the specialist, and complete descriptions, an equal number have not. Without access to the objects themselves, it is difficult for any scholar to undertake a comprehensive study of any aspect of Cypriot writing and seal use. With this in mind, a brief commentary about currently available published information is useful.

There are numerous specialist studies of seals and inscriptions, in the form of either individual articles or specialist reports within larger publications.[154] Compilations of evidence from different sites also exist. Olivier Masson's corpus of Cypriot Syllabic inscriptions, written first in 1961 and updated in 1983, is the most ambitious study to date.[155] A study of Cypro-Minoan by John Franklin Daniel predates the discovery of all lengthy documents in the script.[156] Emilia Masson has published most documents in Cypro-Minoan,[157] but her work is not comprehensive and some parts lack rigorous attention to epigraphical detail and archaeological context.[158] Terrence Mitford produced important studies of Cypriot Syllabic at Kourion and for the general southwestern part of Cyprus.[159] He and Masson together appear as authors and editors of significant compendia of inscriptions, including those from Rantidi.[160] Other scripts have been studied in detail: Phoenician inscriptions by Masson and Maurice Sznycer[161] and Greek alphabetic largely by Ino Nicolaou, such as in her yearly report on inscriptions in the *Report of the Department of Antiquities of Cyprus*. Nicolle Hirschfeld compiled a corpus of published references to inscriptions of all kinds from Cyprus.[162]

Studies of seals in the LBA still hinge on Edith Porada's important 1948 article in the *American Journal of Archaeology*,[163] in which she outlined the major stylistic groups of seals. Individual site and museum group studies of seals by Porada and Victor Kenna add significantly to the known corpus of seals.[164] However, no individual site study is as comprehensive as that for Enkomi published by Jacques-Claude Courtois and Jennifer Webb.[165] Comprehensive in its study of the cylinder seals from Schaeffer's excavations, it analyzes the seals and their stylistic groups critically in terms of function and meaning, significantly drawing on any available contextual information. Studies of Iron Age seals have been treated most comprehensively in published form by John Boardman,[166] but always within the context of stylistic studies of Greek gems, his most important for Cypriot studies being *Archaic Greek Gems*.[167] Site studies of seals from places such as Ayia Irini[168] and Amathus[169] significantly add to our corpus, and considerations of function in site reports for Kition and Amathus are important interpretive contributions.[170] Reyes's consideration of workshops is a rare attempt to address island-wide patterns for the Iron Age.[171]

Comprehensive publications of epigraphic and glyptic material will soon appear. Smith and Hirschfeld have been working to draw together all extant

Cypro-Minoan inscriptions with detailed photographs, drawings, and descriptions, thus making widespread study of the script possible.[172] Bazemore completed a dissertation on Cypriot Syllabic, part of which was the compilation of a catalogue of all inscriptions.[173] This corpus will update Masson's corpus. Reyes has just completed his study of Iron Age seals.[174] It is hoped that a corpus of LBA glyptic will also become a reality.

The archaeological information for scripts and seals has also appeared in published form. Almost all LBA information has been published, at least in a preliminary fashion, such that scholars can know that the information exists, even if in its current published form it is incomplete. The Iron Age information is not as well published in terms of context, although several studies are forthcoming, but individual site studies of inscriptions and seals are significant contributions to the subject. It is, at present, however, easier to study the archaeological contexts of seals and inscriptions in the LBA than it is to study those from the Iron Age based on published information.

There has been, continues to be, and will be considerable progress in all areas of this research. New discoveries and new studies of old finds continue to turn up significant advances. The excavation of a large number of LBA sites, both urban centers and rural sites, over the last 30 years has increased our repertoire of inscriptions and seals and increased the variety of contexts in which they have been found. The total of Cypro-Minoan inscriptions, excluding single-sign potmarks, now totals more than 250. Seals now derive not only from tombs and sanctuaries, but also from well-preserved administrative, storage, and industrial contexts. For the Iron Age, although still more problematic from the point of view of publication and variety of information, we also have significant new information culled over the course of the last 30 years. Increasingly we have seals from the period with well-documented contexts. New and exciting discoveries such as that by Maria Hadjicosti at Idalion promise to change our current picture of the Archaic and Classical periods.[175] Painted inscriptions on ostraca in Phoenician from an administrative building at the site are a notable exception to the sanctuaries and tombs known from the Classical period. It is hoped that studies that integrate Cypriot seal and script use into the larger picture of the Mediterranean and Near Eastern worlds will continue to illuminate patterns both on and off the island.[176]

In Conclusion: Looking toward Integrated Studies

A quick review of the publications and above commentary makes it clear that scripts and seals are published separately, as is information from the Bronze and Iron Age. Often inscriptions and seals form parts of specialist studies that are then not thoroughly incorporated into the context of overall site reports. As the final issue I discuss here, my aim is to encourage a more integrated approach to the scripts and seals of Cyprus and a view toward associations and analogous patterns not only on-island but also in regions east, west, north, and south. Even as we continue to study and publish the specific details of our work, boundaries between script and seal, Bronze and Iron Age, specialist and generalist, and even Cypriot archaeology and other Mediterranean archaeologies need to be overcome.

It is a given that detailed publication of each piece of information is essential for further study. This includes clear photographs, drawings that accurately reflect the observations of the specialist, and complete and clear descriptions of the pieces. Accessible compendia of information, in book form and in electronic database format, will compel both the specialist and the generalist toward more comprehensive study of the available material. Making evidence more accessible may even make it easier for each to understand the other better. The coordination of these efforts toward more accessible publications will also enable us to bridge the gap between Bronze and Iron Age, script and seal, and even better integrate Cyprus into other Near Eastern and Mediterranean archaeologies.

The different languages, scripts, and seal traditions in use on Cyprus once formed part of a whole and was part of a fabric of communication throughout the Mediterranean and Near East that involved many forms of linguistic, written, and iconographical information. Although we cannot fully reconstruct all the fine details of the system of recording and communication on Cyprus, we can begin to take the individually well-defined pieces and work toward that reconstruction. By placing the information in its full context, we can work toward that understanding in every way we can.

In this paper I have discussed problems and prospects in the study of scripts and seals on Cyprus. I have covered a variety of seal and script material from both the LBA and the Iron Age in an effort to illustrate how the objects themselves and their contexts can be studied in order to better understand their functions in society. The brief case studies I have presented emphasize the administrative uses of these objects, for many previous studies have focused primarily on personal and dedicatory purposes. Four of the remaining papers in this volume address specific case studies and point to further ways of understanding the evidence available. These papers each pull together a wide range of information in order to put LBA potmarks (Hirschfeld), Bronze Age seals (Webb), the Cypriot Syllabary (Bazemore), and Iron Age seals (Reyes) into their cultural contexts. Each makes a significant contribution to our understanding of the overall function and significance of glyptic and epigraphic material for the periods discussed, not only administrative, but also as symbols in exchange systems and votive contexts. A concluding paper, by Powell, places these papers and other scholarship in the context of the wider Near Eastern and Mediterranean worlds, making a significant step toward integrating the variety of rich evidence we have for understanding script and seal use in Cyprus during the Bronze and Iron Ages.

NOTES

*Abbreviations for references cited frequently throughout the text are:

AGGems J. Boardman, *Archaic Greek Gems: Schools and Artists in the Sixth and Early Fifth Centuries BC* (London 1968).

ArchRings J. Boardman, "Archaic Finger Rings," *AntK* 10 (1967) 3–31.

Catling H. Catling, "The Seal of Pasitimos," *Kadmos* 11 (1972) 55–78.

Bamboula J.L. Benson, *Bamboula at Kourion: The Necropolis and the Finds* (Philadelphia 1972).

CyRings J. Boardman, "Cypriot Finger Rings," *BSA* 65 (1970) 5–15.

Dikaios I P. Dikaios, *Enkomi, Excavations 1948–1958: The Architectural Remains, the Tombs, volume I* (Mainz am Rhein 1969).

Dikaios II P. Dikaios, *Enkomi, Excavations 1948–1958: Chronology, Summary and Conclusions, Catalogue, Appendices, volume II* (Mainz am Rhein 1971).

Dikaios IIIA P. Dikaios, *Enkomi, Excavations 1948–1958: Plates, 1–239, volume IIIA* (Mainz am Rhein 1971).

GrGems J. Boardman, *Greek Gems and Finger Rings: Early Bronze Age to Late Classical* (London 1970).

ICS O. Masson, *Les inscriptions chypriotes syllabiques. Recueil critique et commenté*[2] (Paris 1983).

K-AD II A.K. South, P.J. Russell, and P.S. Keswani, *Vasilikos Valley Project 3: Kalavasos-Ayios Dhimitrios, volume II: Ceramics, Objects, Tombs, Specialist Studies* (*SIMA* 71:3, Göteborg 1989).

Labels   W.H. Van Soldt, "Labels from Ugarit," *Ugarit-Forschungen* 21 (1989) 375–388.

PyrStamp   J. Boardman, "Pyramidal Stamp Seals in the Persian Empire," *Iran* 8 (1970) 19–45.

Signlist   E. Masson, *Cyprominoica: Répertoires, documents de Ras Shamra, essais d'interpretation* (*SIMA* 31:2, Göteborg 1974).

Smith   J.S. Smith, *Seals for Sealing in the Late Cypriot Period* (Diss. Bryn Mawr College 1994).

[1] Egyptian inscriptions from Cyprus are not covered in detail in this volume. For examples from Cyprus see, e.g., P. Åström, "A Handle Stamped with the Cartouche of Seti I from Hala Sultan Tekke in Cyprus," *OpAth* 5 (1965) 115–21; Egyptian inscribed stone vessels, scarabs, finger rings, and jar handles found on Cyprus appear in I. Jacobsen, *Aegyptiaca from Late Bronze Age Cyprus* (*SIMA* 112, Jonsered 1994) 20, 47–53, 56–59, nos. 79–80, 245–55, 257, 259–62, 266, 279–83, 302–303, 305, 308–310, 314, 322.

[2] Cuneiform inscriptions from Cyprus are not covered in detail in this volume. For examples from Cyprus see, e.g., R.S. Merrillees, "A 16th Century B.C. Tomb Group from Central Cyprus with Links Both East and West," in V. Karageorghis ed., *Acts of the International Archaeological Symposium, "Cyprus Between the Orient and the Occident," Nicosia, 8–14 September 1985* (Nicosia 1986) 114–48, lists imported cylinder seals and their cuneiform inscriptions; other cuneiform inscriptions appear on Cypriot seals, see W. Riedel, "Appendix," in *SwCyprusExp* I, 576–77; P. Åström, D.M. Bailey, and V. Karageorghis, *Hala Sultan Tekke I: Excavations 1897–1971* (*SIMA* 45:1, Göteborg 1976) 17, 33–34, pl. XVIIb–d; E. Porada, "A Theban Seal in Cypriote Style with Minoan Elements," in V. Karageorghis ed., *Acts of the International Archaeological Symposium, "The Relations Between Cyprus and Crete, ca. 2000–500 B.C.," Nicosia 16 April–22 April 1978* (Nicosia 1979) 119–20, pl. XIV.3. An inscribed bowl was also found at Hala Sultan Tekke, P. Åström and E. Masson, "A Silver Bowl with Canaanite Inscription from Hala Sultan Tekke," *RDAC* 1982, 72–76. From the eighth century is the Assyrian Stele of Sargon II, see A.T. Reyes, *Archaic Cyprus: A Study of the Textual and Archaeological Evidence* (Oxford 1994) 50–56; J. Börker-Klähn, *Altvorderasiastische Bildstelen und Vergleichbare Felsreliefs* (*Baghdader Forschungen* 4, Mainz am Rhein) 202–203, no. 175.

[3] Luwian inscriptions from Cyprus are not covered in detail in this volume. For examples from Cyprus see, e.g., a stamp seal with the word for scribe found at Hala Sultan Tekke, P. Åström and E. Masson, "Un cachet de Hala Sultan Tekke," *RDAC* 1981, 99–100, and a gold Hittite stamp seal with words for "man" and "priest" found at Politiko-*Lambertis*, H.-G. Buchholz, "Tamassos, Zypern, 1970–1972," *AA* 88 (1973) 301, fig. 4a, b; H.-G. Buchholz, "Schriftzeugnisse aus Tamassos in Zypern," in A. Heubeck and G. Neumann eds., *Res Mycenaeae: Akten des VII. Internationalen Mykenologischen Colloquiums in Nürnberg vom 6. –10. April 1981* (Göttingen 1983) 66. A cylinder seal from Ayia Paraskevi may also bear the Luwian sign for priest, *Smith* 157.

[4] Although it has inaccuracies and is incomplete, *Signlist* can be used as a standardized and general guide to variations among Cypro-Minoan sign shapes. In this paper, when I refer to

Signlist, I also often make reference to whether the sign observed through my personal study of an artifact finds a parallel among other inscriptions I have studied from the same site.

[5] Phoenician inscriptions from Cyprus are not covered in detail in this volume. For examples from Cyprus see, e.g., Phoenician inscriptions on seals in K. Galling, "Beschriftete Bildsiegel des ersten Jahrtausends v. Chr. vornehmlich aus Syrien und Palästina," *ZDPV* 64 (1941) 121–202; the most comprehensive publication to date is O. Masson and M. Snyzcer, *Recherches sur les pheniciens à Chypre* (Geneva 1972); and an important archive of inscriptions was found at Idalion, see M. Hadjicosti, "The Kingdom of Idalion in the Light of New Evidence," *BASOR* 308 (1997) 58, fig. 24. See also Bazemore, this volume.

[6] Greek alphabetic inscriptions from Cyprus are not covered in detail in this volume. For examples from Cyprus see, e.g., the alphabetic inscriptions published annually by I. Nicolaou in the *RDAC*. See also Bazemore, this volume.

[7] The contextual approach outlined here is not new. In a pivotal article, D.L. Clarke, "Spatial Information in Archaeology," in D.L. Clarke ed., *Spatial Archaeology* (London 1977) 1–32, outlined the principles of spatial archaeology as a broad field that includes the study of archaeological data on several incremental levels. It covers all levels of spatial variation for all spatial elements and the relationships among them.

[8] Clay sealings bearing seal impressions can also be hard to detect; see P. Ferioli and E. Fiandra, "The Importance of Clay Sealings in the Ancient Administration," in W. Muller ed., *Fragen und Probleme der bronzezeitlichen ägäischen Glyptik: Beiträge zum 3. Internationalen Marburger Siegel-Symposium, 5–7 September 1985* (*CMS* Beiheft 3, Berlin 1989) 41.

[9] On the fundamentals of spatial archaeology, see Clarke (supra n. 7). In adapting his pyramid of spatial levels in his fig. 1 (within-site, within-site system, and between-site system) for my study of sealings systems during the LC period, I added an elemental level that derives information about function from the use of space at the level of the artifact. See *Smith* 87–89, fig. 9.

[10] M. Richardson, "The Artefact as Abbreviated Act: A Social Interpretation of Material Culture," in I. Hodder ed., *The Meanings of Things: Material Culture and Symbolic Expression* (*One World Archaeology* 6, London 1989) 172.

[11] Use-wear studies have been particularly prevalent in studies of stone tools, e.g., S.A. Semenov, *Prehistoric Technology: An Experimental Study of the Oldest Tools and Artifacts from Traces of Manufacture and Wear* (London 1964).

[12] See Hirschfeld, this volume, for the analysis of inscribed materials with many known, but often ambiguous contexts.

[13] See below and Bazemore, this volume.

[14] See below and Bazemore, this volume.

[15] See Hirschfeld, this volume.

[16] See Bazemore, this volume.

[17] J.S. Smith, "Cylinder and Stamp Seals from the Phoenician Levels at Kition," in V. Karageorghis, *Excavations at Kition VI. The Phoenician and Later Levels Part II* (Nicosia in press) Area II, no. 508. The long use-lives of seals have received comment elsewhere. For example, see W.L. Rathje, "New Tricks for Old Seals: A Progress Report," in M. Gibson

and R.D. Biggs eds., *Seals and Sealing in the Ancient Near East* (*Bibliotheca Mesopotamica* 6, Malibu 1977) 25–32.

[18] E. Porada, "Cylinder Seals," in T. Dothan and A. Ben-Tor, *Excavations at Athienou, Cyprus 1971–1972* (*Qedem* 16, Jerusalem 1983) 119–21, fig. 54.3, no. 521A.

[19] Porada (supra n. 18) 121.

[20] Porada (supra n. 18) 120. The sign compares to E. Masson's sign 87 in *Signlist* 13–15, figs. 2–4. The correct directional reading of this sign is confirmed by another inscription from the same site, no. 3276, a prefiring inscription on a LC pithos rim discarded in an Iron Age pit, each sign of which was written from left to right, the entire inscription presumably reading from left to right, as do Cypro-Minoan inscriptions generally, see E. Masson, "Cypro-Minoan Inscription and Potters' Marks," in Dothan and Ben-Tor (supra n. 18) 121–23. Personal examination confirmed the presence of sign 87 twice in this inscription, as second and third signs from the left.

[21] On Near Eastern seals with votive inscriptions carved to be read on the seal and not in impression, as were all other Near Eastern seal inscriptions, see M. Gibson, "Summation," in Gibson and Biggs eds. (supra n. 17) 149; D. Collon, *First Impressions: Cylinder Seals in the Ancient Near East* (Chicago 1987) 105, 132–34, no. 564; W.W. Hallo, "'As the Seal upon Thine Arm': Glyptic Metaphors in the Biblical World," in L. Gorelick and E. Williams-Forte eds., *Ancient Seals and the Bible* (Malibu 1983) 9.

A second Cypriot cylinder with an inscription that reads on the cylinder came from a votive context at Ayios Jakovos-*Dhima*. It is a gold-capped hematite cylinder of Elaborate Style, *SwCyprusExp* I, no. 12, pl. CL.9. The inscription was added after the original carving of the cylinder. It is not in Cypro-Minoan but in Akkadian cuneiform and can read in two ways, either as "*Mi-la-ta-ja(wa)* the Prince" or with a Semitic name as "*Şil-la-ta-ja(wa)* the Prince," Riedel (supra n. 2). Riedel's favor of *Mi-la-ta-ja* was based on the absence of "Şil" in the Amarna tablets and in Hittite. However, given the discovery of Semitic inscriptions in Late Bronze Age Cypriot contexts since his study of this inscription, the *Şil-la-ta-ja* is a possibility, see Åström and Masson 1982 (supra n. 2).

[22] J.S. Smith, "The Intersection of Aegean and Middle Assyrian Glyptic in a Seal of Elaborate Cypriot Style (Cylinder Seal K-AD 1738)," in A.K. South et al., *Vasilikos Valley Project 4: Kalavasos-Ayios Dhimitrios III, Tombs 8, 9, 11–20* (*SIMA* 71:4, Jonsered in press).

[23] A.K. South, "Kalavasos-*Ayios Dhimitrios* 1992–1996," *RDAC* 1997, 151–76 contains preliminary comments about Tomb 13.

[24] See Webb, this volume, table 4.

[25] *Smith* 50; Webb, this volume. See below for more on how inscriptions on Cypriot seals would have been used and read.

[26] B.S. Magness-Gardiner, *Seals and Sealings in the Administration of the State: A Functional Analysis of Seals in the Second Millennium B.C. Syria* (Diss. Univ. of Arizona 1987) 77–79. Also on Near Eastern inscribed seals see I.J. Gelb, "Typology of Mesopotamian Seal Inscriptions," in Gibson and Biggs eds. (supra n. 17) 107–126.

[27] Collon (supra n. 21) 110; compare the location of cylinder seal no. B 1626 next to the leg of a skeleton found in Tomb 19:30 at Episkopi-*Bamboula* in *Bamboula* 22–23, pl. 10.

[28] J.M. Webb and D. Frankel, "Making an Impression: Storage and Surplus Finance in Late Bronze Age Cyprus," *JMA* 7 (1994) 5–26; *Smith* 233–313.

[29] First suggested by V.E.G. Kenna in H.W. Catling and V. Karageorghis, "Minoika in Cyprus," *BSA* 55 (1960) 123. Compare the wooden stamps (*typaria*) stamped on modern Cypriot pithoi, similar to wooden stamps used to impress holy bread, G. London, *Traditional Pottery in Cyprus* (Mainz 1990) 70. Rolled impressions were made on modern pithoi with pierced wooden cylinders (*trochoudi*), London, 62, fig. 43.

[30] E.g., E. Porada, "Appendix I: Relief Friezes and Seals from Maa-Palaeokastro," in V. Karageorghis and M. Demas, *Excavations at Maa-Palaeokastro 1979–1986* (Nicosia 1988) pl. E.4; *Smith* 53, 252.

[31] E. Porada, "Cylinder and Stamp Seals," in *K-AD II* 33–34; *Smith* 53.

[32] The only possible location found so far for the production of these minor arts is Room 34 at Enkomi. See *Dikaios I* 99–100. Here both stone and ivory finished and unfinished objects were found together.

[33] Comparisons between Cypro-Minoan writing and writing on wood were noted early on by J.L. Myres, *Handbook of the Cesnola Collection of Antiquities from Cyprus* (New York 1914) 301; S. Casson, *Ancient Cyprus: Its Art and Archaeology* (London 1937) 88.

[34] E. Masson, "Rouleau inscrit chypro-minoen trouvé à Enkomi en 1967," in C. F.-A. Schaeffer, *Alasia* I (Paris 1971) 457–77.

[35] See infra.

[36] Small cylindrical texts were written and used outside of Cyprus, see W. Horowitz, "An Inscribed Clay Cylinder from Amarna Age Beth Shean," *IEJ* 46 (1996) 208–218; W. Horowitz, "The Amarna Age Inscribed Clay Cylinder from Beth-Shean," *BibArch* 60.2 (1997) 97–100.

[37] An example from Voni dates to ca. 500 B.C., *ICS* 265–66, no. 251, pl. XLII.1–2; another stone representation of a tablet appears in O. Masson, "Une inscription étéochypriote probablement orginaire d'Amathonte," *Kadmos* 27 (1988) 126–30.

[38] Powell, this volume; *ICS* 235–44, no. 217; also on wooden tablets see H.T. Bossert, "Sie schreiben auf Holz," in E. Grumach ed., *Minoica: Festschrift zum. 80. Geburtstag von Johannes Sundwall* (Berlin 1958) 67–79; K. Galling, "Tafel, Buch und Blatt," in H. Goedicke ed., *Near Eastern Studies in Honor of William Foxwell Albright* (Baltimore 1971) 207–223.

[39] D. Symington, "Late Bronze Age Writing-Boards and Their Uses," *AnatStud* 41 (1991) 111–23. First proposed by M. San Nicolò, "Haben die Babylonier Wachstafeln als Schriftträger Gekannt?" *Orientalia* 17 (1948) 59–70, waxed writing boards were first found in Iron Age contexts at Nimrud, M.E.L. Mallowan, "The Excavations at Nimrud (Kalhu), 1953," *Iraq* 16 (1954) 59–163; M. Howard, "Technical Description of the Ivory Writing-boards from Nimrud," *Iraq* 17 (1955) 14–20; M.E.L. Mallowan, *Nimrud and Its Remains* I (London 1966) 152–63; D.J. Wiseman, "Assyrian Writing Boards," *Iraq* 17 (1955) 3–13; Iron Age examples were also found at Assur, E. Klengel-Brandt, "Eine Schreibtafel aus Assur," *Altorientalische Forschungen* 3 (1975) 169–71. The earliest writing board found in archaeological context comes from the 14th-century B.C. Ulu Burun shipwreck: G.F. Bass, "A Bronze-Age Writing Diptych from the Sea off Lycia," *Kadmos* 29 (1990) 168–69; R. Payton, "The Ulu Burun Writing-board Set," *AnatStud* 41 (1991)

99–106; P. Warnock and M. Pendleton, "The Wood of the Ulu Burun Diptych," *AnatStud* 41 (1991) 107–108. The loop-and-hook mechanism for closing writing boards like the Ulu Burun example can also be seen in a Neo-Hittite relief from Marash, K. Bittel, *Les Hittites* (Paris 1976) fig. 316.

[40] Symington (supra n. 39) 111.

[41] See Powell, this volume.

[42] A. Lucas, Ancient Egyptian Materials and Industries[3] (London 1948) 7–8.

[43] R.S. Young, *The Gordion Excavations, Final Reports, volume I: Three Great Tumuli* (*University Museum Monograph* 43, Philadelphia 1981) 129–30, nos. MM67–MM69.

[44] It comes from Floor IIIA in Area II at Kition in Temenos A, V. Karageorghis, *Excavations at Kition, volume V: The Pre-Phoenician Levels, Areas I and II, pt. 2* (Nicosia 1985) no. 3330; V. Karageorghis and M. Demas, *Excavations at Kition, volume V: The Pre-Phoenician Levels, Areas I and II, pt. 1* (Nicosia 1985) 65, pls. CXII, CXCI.

[45] Payton (supra n. 39) 102.

[46] K. Niklassen, "A Shaft Grave of the Late Cypriot III Period," in P. Åström, E. Åström, A. Hatziantoniou, K. Niklassen, and U. Öbrink, *Hala Sultan Tekke 8: Excavations 1971–79* (*SIMA* 45:8, Göteborg 1983) 191, no. N1387.

[47] Similar ivory hinges have also been found at sites such as Megiddo, G. Loud, *The Megiddo Ivories* (*Oriental Institute Publications* 52, Chicago 1939) 21, pl. 58: 305–308, and these probably also belong to gaming boards. A bronze hinge similar to those proposed for the boards from Nimrud has been found at Ugarit in the "Archives Sud," C. F.-A. Schaeffer, "Fouilles et découvertes des XVIIIe et XIXe campagnes, 1954–1955," *Ugaritica* 4 (1962) 78, 101.

[48] L. Bell, *Papyrus, Tapa, Amate and Rice Paper: Papermaking in Africa, the Pacific, Latin America and Southeast Asia* (McMinnville, OR 1988) 17. Also on papyrus generally see R. Parkinson and S. Quirke, *Papyrus* (Austin 1995).

[49] W.B. Emery, *Excavations at Saqqara: The Tomb of Hemaka* (Cairo 1938) 14; E.G. Turner, *Greek Papyri: An Introduction* (Princeton 1968) 1, n. 2, P. Berlin 11301; these documents were written with crushed charcoal and other other pigments and special cases stored writing tools, see H. Hodges, *Artifacts: An Introduction to Early Materials and Technology* (London 1964) 157; J. Cerny, *Paper and Books in Ancient Egypt* (Chicago 1977) 11–12; rolled or folded papyrus documents were wrapped with a fibrous cord over which a piece of clay was placed and impressed with a seal, A. Schlott, *Schrift und Schreiber im alten Ägypten* (Munich 1989) 72–73. Documents were not stamped with ink until the Ptolemaic period, though an ink-stamped mark appears on plaster in a tomb of Thutmosis IV of the 15th–14th centuries B.C., P.E. Newberry, *Egyptian Antiquities: Scarabs, An Introduction to the Study of Egyptian Seals and Signet Rings* (London 1906) 12.

[50] R. Dougherty, "Writing upon Parchment and Papyrus among the Babylonians and Assyrians," *JAOS* 48 (1928) 109–135; N. Lewis, *Papyrus in Classical Antiquity* (Oxford 1974); Turner (supra n. 49). A reference to 500 rolls of papyrus in the Tale of Wenamun (J.B. Pritchard, *Ancient Near Eastern Texts Relating to the Old Testament*[3] [Princeton 1969] 28) has been called into question and may refer to clothing instead, H. Goedicke, *The Report of Wenamun* (Baltimore 1975) 94–98.

[51] N. Avigad, *Bullae and Seals from a Post-Exilic Judean Archive* (*Qedem* 4, Jerusalem 1976) 30.

[52] G. Clerc, V. Karageorghis, E. Lagarce, and J. Leclant, *Fouilles de Kition II: Objets égyptiens et égyptisants: scarabées, amulettes, et figurines en pâte de verre et en faïence, vase plastique en faïence, sites I et II, 1959–1975* (Nicosia 1976) 116, Area II/1076. Personal examination showed that a second sealing from the Iron Age levels at Kition has no impression of papyrus, but appears to have been attached to a string, possibly as a nodule attached only to the string tied around a document or other object, Clerc et al., 115–16, Area II/516.

[53] T. Petit, "Syllabaire et alphabet au 'Palais' d'Amathonte de Chypre vers 300 avant notre ère," in C. Baurain, C. Bonnet, and V. Krings eds., *Phoinikeia Grammata: Lire et écrire en Méditerranée, actes du colloque de Liège, 15–18 novembre 1989* (Namur 1991) 485–86, fig. 12; T. Petit, "7. Le Palais," in P. Aupert ed., *Guide d'Amathonte* (Paris 1996) 103; see Reyes, this volume.

[54] F.G. Maier and V. Karageorghis, *Paphos: History and Archaeology* (Nicosia 1984) 230, fig. 205; I. Michaelidou-Nikolaou, "Nouveaux documents pour le syllabaire chypriote," *BCH* 117 (1993) 343–47.

[55] I proposed the possibility that the sealing sealed papyrus, *Smith* 170. E. Porada, "Appendix I: Seals," in *Dikaios II* 790–91 proposed that this object was a wooden box. Whatever was sealed was curved and tied with a string. The object sealed could even have been a fine-grained wooden writing tablet.

[56] J. Weingarten, "The Use of the Zakro Sealings," *Kadmos* 22 (1983) 11–12.

[57] E. Hallager, *The Minoan Roundel and Other Sealed Documents in the Neopalatial Linear A Administration, volume I* (*Aegaeum* 14, Liège and Austin 1996) 137–45.

[58] Dougherty (supra n. 50).

[59] *ICS* 235–44, no. 217; O. Masson, "Eléments de la vie quotidienne dans l'épigraphie chypriote," in *Chypre: La vie quotidienne de l'antiquité à nos jours, Acts du colloque* (Paris 1985) 87–88. On the bronze tablet from Idalion see also Bazemore, this volume.

[60] O. Masson, "Les fouilles américaines à Idalion (1971–1980) et leurs résultats épigraphiques," *Kadmos* 31 (1992) 113–23; Hadjicosti (supra n. 5) 58, fig. 24.

[61] It was found in Level IIB in Area I at Enkomi, *Dikaios II* 254, no. 2052/11; *Dikaios I* 652; *Dikaios IIIA* pls. 130/32, 158/33. This possible palette has no holes for ink. Several small mortars and pestles are found in Late Cypriot contexts, especially in tombs, but whether they were used for crushing pigments for writing is unknown. See H.-G. Buchholz, "Steinerne Dreifusschalen des ägäischen Kulturkreises und ihre Beziehungen zum Osten," *JDAI* 78 (1963) 1–77 on mortars generally. Analysis of one mortar showed that it contained a yellow-gray inorganic substance, possibly ochre, P. Åström and G.R.H. Wright, "Two Bronze Age Tombs at Dhenia in Cyprus," *OpAth* 4 (1963) 299.

[62] See Hirschfeld, this volume.

[63] E. Masson, "Une inscription peinte d'Enkomi en caractères chypro-minoens," *RDAC* 1979, 210–13.

[64] *Dikaios IIIA* pl. 149.2; T.G. Palaima, "Cypro-Minoan Scripts: Problems of Historical Context," in Y. Duhoux, T.G. Palaima, and J. Bennet eds., *Problems in Decipherment* (*Bibliothèque des Cahiers de l'Institut d Linguistique de Louvain* 49, Louvain-la-Neuve 1989) 46, fig. 1.

[65] C. Elliott, "Ground Stone Tools from Kition Areas I and II," in Karageorghis (supra n. 44) 301; C. Elliott, "Ground Stone from Maa-Palaeokastro," in Karageorghis and Demas (supra n. 30) 424.

[66] Ochre in Late Cypriot contexts may have been used for a variety of purposes, including the painting of pottery and dyeing of textiles, see P. Åström, G. Hult, and M.S. Olofsson, *Hala Sultan Tekke 3: Excavations 1972* (*SIMA* 45:3, Göteborg 1977) 64–65; V. Karageorghis and M. Demas, *Pyla Kokkinokremos: A Late 13th Century B.C. Fortified Settlement in Cyprus* (Nicosia 1984) 59; *SwCyprusExp* I, 117, 456, 899, 934, 1116, 1165, 1172; *SwCyprusExp* II, 535, 544, 560, 561; Karageorghis (supra n. 44) 203, 301, 304.

[67] E.g., several pieces of ochre were found in excavations of a Cypro-Archaic sanctuary in Polis, on the site see J.S. Smith, "Preliminary Comments on a Rural Cypro-Archaic Sanctuary in Polis-*Peristeries*," *BASOR* 308 (1997) 77–98.

[68] Supra ns. 56–57.

[69] On the method of inscription for cuneiform documents see, e.g., M.A. Powell, "Three Problems in the History of Cuneiform Writing: Origins, Direction of Script, Literacy," *Visible Language* 15 (1981) 419–40.

[70] On Classical and Hellenistic sealings from Cyprus see supra ns. 52–54. In the Hellenistic period, stamped jar handles also appear in quantity, though there had been a few in earlier periods, see Y. Calvet, *Salamine de Chypre III: Les timbres amphoriques (1965–1970)* (Paris 1972); Z. Sztetytto, *Nea Paphos I: Les timbres céramiques (1965–1973)* (Warsaw 1976).

[71] The brief comments in E. Fiandra and P. Ferioli, "A Proposal for a Multi-Stage Approach to Research on Clay Sealings in Protohistorical Administrative Procedures," *South Asian Archaeology* 1981, 124–27 have had far-reaching implications for archaeological studies of sealings across the Near East, Mediterranean, and Aegean, from prehistoric through historic periods, far too numerous to summarize here.

[72] *Smith* 106–142.

[73] J.M. Webb, "The Cylinder Seals," in J.-C. Courtois and J.M. Webb, *Les cylindres-sceaux d'Enkomi (Fouilles françaises 1957–1970)* (Nicosia 1987) no. 15, inv. no. 1958/69.

[74] Using *Signlist*, the signs on this cylinder read as 1-69-12-(head of figure)-98. Sign 12 is asymmetrical. This sign appears frequently in inscriptions at Enkomi, for example on the inscribed clay cylinder from the site, see Masson (supra n. 34).

[75] I am certain that a third seal also bears an inscription that reads in impression, but evidence for the single asymmetrical sign is slim, and until more is known about it little importance should be placed on this seal, see E. Porada, "The Cylinder Seals of the Late Cypriote Bronze Age," *AJA* 52 (1948) no. 19 and O. Masson, "Cylindres et cachets chypriotes portant des charactères chypro-minoennes," *BCH* 81 (1957) 5. It is in a private collection and has a four-sign inscription placed in a vertical column that divides the Elaborate Style scene. The inscription is original to the carving of the cylinder. The signs are ?-113-50-5 using *Signlist*. Sign 50 indicates the location of the top of the inscription. The first sign is only found again on another cylinder, the inscription on which reads on the seal rather than in impression, B. Buchanan, *Catalogue of Ancient Near Eastern Seals in the Ashmolean Museum* (Oxford 1966) 192, no. 986, pl. 60; J.L. Myres and M. Ohnefalsch-Richter, *A Catalogue of the Cyprus Museum* (Oxford 1899) 135, no. 4504. Yet

another cylinder, L. Delaporte, *Catalogue des cylindres cachets et pierres gravées de style oriental, volume II: Acquisitions, Musée du Louvre* (Paris 1923) pl. 105.22, no. A1177, may have a two-sign inscription that reads in impression, but the existence of the asymmetrical sign in *Signlist* as no. 31 may derive from this cylinder seal, thus making for a circular argument. It may instead be sign no. 13, in which case the inscription reads on the seal.

[76] Late Bronze Age seals from burials, or possibly from burials, with inscriptions that read on the seal surfaces are a cylinder from a tomb excavated by M. Ohnefalsch-Richter, Buchanan (supra n. 75) 192, no. 986, pl. 60; a cylinder with no provenance, H.B. Walters, *Catalogue of the Engraved Gems and Cameos* (London 1926) 15, no. 116, pl. III; a cylinder in a private collection, *GrGems* pl. 206 and I. Pini, "Kypro-ägäische Rollsiegel: ein Beitrag zur Definition und zum Ursprung der Gruppe," *JDAI* 95 (1980) 106, 108, fig. 19; two gold finger rings from Tomb 11 at Kalavasos-*Ayios Dhimitrios*, E. Masson, "Vestiges ecrits trouvés sur le site de Kalavasos-*Ayios Dhimitrios*," in *K-AD II* 38–40, nos. 734 and 795; and a gold ring from Hala Sultan Tekke, Åström, Bailey, and Karageorghis (supra n. 2) 9, 131, fig. 125.3. See *Smith* 157–58, 160–61.

[77] V. Karageorghis, "Two Late Bronze Age Tombs from Hala Sultan Tekke," in Åström, Bailey, and Karageorghis (supra n. 2) 71–72, 78–86; in the same volume are E. Masson, "Les temoinagès epigraphiques," 130–31 and E. Porada, "Appendix IV: Three Cylinder Seals from Tombs 1 and 2 of Hala Sultan Tekke," 99.

[78] The form of this sign is similar to *Signlist* nos. 87 and 88. Although this sign does not occur elsewhere at Hala Sultan Tekke, the pattern among Cypro-Minoan signs is for a single short diagonal stroke to appear to hang off the top right corner of a sign, rather than the top left.

[79] From left to right on the seal surface these signs correspond to nos. 23, 87, and 54 in *Signlist*. Both nos. 87 and 54 are asymmetrical. These asymmetrical signs do not appear elsewhere at Hala Sultan Tekke, but see general rule about short diagonal strokes supra n. 78.

[80] Gelb (supra n. 26).

[81] Porada (supra n. 31) 33, no. 455; the sign equates with *Signlist* sign no. 6. The same sign appears on two loom weights from Kalavasos-*Ayios Dhimitrios*, *K-AD II* fig. 28, nos. 193 and 299, although it is uncertain whether those specific marks are meant to be vocalic signs part of the formal writing system at the site. It also appears once within the formal writing system at the site on one of the clay inscribed cylinders, no. 389, line 11.

[82] A.K. South, "Kalavasos-*Ayios Dhimitrios* 1982," *RDAC* 1983, 103, fig. 3.

[83] South (supra n. 82) 89.

[84] All objects mentioned from this room have been published in *K-AD II*.

[85] J.-C. Courtois, "Le tresor de poids de Kalavasos-*Ayios Dhimitrios* 1982," *RDAC* 1983, 128.

[86] Porada (supra n. 31) 33, pls. XVI, XVII, fig. 36.

[87] I thank Alison South for discussions about this and other contexts at Kalavasos in the spring of 1992.

[88] A.B. Knapp, J.D. Muhly, and P.M. Muhly, "To Hoard is Human: Late Bronze Age Metal Deposits in Cyprus and the Aegean," *RDAC* 1988, pt. 1, 144–45.

[89] Another sealing with the impression of a Cypriot Elaborate Style seal inscribed with a single Cypro-Minoan sign was found at Knossos on Crete; however, although stylistically

and epigraphically connected with Cyprus, the impression of this seal cannot be directly equated with sealing practices on the island of Cyprus itself. See M.R. Popham and M.A.V. Gill, *The Latest Sealings from the Palace and Houses at Knossos* (*British School at Athens Studies* I, Oxford 1995) 20, AECat. no. 20, pls. 12, 29, 42.

[90] *Dikaios I* 178–79, no. 1905/9; *Dikaios II* 813; Porada (supra n. 55) 790–91.

[91] The mark compares to no. 59 in *Signlist*. This sign also appears at Enkomi on small inscribed clay balls of uncertain function, e.g., Enkomi (Schaeffer) 1963/16.27, E. Masson, "Boules d'argile inscrites trouvées à Enkomi de 1953 à 1969," in Schaeffer (supra n. 34), 493, no. 36, fig. 31.

[92] Porada (supra n. 55) 790.

[93] *Smith* 171.

[94] J.-C. Courtois, J. Lagarce, and E. Lagarce, *Enkomi et le bronze récent à Chypre* (Nicosia 1986) pl. XXXI.23, inv. 4.076.

[95] *Dikaios IIIA* no. 1591, pls. 179.5, 180.5, 185.5; Porada (supra n. 55) 792. Porada suggested that this seal was also Mitannian in style, but that it originated on Cyprus because of Mycenaean elements in the portrayal of the lions. The context of 1591 dates to the 13th century B.C., similar to the contextual date for impression no. 1905/9.

[96] Earlier work on Cypro-Minoan inscribed seals appeared in O. Masson (supra n. 75) 6–37. I have discussed inscribed seals elsewhere, *Smith* 142–63. Other Late Cypriot seals not mentioned elsewhere in my discussion here that have Cypro-Minoan signs or possible Cypro-Minoan signs (all symmetrical or probably symmetrical) are A.P. di Cesnola, *Salaminia (Cyprus). The History, Treasures, and Antiquities of Salamis* (London 1884) 128, fig. 128; M. Ohnefalsch-Richter, *Kypros, the Bible and Homer: Oriental Civlization, Art and Religion in Ancient Times* (London 1893) 439, pl. CXXVIII.5; A. S. Murray, A.H. Smith, and H.B. Walters, *Excavations in Cyprus* (London 1900) 36, no. 744, pl. IV; L.P. di Cesnola, *A Descriptive Atlas of the Cesnola Collection of Cypriote Antiquities in the Metropolitan Museum of Art, New York, Volume III* (New York 1903) 301, 434–35, 543, no. 4311, pl. CXVII.2, 4, inv. no. 74.51.4311; L. Delaporte, *Catalogue des cylindres orientaux et des cachets assyro-babyloniens, perses et syro-cappadociens de la Bibliothèque Nationale* (Paris 1910) 269–70, no. 478, fig. 478, pls. XXXII and L; R. Dussaud, *Les civilisations préhelléniques dans le basin de la mer égée*[2] (Paris 1914) 265, 430, fig. 319, AM 1639; *SwCyprusExp* I, 467–68, 474, no. 68; A.H.S. Megaw, "Archaeology in Cyprus, 1949–1950," *JHS* 71 (1951) 258–60, pl. 47.b; C. F.-A. Schaeffer, *Enkomi-Alasia I: Nouvelle missions en Chypre 1946–1950* (Paris 1952) 77–78, fig. 28.1; J. du Plat Taylor, "A Late Bronze Age Settlement at Apliki, Cyprus," *AntJ* 32 (1952) 138, 163, no. 16; V. Karageorghis, "A Late Cypriote Tomb at Tamassos," *RDAC* 1965, 11–29, Tomb 6/11; S. Iakovides, "Ein beschriftete Siegel Zylinder aus Cypern," in W.C. Brice ed., *Europa: Studien zur Geschichte und Epigraphik der frühen Ägäeis: Festschrift für Ernst Grumach* (Berlin 1967); V.E.G. Kenna, "An Unpublished Cypriote Cylinder," *BCH* 91 (1967) 251–54, and E. Porada, "Late Cypriote Cylinder Seals Between East and West," in V. Karageorghis ed., *Acts of the International Archaeological Symposium, "Cyprus Between the Orient and Occident," Nicosia 8–14 September 1985* (Nicosia 1986) 296–97, 299; B. Buchanan, "A Cypriote Cylinder at Yale (Newell Collection 358)," *BCH* 92 (1968) 410–15; V.E.G. Kenna, "The

Kouklia Ring from Evreti," *BCH* 92 (1968) 157–61; V.E.G. Kenna, *Corpus of Cypriote Antiquities, volume 3: Catalogue of the Cypriote Seals of the Bronze Age in the British Museum* (*SIMA* 20:3, Göteborg 1971) no. 83, inv. no. 1966.9–29.2, no. 38, inv. no. 1900.6–15.52; E. Porada, "Appendix A: Glyptics," in *Bamboula* 142–44, pl. 38, no. B1925; E. Porada, "Appendix V: Two Cylinder Seals from Tomb 9 at Kition," in V. Karageorghis, *Excavations at Kition, volume I: The Tombs* (Nicosia 1974) 163–66, Tomb 9, lower burial, no. 10; Pini (supra n. 76) 86, fig. 4, inv. no. 1077; E. Porada, "Appendix I: Seals from the Tombs of Maroni," in J. Johnson, *Maroni de Chypre* (*SIMA* 59, Göteborg 1980) 68–72, no. 45, pl. XII; E. Porada, "The Cylinder Seals Found at Thebes in Boeotia," *AfO* 28 (1981) nos. 1, 5, 6, 11, 21; S.F. Kromholz, *The Bronze Age Necropolis at Ayia Paraskevi (Nicosia): Unpublished Tombs in the Cyprus Museum* (*SIMA-PB* 17, Göteborg 1982) 13–14, 303–304, fig. XXXIII, Tomb 6/369; E. Porada, "Appendix III: Cylinder and Stamp Seals from Palaepaphos-*Skales*," in V. Karageorghis, *Palaepaphos-Skales. An Iron Age Cemetery in Cyprus* (Konstanz 1983) 407–409, pl. CXX (Cypro-Geometric III Tomb 71, nos. 1a, 35, and 46); C. F.-A. Schaeffer, *Corpus I des cylindres-sceaux de Ras Shamra-Ugarit et d'Enkomi-Alasia* (Paris 1983) Chypre A 12 and A 10; J.-C. Courtois, *Alasia III: Les objets des niveaux stratifiés d'Enkomi: Fouilles C. F.-A. Schaeffer* (1947–1970) (Paris 1984) 52, fig. 16/1, pl. VI/7, no. 471, inv. no. 1949/4098; E. Porada, "Cylinder and Stamp Seals from Kition," in Karageorghis (supra n. 44) 251–53, pl. A, nos. 223/1 and 851; E. Porada, "The Cylinder Seals," in E. Vermeule and F. Wolsky, *Toumba tou Skourou, A Bronze Age Potter's Quarter on Morphou Bay in Cyprus* (Cambridge, MA 1990) 339–42, Tomb 2/107, stone 23, pl. 125; P. Amiet, *Ras Shamra-Ougarit IX: Corpus des cylindres de Ras Shamra-Ougarit II, sceaux-cylindres en hématite et pierres diverses* (Paris 1992) 191, no. 454, fig. 82; G.L. Kelm and A. Mazar, *Timnah: A Biblical City in the Sorek Valley* (Winona Lake, IN, 1995) 81, fig. C16, p. 62, fig. 4.29.

[97] Enkomi (Dikaios) nos. 5749/6 and 6032/1 in *Dikaios I* 205, 207, 209, *Dikaios IIIA* pls. 146.2,3,6a, and *Dikaios II* 757, 759. On inscribed loom weights generally see *Smith* 212–32.

[98] Sign no. 102 in *Signlist* may be represented. Alternately, I have suggested that the marks on these weights may illustrate warp-weighted looms, see J.S. Smith, "Changes in the Workplace: Women and Textile Production on Late Bronze Age Cyprus," in D. Bolger and N. Serwint eds., *Engendering Aphrodite: Women and Society in Ancient Cyprus* (*ASOR Archaeological Reports Series,* Boston in press) fig. 8.

[99] Found at Paphos, F.G. Maier, *Alt-Paphos auf Cypern: Ausgrabungen zur Geschichte von Stadt und Heiligtum 1966–1984* (Mainz am Rhein 1985) 19, pl. 8.6a–b, and Polis, found by the Princeton Cyprus Expedition, unpublished. Curiously the impressed weight from Polis bears an impression made with a seal almost identical in design to that impressed on the weights from Paphos. My publication of this weight from Polis will appear elsewhere.

[100] For the two tablets see C. F.-A. Schaeffer, "Commentaires sur les lettres et documents trouvées dans les bibliotheques privées d'Ugarit," *Ugaritica* 5 (1968) 612, 615, figs. 4, 4A, 7, 8, 8A; for the label or tag see C. F.-A. Schaeffer, "Les fouilles de Ras Shamra: cinquième campagne (printemps 1933): rapport sommaire," *Syria* 15 (1934) 118, 123; *Labels* 376, 387; W.H. van Soldt, *Studies in the Akkadian of Ugarit: Dating and Grammar* (*Veröffentlichungen*

zur Kultur und Geschichte des Alten Orients und des Alten Testaments 40, Neukirchen-Vluyn 1991) 542; see also a label in M. Yon, "La Maison d'Ourtenou dans le quartier sud d'Ougarit (Fouilles 1994)," *CRAI* 1995, 439–40, fig. 7a with a two-sign Cypro-Minoan inscription on one side and the impression of a cylinder seal on the other with two bulls facing one another, carved in a fashion similar to a cylinder seal from Kalavasos-*Ayios Dhimitrios*, in Porada (supra n. 31) 33–34, no. K-AD 171, pl. XVI; for another Cypriot cylinder impressed in a non-Cypriot context see E. Porada, "Die Siegelzylinder-Abrollung auf der Amarna-Tafel BM 29841 im British Museum," *AfO* 25 (1974/7) 132–42.

[101] See Reyes, this volume on Cypriot stamp seals from the Late Bronze Age, Geometric, and Archaic periods.

[102] Reyes, this volume and for additional references supra ns. 52–53. Two earlier studies specifically about Cypriot Syllabic inscribed seals are O. Masson, "Quelques intailles chypriotes inscrites," *Syria* 44 (1967) 363–74 and *Catling*.

[103] Phoenician inscribed seals appeared before those of Cyprus or Greece, dating to the eighth century and earlier, see Galling (supra n. 5) 121–202. In Greece, the earliest inscribed seal from the Iron Age known to me comes from Rhodes and dates to the seventh century B.C., J. Boardman, *Island Gems: A Study of Greek Seals in the Geometric and Early Archaic Periods* (*JHS* Suppl. 10, London 1963) M5.

[104] Several examples bear inscriptions that contain only symmetrical signs. These could have been read in impression and/or on the seal surface. See *ICS* nos. 328, 353, 357, 365, 367a (= 463); *Catling* nos. 6, 7, 10, 21, 26, 27; *AGGems* no. 424; *GrGems* 385; *ArchRings* no. N.11; *CyRings* no. 29; *PyrStamp* no. 15. See also a symmetrical Greek Alphabetic example in *AGGems* no. 237. One seal with Cypriot Syllabic characters is not sufficiently published to determine whether the signs read on the seal or in impression, see *ICS* no. 366 and *Catling* no. 23. Additional examples only bear possible Cypriot Syllabic signs, see *ICS* nos. 457, 458, 462; *Catling* nos. 4, 15, 29; T.B. Mitford, *The Inscriptions of Kourion* (Philadelphia 1971) no. 223; *AGGems* nos. 63, 173, 184, 277, 295, 489; *GrGems* fig. 191.

[105] Paris, Bibliothèque Nationale, once collection Tyszkiewicz; Masson (supra n. 102) pl. XX.5; *AGGems* no. 224.

[106] New York, Metropolitan Museum of Art, once Cesnola Collection; Masson (supra n. 102) fig. 3; *AGGems* no. 561.

[107] In London; *GrGems* pl. 688.

[108] Pierides Collection; Galling (supra n. 5) no. 13.

[109] Unknown location; Galling (supra n. 5) no. 49.

[110] Nicosia, Cyprus Museum, inv. no. 125/1a; *ICS* no. 367d; *Catling* 61; O. Masson, "Petites inscriptions chypriotes syllabiques trouvées à Marion," *RDAC* 1964, 187–88; *CyRings* no. 52; Nicosia, Cyprus Museum, inv. no. 1934/I-15/I; *ICS* no. 367; *ArchRings* no. A2; *CyRings* no. 18; the whereabouts of the glass ring are unknown; A.P. di Cesnola (supra n. 96) fig. 76; *ICS* no. 314.

[111] Paris, Musée du Louvre, Département oriental, inv. no. AM 1187; *ICS* no. 361; *Catling* no. 3.

[112] Paris, Collection de Clerq, inv. no. 2795; *ICS* no. 364; *Catling* no. 13; *AGGems* no. 260; *GrGems* pl. 367.

[113] New York, Metropolitan Museum, inv. no. 74.51.4193; L.P. di Cesnola (supra n. 96) pl. XXX, II; Myres (supra n. 33) no. 4193; *ICS* no. 354; *Catling* no. 8; Mitford (supra n. 104) no. 222.

[114] London, British Museum, inv. no. 1949.11-16.1; *ICS* no. 355; *Catling* no. 9.

[115] Péronne, Musée Danicourt, inv. glyptique no. 35; *ICS* no. 363; *Catling* no. 25; *PyrStamp* no. 13; *GrGems* pl. 847.

[116] Nicosia, Cyprus Museum, inv. no. 1935/X-12/2; *ICS* no. 367e; *Catling* no. 24.

[117] For summaries of Cypro-Minoan, its problems and potential see Palaima (supra n. 64) and J.S. Smith and N.E. Hirschfeld, "The Cypro-Minoan Corpus Project Takes an Archaeological Approach," *Near Eastern Archaeology* 62 (1999) 129–30.

[118] See Bazemore, this volume.

[119] A.K. South, "From Copper to Kingship: Aspects of Bronze Age Society viewed from the Vasilikos Valley," in E. Peltenberg ed., *Early Society in Cyprus* (Edinburgh 1989) 315–24 discusses the possible significance of Building X. My full publication of this material will appear in A.K. South ed., *Vasilikos Valley Project 5: Kalavasos-Ayios Dhimitrios IV: the North-East Area (SIMA* 71. 5) (Jonsered in preparation).

[120] E. Masson (supra n. 34).

[121] E. Masson, "Premiers documents chypro-minoens du site Kalavasos-*Ayios Dhimitrios*," *RDAC* 1983, 131–41; E. Masson (supra n. 76).

[122] J.S. Smith, "Unknown? It Must be Sacred! Uprooting the Foundations of Cypro-Minoan (abstract)," *American Schools of Oriental Research Newsletter* 48.2 (1998) A-29; Smith and Hirschfeld (supra n. 117).

[123] Cypriot cylinder seals of clay were found at Enkomi: J.-C. Courtois, "Le sanctuaire du dieu au lingot d'Enkomi-Alasia," in Schaeffer (supra n. 34) 231, 239, fig. 80; Porada (supra n. 55) no. 15. Clay stamp seals also exist, see Porada in *Bamboula* 147, no. B 1640.

[124] See comments by Horowitz in his 1996 article (supra n. 36) 208–209, n. 3; L. Legrain, *The Culture of the Babylonians from Their Seals in the Collection of the Museum* (Philadelphia 1925) 365–66; D.J. Wiseman, "The Nimrud Tablets," *Iraq* 12 (1950) 197; D.J. Wiseman, "The Nimrud Tablets," *Iraq* 14 (1952) 63; J. Nougayrol, "La Lamastu à Ugarit," *Ugaritica* 6 (1969) 404; R.C. Thompson, "A Selection from the Cuneiform Historical Texts from Nineveh (1927–32)," *Iraq* 8 (1940) 109–110; E. Reiner, "Plague Amulets and House Blessings," *JNES* 19 (1960) 154–55; s. v. R.S. Ellis, *Foundation Deposits in Ancient Mesopotamia* (New Haven 1968).

[125] S.A.B. Mercer ed., *The Tell el-Amarna Tablets* II (Toronto 1939) 796, no. 355. See further bibliography in Horowitz 1996 (supra n. 36) 208, n. 3. This text is not covered in detail in either of the standard Amarna publications, J.A. Knudtzon, *Die El-Amarna Tafeln* (Leipzig 1915) or W.L. Moran, *The Amarna Letters* (Baltimore 1992).

[126] Published in two articles by Horowitz (supra n. 36).

[127] *Labels* 379, no. RS 17.72.

[128] H.G. Güterbock, "Die Texte," in K. Bittel and H.G. Güterbock, "Vorläufiger Bericht über die dritte Grabung in Bogazköy," *MDOG* 72 (1933) 38; E. Laroche, *Catalogue des textes hittites* (Paris 1971) 40–41; *Labels* 375–88.

[129] Supra n. 28.

¹³⁰ For the chemical identification of olive oil in addition to locations of storage and production at Kalavasos see A.K. South, "Kalavasos-*Ayios Dhimitrios* 1991," *RDAC* 1992, 133–46; on the centralized storage of olive oil at Kalavasos and other Late Cypriot sites see P.S. Keswani, "Models of Local Exchange in Late Bronze Age Cyprus," *BASOR* 292 (1993) 73–84.

¹³¹ South (supra n. 130).

¹³² A.K. South, "Kalavasos-*Ayios Dhimitrios* 1987: An Important Ceramic Group from Building X," *RDAC* 1988, pt. 1, 223–28.

¹³³ South (supra n. 119) 315–24.

¹³⁴ A.K. South, "Kalavasos-*Ayios Dhimitrios* 1983," *RDAC* 1984, 23.

¹³⁵ South (supra n. 82) 97.

¹³⁶ South (supra n. 82) 100.

¹³⁷ E.g., M. Lang, "Jn Formulas and Groups," *Hesperia* 35 (1966) 397–412; J.S. Smith, "The Pylos Jn Series," *Minos* 27–28 (1992–1993) 167–259.

¹³⁸ R.S. Ellis notes that mutilation is never a feature of foundation deposits (see supra n. 124), pers. comm.

¹³⁹ Pers. comm., D. Pardee and A. Millard.

¹⁴⁰ See Bazemore, this volume.

¹⁴¹ Reyes (supra n. 2) 45–46; remains at Idalion once thought to be evidence for Archaic domestic buildings are now known to date to the third century B.C., see P. Gaber and W.G. Dever, "Idalion, Cyprus: Conquest and Continuity," *The Annual of the American Schools of Oriental Research* 53 (1996) 92–99. A probable Iron Age domestic landscape was located in the region of Tamassos by the Sydney Cyprus Survey Project. See M. Given and J.S. Smith, "6.2 Geometric to Classical Landscapes," in M. Given and A.B. Knapp, *The Sydney Cyprus Survey Project: Social Approaches to Regional Archaeological Survey* (*Monumenta Archaeologica* 21, Los Angeles in press).

¹⁴² Smith (supra n. 67) 91. In the 1997 season industrial installations were found. Geomagnetic survey in 2000 showed that the sanctuary is surrounded by streets and buildings, suggesting that it is not outside of but within the urban fabric of the ancient city of Marion. My work on this sanctuary continues toward its final publication. I thank William A.P. Childs, director of the Princeton Cyprus Expedition, for his continued support of my work.

¹⁴³ *SwCyprusExp* IV.2, figs. XLV.16–18, LVII.21–23, LXIII.10, LXIX.3.

¹⁴⁴ *ICS* fig. 5 shows signs of the Old Paphian script that appear to be most similar to what is found in the Archaic contexts at Polis-*Peristeries*. My reading of this inscription takes the bottom to be the edge where all signs appear to be flush with an invisible common groundline. The sign "*su*" appears in reverse, suggesting that the inscription reads from right to left, rather than left to right.

¹⁴⁵ This practice of labeling storage vessels is more similar to Late Bronze Age Cypriot administrative practices, see Smith (supra n. 67) 91.

¹⁴⁶ Webb, this volume, n. 28.

¹⁴⁷ Webb, this volume, n. 71; Webb (supra n. 73) 28, n. 21. See Hirschfeld, this volume, on numbers of tombs at Enkomi.

[148] South (supra n. 119). Although some of the seals found at Enkomi in LC IIIA and IIIB contexts may have been made earlier, here I compare the quantities of seals deposited in LC IIC contexts.

[149] Webb, this volume, n. 26; Webb (supra n. 73) 26.

[150] Webb (supra n. 73) 26.

[151] On the size of Enkomi see R.S. Merrillees, "The Government of Cyprus in the Late Bronze Age," in P. Åström ed., *Acta Cypria: Acts of an International Congress on Cypriote Archaeology Held in Göteborg on 22–24 August 1991, pt. 3* (*SIMA-PB* 120, Jonsered 1992) 328 and O. Negbi, "The Climax of Urban Development in Bronze Age Cyprus," *RDAC* 1986, 101.

[152] Published seals from Kalavasos appear in Porada (supra n. 31) 33–37; E. Porada, "Stamp Seal," in A.K. South (supra n. 22); and Smith (supra n. 22). My work on the remaining seals from the site will appear in South ed. (supra n. 119).

[153] On the size of Kalavasos-*Ayios Dhimitrios* see Merrillees (supra n. 151) 328 and South (supra n. 119) 319.

[154] Here I do not attempt to cover all publications in this field. The articles in this volume combined, however, do contain most references to currently published material.

[155] *ICS.* On Cypriot Syllabic also see M. Egetmeyer, *Wörterbuch zu den inschriften im Kyprischen Syllabar* (*Kadmos Suppl.* III, New York and Berlin 1992).

[156] J.F. Daniel, "Prolegomena to the Cypro-Minoan Script," *AJA* 45 (1941) 249–82.

[157] *Signlist* is still the most comprehensive study of the script to date.

[158] Palaima (supra n. 64) is a comprehensive survey of publications to 1989.

[159] E.g., Mitford (supra n. 104).

[160] T.B. Mitford and O. Masson, *The Syllabic Inscriptions of Rantidi-Paphos* (*Ausgrabungen in Alt-Paphos auf Cypern* 2, Konstanz 1983).

[161] Masson and Snyzcer (supra n. 5).

[162] N. Hirschfeld, *The PASP Data Base for the Use of Scripts on Cyprus* (*Minos Suppl.* 13, Salamanca 1996).

[163] Porada (supra n. 75).

[164] E.g., Porada (supra ns. 18, 30, 31, 55, 77, 96) and Kenna (supra n. 96).

[165] Webb (supra n. 73).

[166] *GrGems, ArchGems, CyRings, PyrStamp,* and J. Boardman and M.-L.Vollenweider, *Catalogue of the Engraved Gems and Finger Rings I: Greek and Etruscan* (Oxford 1978).

[167] *AGGems.*

[168] E.g., *SwCyprusExp* III, 797.

[169] E.g., A. Forgeau, "Scarabés, scaraboïdes et cônes," in R. Laffineur, *Amathonte III* (*Études Chypriotes* VII, Paris 1986) 135–76; J. Boardman, "Cypriot, Phoenician and Greek Seals and Amulets," in G. Clerc, J. Boardman, O. Picard, and I. Nicolaou, *La nécropole d'Amathonte: Tombes 110–135* (*Études Chypriotes* XIII, Nicosia 1991) 159–70.

[170] E.g., Clerc et al. (supra n. 52).

[171] Reyes (supra n. 2) and Reyes, this volume.

[172] Smith and Hirschfeld (supra n. 117). A corpus of Cypriot potmarks is also under way, see N.E. Hirschfeld, *Potmarks of the Late Bronze Age Eastern Mediterranean* (Diss. Univ. of Texas at Austin 1999).

[173] G.B. Bazemore, *The Role of Writing in Ancient Society: The Cypriote Syllabic Inscriptions, A Study in Grammatology* (Diss. Univ. of Chicago 1998).

[174] See Reyes, this volume, and A.T. Reyes, *The Stamp Seals of Ancient Cyprus* (Oxford 2001).

[175] Hadjicosti (supra n. 5).

[176] See Powell, this volume.

Marks on Pots: Patterns of Use in the Archaeological Record at Enkomi

◈

Nicolle E. Hirschfeld

arks scratched or painted on the Late Bronze Age (LBA) pottery of the eastern Mediterranean are often highly visible elements of the ceramic assemblage because of their bold rendering and prominent placement (fig. 1). Nevertheless, often they have been overlooked. In those instances where they have been noted, interest in them has been primarily epigraphical. Certainly some of the potmarks are connected somehow with contemporary writing systems. But all of them, signs of script or not, have some reason(s) for being painted or incised on certain vases. This paper begins the process of looking systematically for those reasons.

Potmarks may be applied in the process of manufacture, exchange, use, or deposition of a vase, and they may identify potter, workshop, merchant, owner, quality or quantity of contents, price, batch, point of origin, destination, or other information. The potmarks studied in this paper are single signs whose forms give no indication of the value or meaning of the marks. Therefore, a contextual approach is adopted: the marks are examined in terms of the containers on which they appear and the types of deposits in which they were found in order to try to identify patterns of occurrence. Those patterns form the basis for interpreting the significance of the signs boldly painted (fig. 2) or incised (figs. 1, 3, and 4) especially on the pottery found in LBA Cyprus.

Even a subject so seemingly confined as the study of potmarks from LBA Cypriot contexts becomes immense on closer inspection. This paper

Fig. 1. Handle and disk fragment from a large fine ware stirrup jar from an Enkomi tomb with post-firing mark (published in J.-C. Courtois, *Alasia II: Les tombes d'Enkomi—le mobilier funéraire* [fouilles C. F.-A. Schaeffer 1947–1965] [Paris 1981] 285, no. 15, 289, figs. 175.2, 177.6). (Photo by N.E. Hirschfeld)

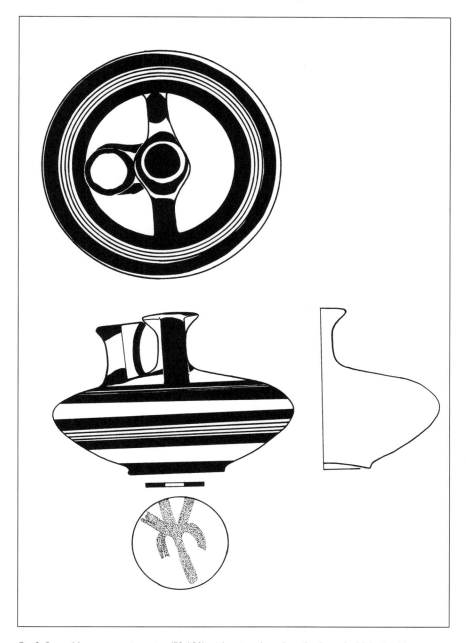

Fig. 2. Squat Mycenaean stirrup jar (FS 180) with painted mark under base (published in V. Karageorghis, *CVA Cyprus 1 Cyprus Museum 1* [Nicosia 1963] A 1632, pl. 22.11, fig. 3.9). (Drawing by N.E. Hirschfeld)

Fig. 3. Fragment of the top of an amphora handle with incised mark (published in P. Dikaios, *Enkomi: Excavations 1948–1958,* volume II (Mainz am Rhein 1971) 726, 891, no. 734/29, pl. 175.10; P. Dikaios, *Enkomi: Excavations 1948–1958,* volume IIIa (Mainz am Rhein 1969) pl. 319.93). (Photo by N.E. Hirschfeld)

Fig. 4. Base of a Red Lustrous Wheelmade spindle bottle with typical prefiring mark (published in P. Dikaios, *Enkomi: Excavations 1948–1958,* volume II [Mainz am Rhein 1971] 778, 891, no. 4702, pl. 319, no. 132; P. Dikaios, *Enkomi: Excavations 1948–1958,* volume IIIa [Mainz am Rhein 1969] p. 149.29). (Photo by N.E. Hirschfeld)

attempts only a beginning and focuses specifically on the material from LBA Enkomi.

History of the Study of Potmarks

Partially because of the high visibility of LBA potmarks and partially because even to the present day no archive or substantial assemblage of formal texts predating the Iron Age has been found on Cyprus, students of Cypriot writing and language have resorted to every scrap of evidence available, including the single signs incised or drawn on the handles, bodies, and bases of Late Cypriot (LC) ceramic containers. Since 1900 these marks have been noted regularly in excavation publications.[1] In addition, synthetic catalogues and discussions of the marks as evidence for formal script have appeared every 20 years or so.[2] Olivier Masson was among the most industrious and thorough collectors of this evidence, and it was his 1957 presentation[3] of the state of knowledge that reinitiated the study of writing on LBA Cyprus after a lull brought about by the sudden death of John Franklin Daniel and the disruptions of the Second World War. The attention paid to potmarks by Masson and his colleagues ensured continued recording of this category of evidence, and my work is possible entirely due to their precedent. Olivier Masson's recent death is a loss to scholarship: I take this opportunity to recognize explicitly the inspiration and challenges that his scholarship has provoked in my own studies of marking and writing systems on LBA Cyprus.

The following study of the potmarks found at the LBA site of Enkomi owes, also, a great debt to the professional and intellectual generosity of another scholar, Jacques-Claude Courtois. It is through his kindness that I was granted access to the entire collection of material, published and unpublished, excavated by Claude Schaeffer at Enkomi and now stored in the basement of the Cyprus Museum in Nicosia. Beyond merely granting me access and publication privileges, Courtois made time to reexamine Schaeffer's inventory records and maps in an attempt to find out as much as possible about the findspots of the marked pottery. Unfortunately, Courtois's untimely death interrupted our collaboration early in the process of study. I dedicate this study of the Enkomi potmarks to the man who worked so hard to present thoughtfully and thoroughly the minutiae of Schaeffer's sweeping glimpses into the history and culture of that Bronze Age site.[4]

The Study of Potmarks at Enkomi

Previous studies of the Enkomi potmarks have concentrated primarily on their possible identification as signs of the LBA Cypriot script, Cypro-Minoan, and, therefore, as evidence of literacy. Already the first publication of discoveries from the site referred to the "Cypriote letters" incised and painted on Mycenaean pottery.[5] The meticulous publications of the Swedish Cyprus Expedition catalogued and discussed the potmarks much more thoroughly, but still almost exclusively in terms of their relationship to formal scripts of the eastern Mediterranean.[6] Dikaios also presented a list of Cypro-Minoan inscriptions that includes every potmark he uncovered, and the potmarks are presented as evidence for literacy in his summary discussions.[7] Schaeffer, too, accepted the equation of the painted potmarks, at least, with signs of the Cypro-Minoan script.[8] But he alone explored the implications of that equation and eventually formulated his theory of the production of Mycenaean pottery on Cyprus based on the evidence of the potmarks.[9] In fact, I do not agree with Schaeffer's conclusions,[10] but I do agree with the direction of his investigations: surely the identification of potmarks with formal script is only a first step, and any such identification demands further inquiry into the patterns and reasons for use of a particular script as a marking device. I extend the process of inquiry in the other direction also and question the initial assumption equating marks with script. Can we truly assume that the marks on pottery from LBA Cyprus are evidence for literacy? As it stands, that claim is based on assumption rather than on methodical evaluation.[11] Furthermore, the study of potmarks from LBA Cyprus is truncated severely by focus on that one question. In their place and context, potmarks functioned as something other than evidence of script. Although my approach to the study of potmarks does not ignore the ties with script and the potential implications, instead it concentrates on attempting to understand the potmarks in terms of their function(s) as marks on pottery. Since we cannot read the marks themselves (they are isolated signs, not deciphered), their meaning must be sought in the patterns of their application on the vases and their deposition in the archaeological record.

This study of the potmarks found at Enkomi is part of a larger-scale project to analyze patterns of potmarking practices found at sites throughout the island during the later Bronze Age. Enkomi was chosen as the starting point because the quantity and range of artifacts and the variety of contexts excavated makes it likely that the material from this site, better than any other single location, might illustrate the kinds and numbers of marked vases in circulation on LBA Cyprus. Enkomi was among the wealthiest, largest, and most powerful of the centers on the island during much of this time. As such, the finds recovered from its tombs and settlement include the full range of objects imported to and produced on the island in the LBA. Enkomi is also the most extensively excavated Late Cypriot site (fig. 5), with major expeditions mounted by British, Swedish, French, and Cypriot

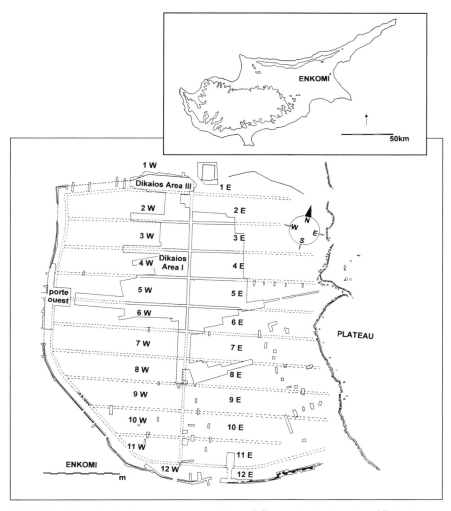

Fig. 5. Enkomi site plan showing areas excavated. Inset of Cyprus showing location of Enkomi.

archaeological missions. Final accounts of the work undertaken by the Swedes and Cypriots have been published, and the results of the British expedition have been summarily documented, while the work done by the French has been haphazardly reported.

The Sample

The four archaeological expeditions excavated approximately 200 tombs and about one-quarter of the 15-ha settlement, recovering at least 250 marked vases.[12] Figure 5 illustrates the general layout of the settlement at Enkomi, with excavated areas demarcated. Table 3 presents the tombs excavated by the various missions, distributed according to the sector of the site in which they are located. Only tombs with marked vases are listed specifically. Table 2 lists the numbers of marked vases found in each sector (quartier), specifying also the excavator and funerary/nonfunerary contexts.

British Museum Turner Bequest Excavations, 1896

> Number of tombs excavated: ca. 100
> Number of tombs with marked vases: 13?
> Number of settlement areas: 0

Extensive plundering of Enkomi's tombs had revealed the archaeological potential of the site long before the British Museum commenced the first systematic excavations there, in 1896. The team dug up approximately 100 tombs. The published records of those tombs and their contents are very brief and incomplete, focusing especially on the luxury objects and Mycenaean pottery.[13] They sometimes note the appearance of painted and incised marks on individual vases. Occasionally the marks are illustrated; however, no detailed descriptions of the marks are provided, and it is clear that the listing of marks was not exhaustive, particularly with respect to those on vases stored in the Cyprus Museum.[14] As a result of sporadic initial recording and the subsequent dispersal and loss of significant amounts of material, there is no way to ascertain to what extent the marked vases now known accord with the patterns of marking in the original tomb depositions. In particular, painted marks (often very faint) and any marks on plain and coarse wares may be significantly underrepresented. Of the approximately 100 tombs, we know of marked vases from 13 only, most containing 1, some with 2 marked vases. The total number of marked vases known to have been recovered by the British Museum expedition to Enkomi: 18 Mycenaean[15] and 2 local (Plain White Wheelmade jugs).

The Swedish Cyprus Expedition, 1930
    Number of tombs excavated: 22
    Number of tombs with marked vases: 6
    Number of settlement areas: 0

Three decades later, in 1930, the Swedish Cyprus Expedition excavated 22 mostly-intact tombs at Enkomi. The Swedes excavated, recorded, and published in meticulous detail.[16] Even so, subsequent work in museum storerooms has brought to light additions to the published inventories of objects from each tomb.[17] These finds consist mostly of sherds; evidently, only fairly complete vases were included in the original published catalogues. In general, these recent (re)discoveries do not markedly alter the interpretation of the wealth, kinds of objects, or number of individuals buried in each tomb. There is no reason to doubt that the presently known distribution of marked vases presents a fairly accurate picture of the types and quantities of marked vases deposited in these funerary assemblages. Only 6 of the tombs excavated by the Swedish Cyprus Expedition contained vases marked with single signs; a 7th held a vase with a multisign inscription incised into the handle. Finally, an unprovenanced handle fragment probably also comes from a burial, since the Swedes excavated only tombs. The number of marked vases found in any one tomb ranged from 1 to 3, with the remarkable exception of Tomb 18, which contained 16 marked vases. The total number of marked vases recovered by the Swedish Cyprus expedition to Enkomi: 27 Mycenaean and 5 local.

Claude F.-A. Schaeffer, 1934–1972
    Number of tombs excavated: 23+
    Number of tombs with marked vases: 9+?
    Number of settlement areas: see figure 5

The British and Swedish expeditions excavated only tombs at Enkomi; Claude F.-A. Schaeffer, director of the French mission to Enkomi, first recognized the presence of a settlement at the site. In the course of almost 40 years (1934–1972, intermittently) of excavations on a grand scale, Schaeffer uncovered great tracts of the settlement that included domestic, ritual, and industrial, private and public, elite and humble spaces. Figure 5 illustrates the layout of the site as uncovered by Schaeffer: the area enclosed by a circuit wall,

bounded by cliffs, divided into eastern and western halves by a central
north–south road, and further subdivided by a series of cross-streets.
Schaeffer designated the subdivisions "quartiers," numbering them 1–12
(north to south); thus the sectors of the site are referred to as Quartier 1E,
1W, 2E, etc. Schaeffer also uncovered at least 23 (but probably many more)
tombs. Thus, Schaeffer's work at Enkomi, in contrast to that of his predecessors, uncovered material from a range of functional contexts and offers an
opportunity to study the appearance of potmarks in nonfunerary contexts.

Unfortunately, publication of Schaeffer's discoveries has been erratic, and
much material and information are now lost.[18] Although a large collection of
inventoried finds is still stored in the basement of the Cyprus Museum in
Nicosia, the bulk of the archaeological assemblage was culled long ago. The
kindness of Schaeffer's colleagues did make it possible for me to look
through all the extant finds in Nicosia. That search allowed me to increase
by one-third the known assemblage of marked vases found by Schaeffer.[19]
There is no way to ascertain how completely this collection of marked vases
represents the total number of marked vases uncovered by the French mission. There are some indications that the assemblage might be reasonably
complete, at least insofar as it may preserve the bulk of marks noted by
Schaeffer and his team. Schaeffer's research interests[20] as well as the inclusion
of so many marked handles among the inventoried objects make clear that
marks—even simple crosses or strokes on plain wares—were collected by the
excavator and his team. The inventory dates associated with the marks span
many of the years of fieldwork and indicate that this collection is not selec-
tive according to field season or area of excavation. These indications are,
however, tenuous arguments for arguing that the finds in the museum represent the complete collection of potmarks recognized by Schaeffer. In any
case, given the magnitude of his operations and the demonstrable lapses in
recording and storing, it is clear that some quantity of marked pottery
escaped the notice of the excavator and his team. Although the collection
cannot be assumed to be complete, it does, nevertheless, provide valuable
evidence for the variety of marks and marked vases.

It also serves to demonstrate at least the minimum dispersal of marked vases
in the nonfunerary contexts. Again, the sparse publication and cataloguing
procedures hamper full evaluation of the material, but thanks to the efforts of
the ever-generous and diligent Courtois, the proveniences of as many of the
marked vases as possible were pinpointed. Inclusion of settlement areas in the

analysis of potmarks adds a new category of marked vases, namely amphoras (Canaanite jars), as well as adding substantially to the numbers and varieties of marked local wares. The total number of marked vases recovered by the French expedition to Enkomi: ca. 24 Mycenaean, 36 amphoras, and 31 local.

Porphyrios Dikaios (Department of Antiquities, Cyprus), 1948–1958

> Number of tombs excavated: 25 + 5 other burials
>
> Number of tombs with marked vases: 0
>
> Number of settlement areas: Area III/Quartier 1W, Area I/Quartier 4W

In 1948 Porphyrios Dikaios, at that time curator of antiquities of the Cyprus Department of Antiquities, commenced 11 seasons of excavation in northern (Area III = Quartier 1W) and central (Area I = Quartier 4W) sectors of the site (fig. 5). Those excavations, which included a variety of settlement and funerary deposits, have been published fully. Like his predecessors, this excavator took an interest in the potmarks as traces of Bronze Age writing. He took pains to inventory and publish in detail the painted and incised signs.[21] As a result, much information is available concerning not only the marks themselves but also the date and function of their findspots. In spite of Dikaios's interest and care, I found several unrecorded examples of marked handles while checking the trays of uninventoried finds from Enkomi. While the marks on Mycenaean wares are less likely to be missed, because of the attention given to this class of pottery, it should be kept in mind that those occurring on plain and coarse wares are probably underrepresented in most collections and publications of archaeological material. The total number of marked vases recovered by the Cypriot expedition to Enkomi: ca. 9 Mycenaean, 1 Bichrome, 41 amphoras, and 57 local.

Finally, a few marked vases in various collections are thought or suggested to be from Enkomi, probably looted from tombs.[22]

In total, about 250 marked vases can be identified among the finds recovered from Enkomi. That sample is at the same time both large and small. It is large in terms of quantity, outnumbering all assemblages of marked vases known from any other LBA Cypriot site. It is also qualitatively large: all types of marks are represented—painted (fig. 2), incised (figs. 1, 3, and 4), and impressed; pre- and postfiring; single signs, multisign inscriptions, graffiti, and even a scarab impression—appearing on bases, handles, shoulders, and bodies of all sorts of shapes in a variety of wares, from a range of chronological and functional contexts. Thus, the number and range of marked vases from Enkomi make this a good sample from which to commence analysis of marking patterns on Cyprus. On the other hand, considering the area of ground excavated, the 200 or so tombs excavated by archaeologists, and the tens of thousands of ceramic vases and sherds uncovered, 250 marked pots is a modest number. Of course, the documented sample is not comprehensive. Many examples must have been lost among the booty of tomb robbers or in the piles of discarded plain and coarse wares. Some may simply have gone unnoticed. In spite of these lacunae, the impression that marked vases were relatively scarce features in the LBA ceramic assemblage is probably valid. This general impression is corroborated by the small numbers of marked vases recovered at Enkomi in the course of the controlled excavations of both tombs and settlement by the Swedish and Cypriot missions.[23] The sample of marked vases from Enkomi, then, may be understood to demonstrate, in broad outline, the range and rarity of marks on vases from the site. To what extent this is a truly representative sample of the use and appearance of marked vases at the LBA site is impossible to ascertain.

The Marks

Vases at Enkomi are marked in a variety of ways: multisign inscriptions and isolated, single marks that may be incised, painted, or impressed on the handles, shoulders, and bases of open and closed, local and imported, fine and coarse, plain and decorated vases. This study examines closely most, but not all, marked vases. Certain kinds of markings appear to be fundamentally different in nature from the general corpus of postfiring single potmarks found at the site. They require further study in their own right; here, they are identified and discussed mainly in comparison and in contrast to the usual range of potmarks.

One such group contains the vases that carry inscriptions. Two or more marks located adjacent to one another, in alignment, and made using the same tool are considered to be an (Cypro-Minoan?) inscription.[24] By this definition, approximately 25 vases with inscriptions have been found at Enkomi, primarily plain ware jars with two or three signs incised into the handle, often before firing. It is possible that there is some connection between inscriptions and potmarks on vases. This question will be examined in detail in a separate paper. Here simply note that the function(s) of the (undeciphered) inscriptions are not known and therefore do not offer suggestions for the purpose of potmarks. There are also no obvious patterns of clustering in the spatial distributions of vases with inscriptions and those with potmarks (fig. 6.1–6.11).

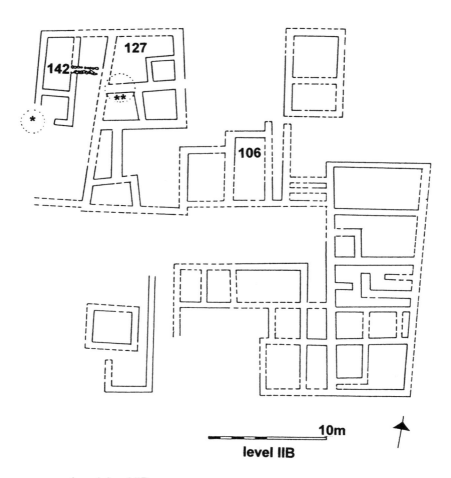

level IIB

Area I, level IIB

room 142	5897/4	plain	+
	5902/4	amphora	☆
	5903/4	local (cw SJ)	Ａ··
room 106	2130	plain	I
room 127	1972	plain	+ (BF)
* = OP 0-2	6009/5	Aegean (cw SJ)	·¬ ·¬··
** = tomb 19	2199	amphora	⚟···

Fig. 6.1. Distribution of marked vases from Enkomi, Dikaios Area I Level IIB

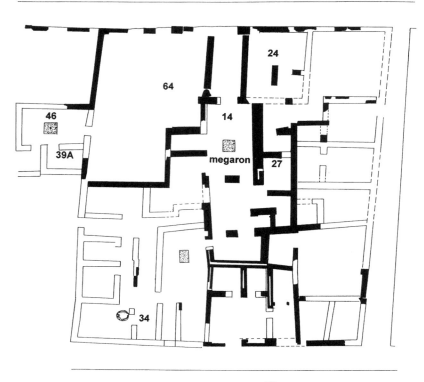

10m

level IIIA

Area I, level IIIA

room 46	1687	tablet	
room 39A	5791/1	Aegean (cw SJ)	⅄ʌ
room 64	930	plain	Λ ψ
		1 *boule*	
room 14	1944	amphora	坫
room 24	1906	plain	手
room 27	5590/3	amphora	ψ ψ
room 34	5902/2	amphora	手

Fig. 6.2. Distribution of marked vases from Enkomi, Dikaios Area I Level IIIA

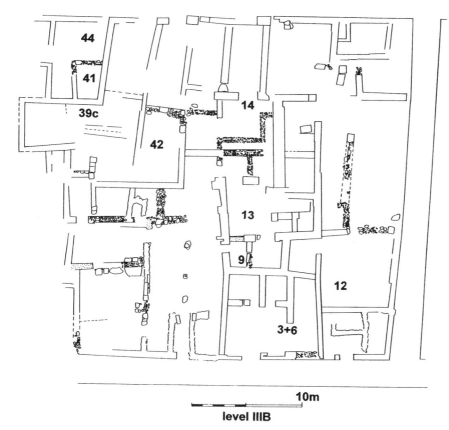

10m

level IIIB

Area I, level IIIB

room 44	5926/4	plain	⤬
room 41	5819/5	amphora	𐤰𐤰
	5819/6	amphora	Ⳗ
room 39c	6098A	amphora	▽
room 42	1085	plain	↳ ⏐ 米
	5837/20	Myc IIIC:1b	三
room 14	1020/4	amphora	+
room 13	760/12	amphora	⊥
	265	plain	+
room 9	5183/4	amphora	⌐𝖳⌐
room 3+6	734/29	amphora	♯
	717/8	plain	⊥
	718/7	amphora	⊕ painted
room 12	5240/1	plain	丼

Fig. 6.3. Distribution of marked vases from Enkomi, Dikaios Area I Level IIIB

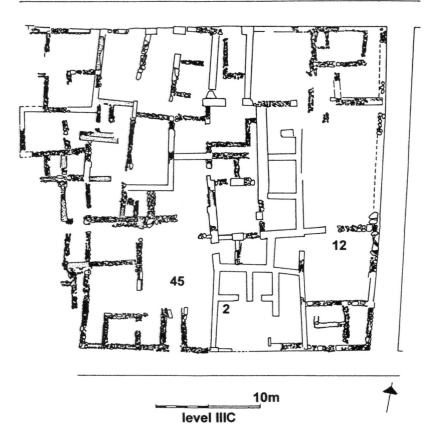

10m

level IIIC

Area I, level IIIC

room 45	5985/2	amphora	=
	5972/3	amphora	_Ⅲ_..
room 2	4936/5	Black Slip	_Ⅲ_--
room 12	*boule*		

Fig. 6.4. Distribution of marked vases from Enkomi, Dikaios Area I Level IIIC

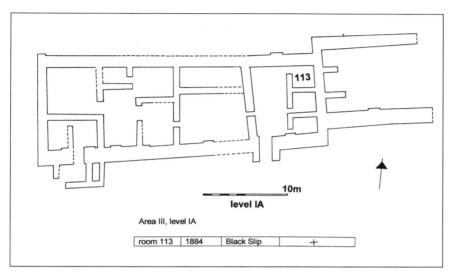

Fig. 6.5. Distribution of marked vases from Enkomi, Dikaios Area III Level IA

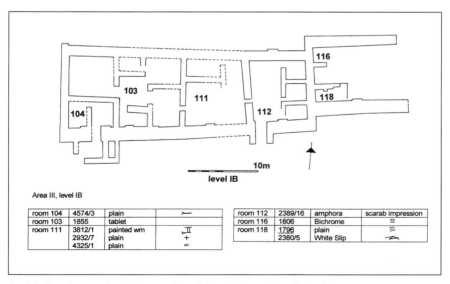

Fig. 6.6. Distribution of marked vases from Enkomi, Dikaios Area III Level IB

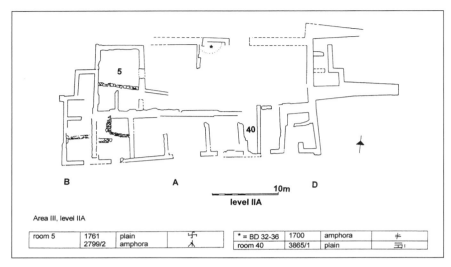

Area III, level IIA

| room 5 | 1761 | plain | 卆 |
| | 2799/2 | amphora | 人 |

| * = BD 32-36 | 1700 | amphora | ≠ |
| room 40 | 3865/1 | plain | 尹 ı |

Fig. 6.7. Distribution of marked vases from Enkomi, Dikaios Area III Level IIA

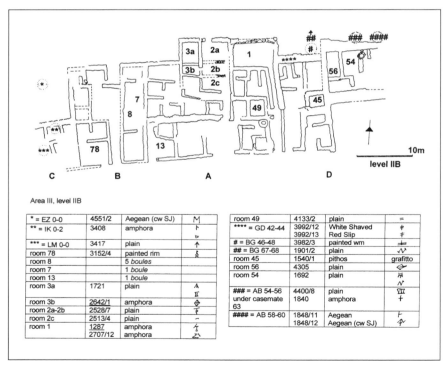

Area III, level IIB

* = EZ 0-0	4551/2	Aegean (cw SJ)	M
** = IK 0-2	3408	amphora	ト
			ᶭ
*** = LM 0-0	3417	plain	↑
room 78	3152/4	painted rim	ᶭ
room 8		5 boules	
room 7		1 boule	
room 13		1 boule	
room 3a	1721	plain	Λ
			Ⅱ
room 3b	2642/1	amphora	⊕
room 2a-2b	2528/7	plain	∓
room 2c	2513/4	plain	¯
room 1	1287	amphora	ᵴ
	2707/12	amphora	Łᴧ

room 49	4133/2	plain	=
**** = GD 42-44	3992/12	White Shaved	≠
	3992/13	Red Slip	≠
# = BG 46-48	3982/3	painted wm	≠
## = BG 67-68	1901/2	plain	Λᴧ
room 45	1540/1	pithos	grafitto
room 56	4305	plain	⊘
room 54	1692	plain	ﬁ
			N
### = AB 54-56	4400/8	plain	Ⅶ
under casemate 63	1840	amphora	+
#### = AB 58-60	1848/11	Aegean	⊢
	1848/12	Aegean (cw SJ)	⬘

Fig. 6.8. Distribution of marked vases from Enkomi, Dikaios Area III Level IIB

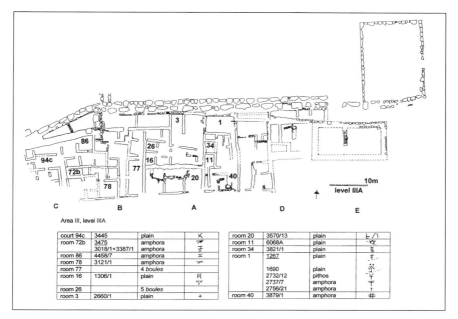

Fig. 6.9. Distribution of marked vases from Enkomi, Dikaios Area III Level IIIA

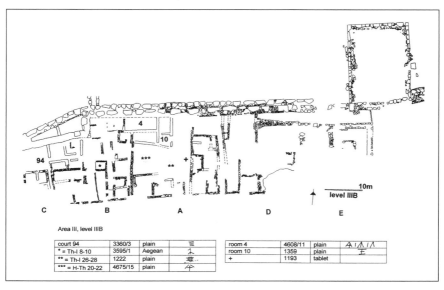

Fig. 6.10. Distribution of marked vases from Enkomi, Dikaios Area III Level IIIB

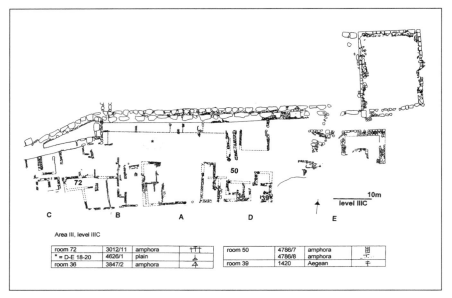

Fig. 6.11. Distribution of marked vases from Enkomi, Dikaios Area III Level IIIC

Included in the discussion of potmarks, however, are those painted marks consisting of the same sign, repeated twice. Such immediate repetition of signs is not a feature of Cypro-Minoan writing as far as we now know; therefore, these doubled signs on vases, even though they can sometimes be identified as Cypro-Minoan characters, fall somewhere in between multisign combinations and the single potmarks.

The potters' marks that occur frequently on Red Lustrous Wheelmade (RLWM) vases (fig. 4) are very clearly a distinctive and self-contained marking system, unrelated in every aspect to the potmarks on all other vases from the site. Although I return to the subject of the RLWM marks later, they are not tabulated in the general sign lists discussed below.

Two impressed (prefiring) marks and an impressed scarab are unusual features and differ from the general marking patterns in use at the site.[25]

The central column of table 1 is a list of known potmarks from vases found at Enkomi. The tremendous variety is immediately striking. Most of the potmarks are simple forms and can be identified with signs appearing in several of the scripts and marking systems current in the LBA eastern Mediterranean.[26] They may just as easily have been developed completely independently of the influence of any external systems of notation. It is only

Table 1. Potmarks from Enkomi: comparison with formal scripts and distribution on vases. P=painted, BF=before firing, cwSJ=coarse ware stirrup jar, WhSh=white shaved, BR=base-ring.

scripts*				vase types			
other	Linear B	Cypro-Minoan	**MARK**	amphora	local	Aegean	other
	10		—		1		
	20		═	7	2		
	30		≡	4			1 Myc.IIIC:1b
	40		≣	1	2		
			▆	1			
	1		|	1	3		
		∧ 12	∧			1	
			ʓ	1			
			∱	1+1?			
			⤐	1		1ᴾ	
AB 01 ⊦	⊦ da	⊦ 4	⊦ ⊤ ⊥		2	7+3ᴾ	
A 319 ⊤			⊤	1	2		
		Ⅲ	Ⅲ	2			
			⊥	1			
			⟙		1		
			⊥	1			
			⫪	1?			
			⟊	1			
			⟒		1		
			ſ		1 ᶜʷ ˢᴶ		
AB 05 ⟊	⟊ to	⟊ 8 ⟊ 9	⟊ ⟊ ⟊	1	2	5	
AB 03 ⟊	⟊ pa	⟊ 6	⟊	2	4+1 ᵂʰˢʰ	5+1 ᵈⁱˢᵏ	
			⟊		1		
			⟊		1		
			⟊		1		

* AB (Linear A and B) and A (Linear A) designations as in L. Godart and J.-P. Olivier, *Recueil des inscriptions en Linéaire A* vol. 5: *Addenda, corrigenda, concordances, index et planches des signes* (*Études Crétoises* XXI:5 Paris 1985). Linear B as in M. Ruipérez and J.L. Melena, *Oi Mykenaioi Ellenes* (Athens 1996) 84–85. Cypro-Minoan as in E. Masson, *Cyprominoica: répertoires, documents de Ras Shamra, essais d'interprétation.* (*Studies in the Cypro-Minoan Scripts 2, SIMA* 31:2 Göteborg 1974) 12–15, figs. 1–4.

Table 1 continued on the following page

Table I *continued from the preceding page*

scripts			MARK	vase types			
other	Linear B	Cypro-Minoan	**MARK**	amphora	local	Aegean	other
AB 24	‡ te	‡ 7	‡ +++			9+1^P	
AB 24 ⟂	te		⟂	1	2	1	
			‡	1			
			⟂			1	
AB 02 +	+ ro	+ 5	+	10	5+2^BF	1^P?	
			⊬ ⊬		1	1	
			(+)			1^P	
			⊬"			1	
		⊓ 78	++	1	1?		
		⊔ 60	⊓		1^BF		
			‡‡	2	1		
			卅 varia	2	2		
		⊟ ⊽ 77	⊽	1			
		⊟ 69	⊟		1		
			⊟ ⊟		2		
			☐		1		
		Φ 3	⊘			1^P	
AB 77 ⊕	⊕ ka		⊗ ⊕ ⬦	1+1^P		1^P	
		◇ 15	◇	1			
		∧ 21	∧ ∨ ⟩	3		2	
			∇ ◁	2	1+1?		
AB 37	∧ ti	∧ 23	∧	1	2		
AB 38 ⋀	e (variant)		⋀			1	
		⋀ 25	⋀	1	2		
			⋀			2	

Table 1 continued on the following page

Table I *continued from the preceding page*

scripts			MARK	vase types			
other	Linear B	Cypro-Minoan		amphora	local	Aegean	other
			(symbol)	1			
			(symbol)	1			
			✕	2	3+2^{BF}+1^{BR}		
A 318 (symbol)			(symbol)		1		
AB 46 (symbol)	(symbol) je		(symbol)			1	
			(symbol)			1?	
		(symbol) 104	✕ ✕		1	1?	
AB 44 45 (symbols ke / de)	(symbols)	(symbols) 107	(symbol)			1^{P}	
AB 44 45	ke de	107	(symbol)			2	
			(symbol)	1			
			(symbol)	1			
AB 09 (symbol)	(symbol) se	(symbol) 44	(symbol)			1	
			(symbol)		1		
			(symbol)		1		
		(symbol) 87	(symbol)			1	
		87	(symbol)			1^{P}	
			(symbol)		1		
AB 27 (symbol)	(symbol) re	(symbol) 82	(symbols)	2	1+1?		
			(symbol)			1^{P}	
			(symbols)			1^{P} + 1^{P}?	
		(symbol) 26	(symbol)		1	1	
		(symbol) 31	(symbols)		1	1	
		(symbol) 36	(symbol)		1		
A 312 (symbol)		(symbols) 27	(symbol)			3+1?+1^{P}	
		27	(symbol)			2^{P}	
		variant 27?	(symbol)			1^{cwSJ}	
			(symbol)	1			

Table 1 continued on the following page

Table 1 *continued from the preceding page*

scripts				vase types			
other	Linear B	Cypro-Minoan	**MARK**	amphora	local	Aegean	other
		ᗯ 104	ᗯ ᗯ		2		
		⋁ 87	⋁		1+1?		
			И		1		
		Ѵ 19 Ѵ*	Ѵ		1		
		ᙢ 20	ᙢ		1		
cuneiform ?			⋀⋀	1			
cuneiform ?			⨂	1			
			⊿⊿	1			
			ᙡ		1		
			✳	1	1		
			⟊	1			
			⟍⟋	1			

by means of the more complex marks that one may assess whether (some of) the potmarks are related to any specific script or marking system. The left-hand set of columns in table 1 records possible parallels for the potmarks. Concentrating on the more significant parallels, namely, those among the comparatively complex signs, it is readily apparent that relatively few identifications are possible. In other words, as a group these potmarks are not connected strongly with any script or known contemporary LBA marking system. The traditional equation of these potmarks with signs of the Cypro-Minoan script or as indications of literacy should not be made automatically.[27] On the other hand, that tradition is not completely without merit, since it is almost solely with Cypro-Minoan that any parallels between complex potmarks and script signs can be made.[28] The number of these parallels may increase as more examples of Cypro-Minoan writing are discovered and the script becomes better understood.[29] Only one complex potmark may be identified possibly with a Linear B sign.[30] That identification is very tenuous, and there exists also a Cypro-Minoan counterpart for that mark. Given the lack of any other Linear B comparanda among the complex marks as well as the certain identification of several Cypro-Minoan signs among the potmarks, the identification of the possible Linear B mark with Cypro-Minoan seems more likely. There is no reason to propose any close connection between the Mycenaean script and any of the marks on the vases found at Enkomi, including the ceramics imported from the Aegean.

Macro-Context: The Site

Figure 5 outlines the areas excavated by the Cypriot and French missions; the tombs excavated by the British and Swedish expeditions are scattered within and outside these boundaries. The figure is composite, including features from several different periods of the site's existence. Enkomi, of course, changed substantially through time. Certain aspects of those changes are well documented; many others remain murky.

Table 2 presents the distribution of marked vases according to the sector of the site in which they were found. It can be seen that marked vases were found in all excavated areas of the site. The high numbers of marked vessels recovered from Quartiers 1W and 4W reflect the careful work of Dikaios. They probably should be viewed as indications of the amount of evidence lost in the excavation and documentation of material from other areas of the site rather than as unusual concentrations of marked pottery in these particular areas. Large numbers of marked vases from Quartier 5W may also be more the result of recovery and publication than original deposition, since the bulk of material from this area comes from two tombs (Swedish Tomb 18 and French Tomb 110) that happen to have been published thoroughly. One wonders if similar concentrations of material in other sectors would have been apparent had other tombs been documented similarly. Finally, Quartier 6W is the one other sector from which a comparatively large quantity of marked vases has been retrieved; most of these finds come from the "maison aux couteaux." The haphazard nature of Schaeffer's records make it difficult to determine whether the apparent concentration of finds in this building is also real, or whether it is the result of methodological happenstance (these particular rooms more carefully excavated, or the finds more diligently inventoried, for example). Several of the buildings excavated by Dikaios contained similarly large numbers of marked vases, suggesting that the quantity in the "maison aux couteaux" was not unusual. The finds scattered throughout the site, then, indicate that marked vases were deposited in all areas. The fact that the significantly higher numbers of marked vases in some sectors correlate (for the most part) with detailed publications of features in those areas suggests that the quartier totals reflect the documented rather than the depositional record. No weight can be given to the relative numbers of marked vases recorded in the various sectors.

Table 2. Distribution of marked vases at Enkomi.

quartier	vase type	tombs BM	SCE	Schaeffer	Dikaios	tomb totals	non-funerary Schaeffer	Dikaios	non-funerary totals	quartier totals
1 W	Aegean					0		5	5	5
	amphora					0		18	18	18
	local					0		41+1 incl: 7 inscr 1 WhSh 1 WS	41+1?	41+1?
	other					0		5 incl: 1 bichrome 2 BF (1 Myc, 1 local) 1 scarab (amph) 1 grafitto	5	5
						0			69+1?	69+1?
rue 1E	Aegean	2ᴾ				2ᴾ			0	2
2W + rue 2W	Aegean			2		2			0	2
	local			3		3			0	3
										5
3 W	Aegean		5			5			0	5
	amphora					0	2		2	2
	local		2			2	3 Incl: 1 cw SJ		3	5
										12
3E + rue 3E	Aegean	3 Incl: 1P 1P inscr?				1+2ᴾ	1+2ᴾ		1+2ᴾ	6
	amphora					0	1		1	1
	local					0	1		1	1
										8
4 W	Aegean	1ᴾ				1ᴾ		3	3	4
	amphora					0		16	16	16
	local					0		10 Incl: 2 inscr	10	10
	other					0		1 Myc IIIB 2 BF: 1 local 1 inscr 1 ostrakon	4	4
						1ᴾ			33	34

Table 2 continued on the following page

Table 2 *continued from the preceding page*

quartier	vase type	tombs				tomb totals	non-funerary		non-funerary totals	quartier totals
		BM	SCE	Schaeffer	Dikaios		Schaeffer	Dikaios		
4 E	Aegean	1^P				1^P	2		2	3
	amphora					0	2		2	2
	local					0	2 / Incl: 1 inscr		2	2
	other					0	2^{BF amph}		2	2
						1			8	9
5 W	Aegean	2+3^P	12+ 4^P+ 1^{l/P}	2^P+ 4^P+ 1		14+ 1? 9^P+ 4^P? 1^{l/P}	1		1	15+1? 9^P+4^P? 1^{l/P}
	amphora					0	1		1	1
	local		1 / Incl: 1 WS	1		2	2		2	4
	other			1^{BF} local		1	1^{BF} local		1	2
						27+ 5?			5	32+5?
5 E	Aegean			1		1	2		2	3
	amphora					0	4		4	4
	local			1+ 1?		1+ 1?	4 / Incl: 1 cooking pot 2 inscr		4	6
										13
6 W	Aegean					0	1		1	1
	amphora					0	10		10	10
	local		1?	1		1+ 1?	2 / Incl: 1 BR		2	3+1?
	other					0	1^{BF} local		1	1
						1+ 1?			14	15+1?

Table 2 continued on the following page

Table 2 *continued from the preceding page*

quartier	vase type	tombs				tomb totals	non-funerary		non-funerary totals	quartier totals	
		BM	SCE	Schaeffer	Dikaios		Schaeffer	Dikaios			
7 W	Aegean	2^P+ $1^{I(P?)}$	$1+$ 1^P	$1^{P?}$		1 3^P+ $1^P?$ $1^{I(P?)}$			0	$5+$ $1?$	$7+$ $1?$
	local		$1+\underline{1}$ local?						0	2	
9 W	Aegean	1^P				1^P			0	1	
?	Aegean					0			0		
	local			$\underline{3}$ Incl: 1each inscr WhSh		3			0	3	
	other					0			0		

abbreviations:	BM = British Museum	BR = Base Ring
	SCE = Swedish Cyprus Expedition	WhSh = White Shaved
	P = Painted Mark	WS = White Slip
	I = Incised Mark	Myc = Mycenaean
	BF = Before firing mark	cw SJ = coarse-ware stirrup jar
	inscr = inscription	amph = amphora

Marked vases have been found in every type of context: funerary, ritual, domestic, storage, and industrial. The following discussion separates these contexts into two main categories: funerary and nonfunerary.

Archaeological Contexts: Funerary Deposits

Perhaps 1,000 tombs at the Enkomi site have been located and explored. Not even 200 have been excavated by archaeologists, and of these we have thorough records of the architecture and contents for only one-third. The incomplete and skewed nature of the sample should be kept in mind in reviewing the observations offered below.

It is fair to say that many more tombs did not have marked vases among their assemblages than did. This is clear from the careful work of the Swedish and Cypriot expeditions. Six (of 22) tombs excavated by the Swedes contained vases marked with single signs; a seventh tomb held a vase with a long inscription on its handle. None of the 30 funerary deposits excavated by Dikaios included marked vases. It is more difficult to evaluate the tombs excavated by the British and French expeditions, since the former are only briefly published and the latter sporadically. But here, too, the presence of marked vases seems to be the exception rather than the rule. Marked vases are recorded for 13 of the 100 tombs excavated by the British. Approximately half of the tomb groups were brought back to England and subsequently catalogued and published in the form of both brief inventories and detailed descriptions of individual vases.[31] Attention was paid to marks in both publications, particularly in the catalogue of vases. Only six of the tomb groups now in the British Museum include vases with marks, and this can be assumed to reflect fairly accurately the depositional record. The tomb groups that remained in Cyprus were less thoroughly inventoried, and most of the marks have been identified in the course of subsequent, unrelated, studies.[32] No systematic search for marks has been made. For these reasons, it may be that the small number of marked vases known (8, from 5 different tombs) underrepresent the actual number of marked vases originally deposited in these tomb groups. Because so few of the minimum 37 tombs excavated by Schaeffer have been fully documented, it is not possible to assess the significance of the fact that 9 (possibly 11) have been noted as containing one or more marked vases.

Table 3 illustrates the distribution of tombs containing marked vases in relationship to the total number of tombs excavated in each sector of the site.[33] It can be seen that tombs containing marked vases are scattered across the entire site. Sectors with higher numbers of tombs with marked vases are also the sectors in which greater numbers of tombs have been excavated. In other words, there is no significant clustering of tombs with marked vases, and marked vases in funerary contexts cannot be associated with any particular area of the site. Two observations may throw some doubt on this generalization but, in my mind, do not negate it: First is the absence of any marks in the tombs of Quartier 1W, in spite of the careful excavation and documentation of 10 tombs in that sector. Second is that only one of the 26 tombs excavated in Quartier 4W contained a marked vase. Because of the large numbers of tombs carefully excavated, one would expect larger numbers of marked vases to have been found in each of these sectors. The fact that Dikaios was responsible for excavating all or most of the tombs in these two quartiers makes it impossible to suggest that negligence or oversight could explain the dearth of marked vases in tombs. The significance of these lacunae is not clear, although some possible explanations are offered below.

There are few patterns in the kinds of burials in which marked vases have been found. Chamber tombs are by far the most common types of graves at

Table 3. Distribution of tombs and tombs with marked vases at Enkomi.

W — Tombs with Marked Vases	Total Number Tombs Excavated	E — Tombs with Marked Vases	Total Number Tombs Excavated
1	**10** C	1 —BM T.67—	**1** BM
— rue 1 —			
2 F T.1851	**2** 1 F / 1 BM	2	**1** BM
— rue 2 — F T.1907 —	**1**		
3 ?SCE T.3 / ?SCE T.6	**3** F / 1 BM **+ 7?** / 1 SCE SCE / 1 F	3	**5** 1 F / 4 BM
— rue 3 —		—?BM T.68—	**1** ? BM
4 BM T.91	**26 + 2?** / 6 BM BM / 20 C	4 BM T.66 / ?F T.1409, dromos	**12** ? BM **+ 1?** / 3 F BM / 9 BM
			3 BM
5 SCE T.18 BM T.43 / F T.110 BM T.45 / ?F T.12 BM T.48 / ?SCE T.19	**19 + 8?** / 13 BM 4 SCE / 2 SCE 4 F / 4 F	5 F T.5 / ?F T.1336, dromos	**5** F
6 F T.p.t.134 / ?SCE T.13	**10 + 4?** / 7 BM SCE / 3 F	6	
7 BM T.78 / BM T.83 / ?SCE T.11 / ?SCE T.7A / ?F T.7	**3 + 7?** BM SCE	7	
			2? F
8	**2?** SCE	8	**1** F
	3? F		
9 ?BM T.94	**3?** BM	9	**10?** BM
			1? BM
10		10	**1?** BM
11		11	
12		12	**1** F

abbreviations: BM = British Museum   C = Cypriot Expedition (Dikaios)
SCE = Swedish Cypress Expedition   T = Tomb
F = French Expedition (Schaeffer)

Enkomi, and, not surprisingly, most marked vases in funerary contexts come from chamber tombs. Marked vases are not limited to this burial type; examples have also been found in ashlar-built tomb(s) and perhaps in two different tholoi.[34]

Multiple burials were the general practice, and in all cases where records are available, marked vases come from tombs with more than one interment. The number of burials varies tremendously, from a minimum of three to at least 55.

All graves with marked vases exhibit some degree of wealth (indicated by the presence of imports or objects of precious materials), but it is difficult to evaluate relative richness.[35] This may explain the lack of marked vases in the tombs excavated by Dikaios, which, with only two exceptions,[36] had few bodies and only a small number of associated finds. Half of Dikaios's tombs had been looted or emptied, but the other 14 were intact. The paucity and nature of finds in the latter presumably reflect low-status burials; the lack of marked vases in these tombs suggests that marked vases circulated (only?) in contexts of prosperity.

The other consistent characteristic among the tombs that contain marked vases is that almost every one is dated to the earlier phases of the Cypriot LBA, i.e., pre-LC IIIA (table 4).

To some degree, the last two observations discussed in the paragraphs above—the wealth and dating of the tombs with marked vases—rely on circular reasoning. In tombs most marks occur on the same Mycenaean vases that serve both as indicators of wealth and particularly as the primary chronological criterion for dating most of these tombs. However, the other objects associated with each funerary assemblage do provide some independent confirmation of both wealth and date.

More than two-thirds of the marked vases known to have been found in funerary contexts at Enkomi are Aegean.[37] This proportion may be artificially elevated because Mycenaean pottery traditionally has received much greater attention than the plain local wares. So, for example, the Mycenaean pottery recovered in the British tombs has been published in much more detail than the plain wares, which must have been found in much greater quantities than indicated by the occasional cursory mentions in the catalogues. The range of marked Mycenaean shapes includes open and closed, large and small varieties. Kraters,[38] piriform jars,[39] and many kinds of stirrup

Table 4. Chronology of tombs and tombs with marked vases at Enkomi.

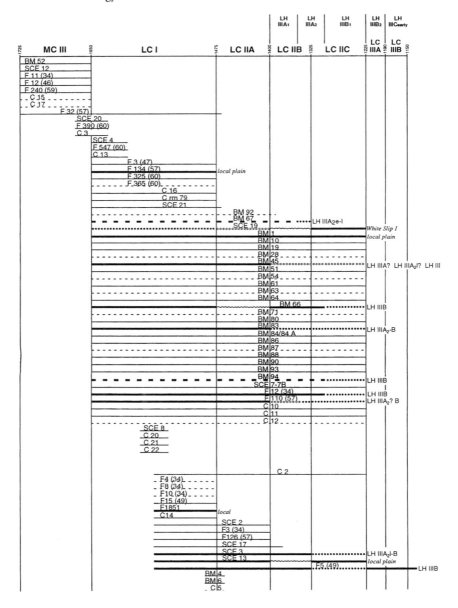

Table 4 continued on the following page

Table 4 *continued from the preceding page*

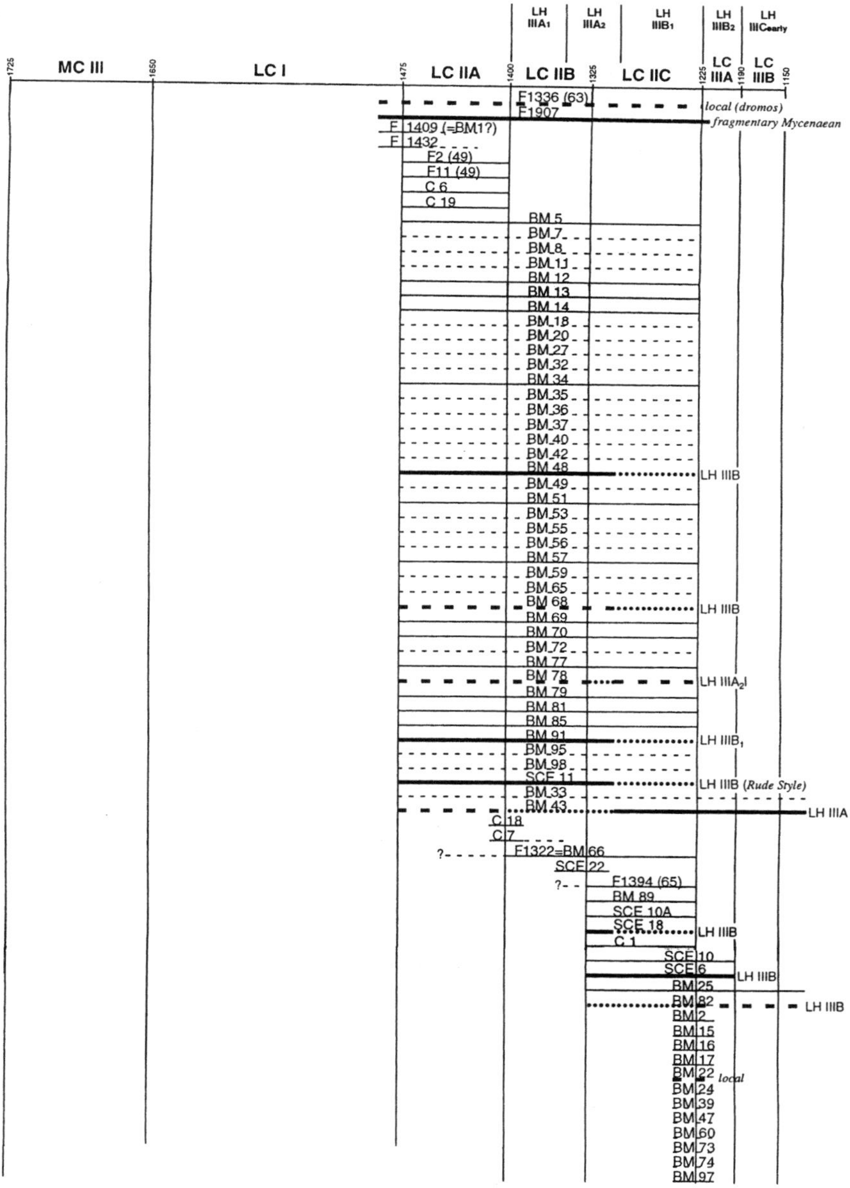

				LH IIIA₁	LH IIIA₂	LH IIIB₁	LH IIIB₂	LH IIICearly

Column headers across the chart (with date markers):

1725 — MC III — 1650 — LC I — 1475 — LC IIA — 1400 — LC IIB — 1325 — LC IIC — 1225 — LC IIIA — 1190 — LC IIIB — 1150

Entries (left to right, by period):

- F1336 (63) — *local (dromos)*
- F1907 — *fragmentary Mycenaean*
- F 1409 (=BM1?)
- F 1432
- F2 (49)
- F11 (49)
- C 6
- C 19
- BM 5
- BM 7
- BM 8
- BM 11
- BM 12
- BM 13
- BM 14
- BM 18
- BM 20
- BM 27
- BM 32
- BM 34
- BM 35
- BM 36
- BM 37
- BM 40
- BM 42
- BM 48 — LH IIIB
- BM 49
- BM 51
- BM 53
- BM 55
- BM 56
- BM 57
- BM 59
- BM 65
- BM 68 — LH IIIB
- BM 69
- BM 70
- BM 72
- BM 77
- BM 78 — LH IIIA₂-I
- BM 79
- BM 81
- BM 85
- BM 91 — LH IIIB₁
- BM 95
- BM 98
- SCE 11 — LH IIIB (*Rude Style*)
- BM 33
- BM 43 — LH IIIA
- C 18
- C 7
- ? F1322=BM 66
- SCE 22
- ? F1394 (65)
- BM 89
- SCE 10A
- SCE 18 — LH IIIB
- C 1
- SCE 10
- SCE 6 — LH IIIB
- BM 25
- BM 82 — LH IIIB
- BM 2
- BM 15
- BM 16
- BM 17
- BM 22 *local*
- BM 24
- BM 39
- BM 47
- BM 60
- BM 73
- BM 74
- BM 97

Table 4 continued on the following page

Table 4 *continued from the preceding page*

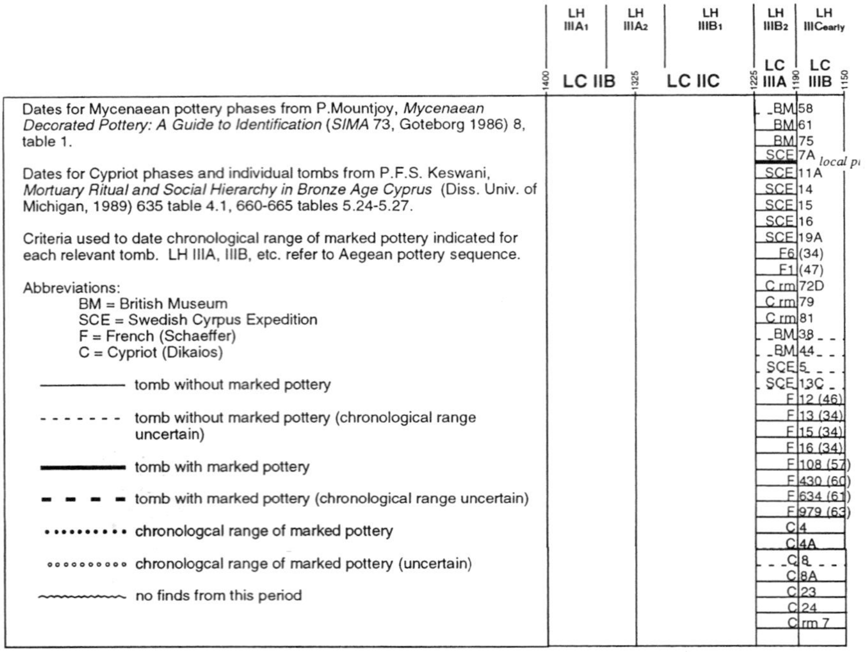

	LH IIIA1	LH IIIA2	LH IIIB1	LH IIIB2	LH IIICearly
	1400 LC IIB	1325 LC IIC	1225	LC IIIA 1190	LC IIIB 1150

Dates for Mycenaean pottery phases from P.Mountjoy, *Mycenaean Decorated Pottery: A Guide to Identification (SIMA 73, Goteborg 1986)* 8, table 1.

Dates for Cypriot phases and individual tombs from P.F.S. Keswani, *Mortuary Ritual and Social Hierarchy in Bronze Age Cyprus* (Diss. Univ. of Michigan, 1989) 635 table 4.1, 660-665 tables 5.24-5.27.

Criteria used to date chronological range of marked pottery indicated for each relevant tomb. LH IIIA, IIIB, etc. refer to Aegean pottery sequence.

Abbreviations:
    BM = British Museum
    SCE = Swedish Cyrpus Expedition
    F = French (Schaeffer)
    C = Cypriot (Dikaios)

————————— tomb without marked pottery

- - - - - - - tomb without marked pottery (chronological range uncertain)

━━━━━━━ tomb with marked pottery

━ ━ ━ ━ tomb with marked pottery (chronological range uncertain)

• • • • • • • • • chronologcal range of marked pottery

∘ ∘ ∘ ∘ ∘ ∘ ∘ ∘ ∘ chronologcal range of marked pottery (uncertain)

〜〜〜〜 no finds from this period

Right column tomb entries:

BM 58
BM 61
BM 75
SCE 7A *local pi*
SCE 11A
SCE 14
SCE 15
SCE 16
SCE 19A
F 6 (34)
F 1 (47)
C rm 72D
C rm 79
C rm 81
BM 38
BM 44
SCE 5
SCE 13C
F 12 (46)
F 13 (34)
F 15 (34)
F 16 (34)
F 108 (57)
F 430 (60)
F 634 (61)
F 979 (63)
C 4
C 4A
C 8
C 8A
C 23
C 24
C rm 7

jars[40] form the bulk of marked shapes. Others include shallow cups, jugs, a patera, a deep bowl, and possibly a flask. Except for a single large stirrup jar, all are fine ware. All are decorated. Motifs vary, from simple linear arrangements to elaborate pictorial representations.

Nineteen Cypriot vases carried marks. With two exceptions, these are all small to medium-sized jugs or jars.[41] Ten of the jugs are identified as Plain White Wheelmade ware, the standard LC plain fabric. An assortment of wares make up the rest of the jars: three Black Slip, one Monochrome, one Painted Wheelmade, and one Base-Ring.

The one class of vase conspicuously missing from the list of marked vases found in tombs is the amphora, often called a Canaanite jar (fig. 3). Marked amphoras, as will be seen below, form a significant proportion of the marked vases found in nonfunerary contexts. No amphoras at all, marked or unmarked, were noted in the tombs excavated by any of the expeditions.[42] Otherwise, the kinds of marked vases found in tombs do not differ significantly from the range of marked vases excavated in nonfunerary contexts at Enkomi.

A variety of marks is found on the vases from tombs. Many are the same as those on vases from nonfunerary contexts, but there exists also one class (the painted marks, discussed below) specific to tombs. One vase from the LBA tombs is marked by means of three holes drilled into the handle; all the other marked vases bear painted or incised signs. Most of these are applied or cut after firing, and most commonly they consist of a single mark only (fig. 1). The incised signs, whether single marks or multisign inscriptions, do not differ from the kinds of marks found in nonfunerary contexts except, of course, that the range of marks found on amphoras is missing from the tomb finds. Painted signs (fig. 2), however, are special to funerary deposits. Of 39 painted marks recovered from Enkomi, only 3 were found in nonfunerary contexts.[43] All the rest were recovered from tombs, and all of these occurred on Mycenaean vases. The connection between painted marks and Aegean vases is striking and will be discussed in further detail below. Here, in the discussion of findspots, it should be noted that since Aegean ceramics traditionally are given close attention, it is fair to assume that marks on Mycenaean vases were more likely than not to be noticed and recorded. The fact, therefore, that only one painted mark has been noted on the hundreds of Mycenaean vase fragments found in nonfunerary contexts reflects a real difference between funerary and nonfunerary deposits and suggests that painted marks somehow were connected directly with the deposit of these vases in tombs.

Thirteen of the 28 to 30 tombs in which marked vases were found contained more than one such vessel (table 5). With one exception, Swedish Tomb 18, which will be discussed separately (below), the number of marked vases found in any one tomb is limited to two or three. As can be seen in table 5, there are no consistent patterns of marking in the tomb assemblages: The number of marked vases bears no relation to the number of interments. The marked vases in any tomb differ in shape, decoration, and even fabric. The marks found in a particular tomb vary in shape and type (painted, incised; single, multiple) and placement; there is no repetition. In other words, there are no patterns in the marks found in a tomb, and thus there is no discernible evidence for an explicit connection between a particular mark and either individual burials or tomb groups as a whole.

The exception to this generalization is Swedish Tomb 18, whose unlooted contents included 16 vases marked with some consistency. It is worth examining this tomb's contents carefully, both because of the intrinsic importance

Table 5. Enkomi tombs containing multiple marked vases. Ø=no mark, NP=not preserved, P=painted, BF=before firing, PWWM=Plain White Wheelmade.

Enkomi BM tomb 22

#	handles	base	other	shape	decoration
97.4-1.878	⋈		≡ (rim)	PWWM I jug	none
97.4-1.879	⋇			PWWM I jug	none

Enkomi BM tomb 45

#	handles	base	other	shape	decoration
97.4-1.928		(mark) P		amphoroid krater (FS 54)	pictorial: warrior procession, vegetal, sphinxes
97.4-1.932	A ≠ ∅			amphoroid krater (FS 36)	double row of joining semicircles (FM 42) frames field above and below; dotted rosettes (FM 27, "sea anemone") in center

Enkomi BM tomb 48

#	handles	base	other	shape	decoration
97.4-1.967	⋔ ⊢			large fine stirrup jar (FS 164)	linear
97.4-1.970			⊢ body P	stirrup jar (FS 185)	concentric semicircles

Enkomi BM tomb 67

#	handles	base	other	shape	decoration
97.4-1.1088	∅ NP		⊳ ⊢⊳ interior rim P	amphoroid krater (FS 54)	floral
97.4-1.1089			Ψ Ψ body P	ring-based krater (FS 7)	zigzag (FM 61:15)

Enkomi BM tomb 68

#	handles	base	other	shape	decoration
1646			∧⋮V ⅡY body P	amphoroid krater (FS 55)	pictorial: chariot
1650	⧧ ⊢ NP			three-handled piriform jar (FS 36)	pendant scale pattern (FM 70)
1650b ?	≠ ∧ ⋇			three-handled piriform jar (FS 36)	pendant scale pattern (FM 70)

Enkomi BM tomb 83

#	handles	base	other	shape	decoration
97.4-1.1149			)⋋(≠ interior P	amphoroid krater	octopi
97.4-1.1162		(mark) P		small globular stirrup jar (FS 178)	flowers

Table 5 continued on the following page

of the evidence and because Persson's initial publication and interpretation of that evidence has played an important role in the study of potmarks and writing on LBA Cyprus.[44] In brief, Persson argues, based on the repeated appearance of specific combinations of signs on the vases from this tomb,

Table 5 *continued from the preceding page*

Enkomi SCE tomb 11 [21+ burials]

#	handles	base	other	shape	decoration
24	(marks)			three-handled piriform jar (FS 36)	pendant scale pattern (FM 70)
33		(mark) P		amphoroid krater (FS 54)	pictorial: chariot, vegetal, fish
115	+			monochrome jug with trefoil mouth	none
acc. 708		(mark) ??		deep bowl (FS 284)	vegetal

Enkomi SCE tomb 18, side chamber 1 [3? burials]

#	handles	base	body	shape	decoration
6	(marks)	(mark)		amphoroid krater (FS 55)	pictorial: bulls & birds
53	(marks)			large fine-ware stirrup jar (FS 164)	linear
48	(marks)			bell krater (FS 281)	panel decoration (FM 75) with U-pattern (FM 45); below the handles: bulls
31	(marks)			three-handled piriform jar (FS 36)	two rows of joining semicircles (FM 42:14) frame field above and below; half-rosettes (FM 74) in center
58	(marks)			three-handled piriform jar (FS 36)	vertical wavy lines (FM 53:32)
77	(marks) NP			three-handled piriform jar (FS 36)	single row of joining semicircles (FM 42) frames field above and below; dotted rosettes (FM 27, "sea anemone") in center
5	(marks)			jug (FS 110)	pictorial: single bull (filled with "T's", circles on hindquarters)
74	(marks)			jug (FS 110)	pictorial: two bulls (stars on neck, dot-rosettes and crossed ladders on hindquarters)
54	(marks)			large fine-ware stirrup jar (FS 164)	linear

Table 5 continued on the following page

that the sign groups refer to the names of the individuals buried here.[45] There is then, according to Persson's interpretation, a direct correlation between archaeological context (individual burials) and the marked vases. But the details and methodology of Persson's argument are not satisfactory,[46] and a re-examination of the evidence from Tomb 18 is in order.

The Swedish Cyprus Expedition excavated Tomb 18 in characteristically meticulous fashion. Plans, stratigraphy, and a complete list of finds were recorded and published.[47] The tomb is a typical LC example, with a dromos, stomion, main chamber, and two smaller subsidiary chambers. It was not looted. The stratification of the main chamber shows two different burial

Table 5 *continued from the preceding page*

#	handles	base	other	shape	decoration
55				large fine-ware stirrup jar (FS 164)	linear
47				rong-based krater (FS 281)	pictorial: water birds
57				three-handled piriform jar (FS 36)	horizontal wavy lines (FM 53)
19		P		three-handled piriform jar (FS 48)	quirk chain (FM 48)
26		P		small stirrup jar (FS 180)	multiple stem (FM 19)
45		P		ring-based krater (FS 281)	fish flanking panelled pattern (FM 75) with chequers (FM 56)
43		P		ring-based krater (FS 281)	heraldic goats(?) frame panelled pattern (FM 75) with chequers (FM 56)/alternate squares with diagonal cross-hatching
59		P	P	three-handled piriform jar (FS 40)	two rows of joining semicircles (FM 42:14) frame field above and below; horizontal wavy line (FM 53)

Enkomi SCE tomb 3 [15+ burials]

#	handles	base	other	shape	decoration
218				PWWM I jug	none
272				amphoroid krater (FS 54)	pictorial: chariot
?	NP			amphoroid krater (FS 54)	pictorial: chariot

Enkomi SCE tomb 6* [19+ burials]

#	handles	base	other	shape	decoration
48		P		patera (FS 250)	quirk frieze?
52		P		deep bowl (FS 284)	quirk frieze
77			rim	PWWM jug	none
?		P		small stirrup jar (FS 172?)	

*Present location of these objects unknown; not seen by NEH.

Table 5 continued on the following page

periods separated by a layer of fill, the lower one dating to LC IIC, the upper one to LC IIIA. Skeletons and associated finds were fairly well preserved for the upper burial, but only jumbled remains were found in the lower level. With regard to the lower deposit, the excavators mention one skull (possibly two), ribs, and a femur as well as 25 vases. Side Chamber 1 was evidently

Table 5 *continued from the preceding page*

Enkomi French tomb 1907E [24 burials]

#	handles			base	other	shape	decoration
20.229	⌐⌐E⌐	NP		NP	NP	krater?	
20.230	⊔⊔	NP	NP	NP	NP	three-handled piriform jar	
20.56	𝓧 (T/Λ)					PWWM I jug	none
20.199	X					Base Ring I pitcher	none

Enkomi French tomb 5 [55+ burials]

#	handles	base	other	shape	decoration
4.529		X, ? P		stirrup jar (FS 171)	linear; spiral on disk
5.199	⊢T			plain handmade jug with trefoil mouth	none

Enkomi French tomb 110 [3+ burials]

#	handles	base	other	shape	decoration
282			⟁⊥ interior P	shallow cup (FS 220)	stemmed lozenges (FM 73)
283			X interior P BF?	shallow cup (FS 220)	foliate band (FM 64)
267		P?		squat stirrup jar (FS 180)	multiple stem (FM 19)
266		P?		squat stirrup jar (FS 180)	linear
260		P?		horizontal flask (FS 191?)	linear
246		P?		three-handled piriform jar (FS 45)	foliate band (FM 64)
296	⊥I			Black Slip jug	
268	o o o BF			Black Slip jug	

used to house the remains of burials from the lower level of the main chamber that had been swept aside to make room for subsequent interments. Scattered fragments of about three skeletons were found in this chamber along with 70 "Levanto-Helladic" vases, 7 bronze bowls, 17 pieces of gold jewelry, 2 glass bottles, fragments of an ostrich egg, and only a handful of local ceramics. The high proportion of imports and general richness of this assemblage is noteworthy. The second side chamber was probably intended for the same use but for some reason never was used. In summary, the finds from Side Chamber 1 of Tomb 18 can be considered as a coherent, if scrambled, assemblage of bones and objects deposited as secondary interments. Whether those secondary burials were installed individually or deposited together as part of a general clearing operation is unclear. For this reason it is also not certain whether any of the vases recovered from the lower deposit of the main chamber might originally have been associated with burial groups transferred into Side Chamber 1.

None of the vases from the main chamber were marked in any way; of the 79 vases found in the side chamber, 16, that is, one-fifth, are marked (table 5). The proportion would be slightly less if the vases in the lower stratum of the main chamber should be considered part of the assemblage in the side chamber. The marked vases include a range of shapes: one large amphoroid krater, three bell kraters, three large fine-ware stirrup jars (FS 164) and one smaller squat version (FS 180), six piriform jars (three FS 36), two jugs. Two of the bell kraters, the two non-FS 36 piriform jars, and the small stirrup jar carry painted signs; all the others have incised signs on their handles or bases. There are no surprises here—the kind of mark (painted or incised) carried by each of these vase shapes conforms to general patterns. The individual marks, too, are not unusual in any way and parallels for all the completely preserved signs are easily found.

What is unusual, as Persson noted, is the repetition of certain signs and combinations of signs on many of the marked vases found in this tomb. Eleven of the 12 incised vases all have one sign in common, ‡. Most of these vases carry two-sign inscriptions, with the second sign being either a ⌐ or a ⸐. It is likely that FS 36 piriform jar no. 77 also fit into one of these categories[48] and that the inscription on the base of krater no. 47 consisted of only the two signs, ‡ ⸐.[49] One vase, FS 36 piriform jar no. 31 carries a third sign. In sum, almost all the vases in this tomb with incised marks fall into one of two categories of sign combinations, ‡ ⸐ or ‡ ⌐. There is one exception: FS 36 piriform jar no. 57, incised on all three handles with signs that are not found on any other vessel in this tomb.

It is possible that one of the vases with painted marks may also fit the pattern observed above. The mark painted on the base of piriform jar no. 59 is the one common to most of the incised vases, and Persson suggests that the painted version should be interpreted as serving the same function as its incised counterparts. Exciting as it is to think about the implications of that statement, it should also be remembered that the sign under consideration is very common in both the painted and incised potmark repertoires. Although it is seductive to view the sign painted on the base of no. 59 as related to the incised marks, it is equally possible that its co-occurrence is coincidental.

The four other painted marks (on vases nos. 19, 26, 43, and 45) are badly preserved and it is difficult to discern their forms. The traces that are still visible do not seem to match any of the signs common to the other vases from this tomb, nor do they appear to be similar to one another. Thus, these painted signs seem to be a collection of renegade singles, unrelated to each other or to the incised marks. This observation bolsters the argument that the sign painted on the base of no. 59 should be considered as unrelated to the incised marks found in this tomb.[50] It also removes the reason for suggesting that painted and incised marks had similar functions in the context of this tomb. The painted marks from Tomb 18 appear on a variety of shapes, variously decorated. There is no pattern among these painted marks or the vases on which they appear to suggest any specific connection with each other, or with vases marked by means of incised signs.

Persson suggests that there may be a connection between the incised marks and their funerary context. This reasoning is based partly on elimination: There is nothing about the signs or the vases upon which they are inscribed to suggest a reason for their repeated occurrence. Differences in the renderings of marks within each of the two sign groups indicate that neither sign combination can be associated exclusively with a single inscriber.[51] Neither are the sign groups associated with particular types of vessels; each occurs on a range of shapes, open and closed, variously decorated. The one feature common to all the vases in each sign group is their depositional context—the tomb. Persson suggests that each of the three sign groups (the third being the single example, no. 57) should be correlated with the three (preserved) burials in the tomb, and that the marks signify ownership.[52] The material from Tomb 18 fits this theory, but does not prove it. First, the evidence from the tomb is too fragmentary and jumbled to allow a certain correlation between number of sign-groups and number of interments, a correlation that would strongly support the identification of the incised signs as marks of ownership. Second, owners' marks do not form the only explanation that fits the evidence. It is possible, for example, that the marks indicate lots of vases sold or transported or bought and eventually deposited together. Thus, the same set of marks on very similar vases (nos. 5 and 74, or 54 and 55) may reflect the acquisition and movement of these vases in a group.

In summary, examination of all the possible variables among marks, vases, associated finds, burials, and tomb types reveals that the practices of marking vases and burying them in tombs are certainly connected only with reference to the painted marks. At Enkomi, painted marks are found almost exclusively on Mycenaean pottery deposited in tombs. A survey of all the ca. 115 vases with painted signs found on Cyprus corroborates the pattern noticed at Enkomi: with perhaps only half a dozen exceptions, all Mycenaean vases with painted marks whose context has been recorded[53] were found in tombs. The absence of painted marks in nonfunerary contexts cannot be explained by a lack of appropriate pottery found there. This pattern strongly suggests that painted marks are somehow associated with their funerary contexts.

Incised marks, on the other hand, are not exclusive to tombs and, with one exception, there are no indications that the reason(s) for incising marks was connected with their eventual deposit in tombs. The one exception (Swedish Tomb 18) should not be relegated to a footnote because its evidence, if further supported or somehow corroborated, would refute the preceding statement. At present, however, the evidence is inconclusive.

Other observations that can be made about tombs, funerary assemblages, and marked vases at Enkomi do not aid in elucidating the purpose(s) of the marks: all the tombs with marked vases contained multiple burials and relatively rich deposits of funerary goods. The tombs were of various types and scattered throughout the site. A wide range of marked ceramic types were found in the tombs, excepting amphoras, which were not present at all.

Finally, it should be noted that any possible connections between funerary context and marked vases were apparently severed in the transition from LC IIC to IIIA, after which the deposit of any marked vases in tombs ceased altogether.

Archaeological Contexts: Nonfunerary Deposits

Enkomi seemed an excellent site to test possible associations between marked vases and nonfunerary contexts because of the large areas and varied deposits (ritual, industrial, domestic, public, and private) excavated by the French and Cypriot missions. Incomplete publication and secondary contexts, however, have rendered the evidence less useful than had been hoped. (Published) records of Schaeffer's work are not complete and yield only limited contextual information for much of the material. Dikaios's complete and detailed report, on the other hand, provides a great deal of contextual information for nearly every marked piece. Unfortunately, most of the marked vase fragments were found in secondary contexts (between floors, in dumps, pits, and fill) and thus removed from the contexts to which the marks on the vases may have had relevance. Still, some observations about findspots can be made.

It has already been remarked that the kinds of marked vases found in tombs and in nonfunerary contexts differ (table 2) in that painted marks are particularly characteristic of the former while marked amphoras are found only in the latter. Local vases, of whatever types, marked in whatever way, are much more abundant in nonfunerary contexts than in burial deposits, but they are not unusual in the tombs. In general, the total number of marked vases found outside of tombs at Enkomi is about three times the number found associated with burials. But it is impossible to assess whether the relative proportion of marked to unmarked is greater in one type of context than the other because so much material has not been recorded.

Jacques-Claude Courtois spent many long hours helping me to locate—on Schaeffer's state plans and in the inventory notebooks—the findspots of as many marked vases recovered by the French as possible. Many proveniences could not be traced; other findspots have been located, but very little information is readily available concerning the associated remains, date, or function of the area. There is some obvious clustering of marked pottery in certain areas, notably the "maison aux couteaux" and "sondage XLI," but it is not possible to examine this in further detail because both contexts are unpublished and even the location of the latter is now unknown. The marked vases from those contexts display no consistency in kinds of marks or in types of vases marked.

Dikaios worked in Quartiers 1W and 4W, each area including a substantial building that housed domestic, industrial, public, and ritual spaces in the middle and later phases of the LBA. Figures 6.1–6.11 illustrate the distribution of marked vases and discoveries of traces of formal writing in each area, in each period. The relatively few marked vases found in primary contexts are noted specifically by means of underlining in the chart accompanying each map. It can be seen readily that the only clustering of marks occurs in certain periods, that is, chronologically (see below). Otherwise, the distribution of marked vases shows no patterns; they are found sporadically throughout the area uncovered, and there is no consistency in type of vase or kind of mark discovered in proximal areas. Examination of the findspots reveals no connection among marks, the vases on which they occur, and function of space.

The evidence from nonfunerary contexts at Enkomi suggests no strong correlations between nonfunerary context and marked vases or specific marks. However, this conclusion must be regarded as very tenuous. Most of the marked vases uncovered by Dikaios were found in secondary contexts; thus, whatever connection there may have been between mark and place of use of the vases is not reflected in the depositional record. There are hints of connections between findspots and some marked vases in Schaeffer's material, but unfortunately the information needed to examine this further is not available. The correlation between potmarks and archaeological contexts must be examined at other Late Cypriot sites. This process is currently under way.

Micro-Contexts: The Vases

The immediate context of the marks is the vases on which they appear. Significant correspondences between specific vase types and certain marks might suggest that the reason for marking was directly connected with the container itself, especially in the absence of correlations between mark and depositional context. Table 1 documents the marks in relationship to the types of vases on which they appear. The category labeled "local" includes all types of pottery traditionally recognized as Cypriot, that is, manufactured on the island. In fact, most of the marked local vases are plain and Plain White Wheelmade (semicoarse) jars; other kinds of local pottery are labeled specifically. As noted above, *amphoras* refer to the two-handled transport jars typical of the LBA eastern Mediterranean, often called Canaanite jars (fig. 3). Many Canaanite jars may actually have been produced on Cyprus.[54] Technically, this category overlaps the "local" column, but until closer study of these jars sorts out their various places of origin, here they are included in a single category whose criteria are a specific shape and function (transport/storage jar). The third category of vase types, Mycenaean, includes both the fine ware decorated vase types traditionally labeled Mycenaean as well as coarse ware (Minoan?) stirrup jars (figs. 1 and 2). Like the amphoras, Mycenaean pottery was produced in a number of regions, including locations outside the Aegean and perhaps even Cyprus itself. Thus, the "Aegean" and "local" columns are not necessarily entirely discrete in terms of place of origin of the vases. There is some overlap, also, in terms of function, between the Aegean large stirrup jars and the amphoras. However, for the most part, the kinds of Mycenaean vases that are marked are very different in shape (and function) from the local jugs and the amphoras.[55] Thus, although there are some inconsistencies in sorting vases into these particular categories, these designations do in general reflect basic differences not only in the origins of the vases, but also in their use.[56]

The central column of table 1 lists the known potmarks from vases found at Enkomi. The tremendous variety of signs and the lack of repetition is striking. No sign is found on large numbers of vases, the majority occur on fewer than five vases, and most signs appear on only one or two vases. Nevertheless, some patterns emerge.

Marks that can be associated certainly with the Cypro-Minoan script are found on local and Aegean vases only, never on amphoras. In fact, aside from the simple signs that cross all boundaries, it is apparent that, while there is some overlap between the signs appearing on local and Aegean vases, there is practically none between either of these categories and the amphoras.[57] These two observations lead to the hypothesis that, while marks on local and Aegean pottery may borrow from the Cypro-Minoan repertory, the marks on amphoras do not. Different marking systems were evidently in use on the different vase types.

RLWM spindle bottles, also found in LBA contexts at Enkomi, lend support to this hypothesis. These vases, distinctive in fabric and shape, are often marked, always in a singular fashion: small-scale, simple patterns of curved lines, short strokes and dots, drawn into the wet clay bases (fig. 4).[58] The consistent form and application of the marks makes it possible to speak of a marking system. Because the marks were made before firing and are inconspicuous in appearance and location, by ethnographic analogy[59] it is possible to suggest that these are truly potters' marks, somehow related to the manufacturing process. If indeed RLWM vessels were made and marked on Cyprus,[60] then their marks are further evidence that Cypriots had developed different marking systems for use in different ceramic contexts.

The observation that local and Aegean ceramics carried marks based on the Cypriot script while amphoras did not implies that those people marking the local and Aegean vases were accustomed to using the Cypro-Minoan script to keep track of objects, while amphora markers either were not familiar with Cypro-Minoan or chose not to use it. Somehow Aegean and local vases moved through similar channels or were used for similar purposes, while amphoras were accounted for differently.

The Cypro-Minoan-related marks must have been made by people familiar with the Cypro-Minoan script, very likely (although not absolutely necessarily) Cypriots. Non-Cypro-Minoan signs on amphoras, however, do not necessarily indicate non-Cypriot inscribers.

Conclusions

Potmark studies in LBA Cyprus have so far been one-dimensional in that they have concentrated almost exclusively on the identification of marks with signs of the formal script(s). This approach is doubly shortsighted. First, the repertoire of Cypro-Minoan signs is hardly known, and it is often difficult to ascertain whether or not any mark occurring in isolation indeed belongs to or was derived from the formal script. Even if one can be sure that a mark is indeed Cypro-Minoan, the script is not yet deciphered and the import of any one sign is unknown. Second, concentration on marks merely as writing ignores a wealth of other evidence pertaining to the function(s) and writers of these signs. Not only the form of the sign, but the manner of its application, its position on the vase, the kinds of vases on which it appears, its chronological and depositional context, and its distribution by site and region are all clues to the reasons vases were marked.

Of course, the connection between mark and script is important, and it is certain that at least some of the marks are based on Cypro-Minoan signs. At present, because the Cypro-Minoan script is undeciphered and its structure poorly understood, it is not immediately possible to use the script to understand the meaning of the marks. Nevertheless, examination of the placement of the potmarks that also appear in formal texts may yield significant information. If, for instance, such marks commonly appear as initial signs or perhaps ideograms in the texts, this would suggest a definite relationship (rather than haphazard borrowing) between potmarks and writing. An analysis of the appearance and function of potmark signs in the Cypro-Minoan texts is currently in progress.

However, even now, the simple observation of some sort of connection with Cypro-Minoan can be taken further by looking more closely at the marks themselves and the vases on which they occur. When marks are looked at in conjunction with the types of vases on which they appear, then it becomes clear that, while (some of) the signs on Aegean pottery and on local plain wares are based on Cypro-Minoan signs, there appears to be no connection between the Cypriot script and the marks on the amphoras. It should be emphasized that this conclusion is based on a pattern of marking that is suggestive but certainly not conclusive. As it stands, the implication is that marks based on different sign repertories were used on different sorts of pottery.

An obvious example of a close association between a recognizable group of marks and a specific category of ceramic vases is provided by the RLWM spindle bottles. Here, the consistent form and application of the marks makes it possible to speak of a marking system.

Consistencies in the marks incised on local plain ware jugs and imported Aegean vases (fig. 1) suggest that these two wares may share a common marking system. The repertoires of incised marks on local and Mycenaean vases overlap. Both incorporated at least some Cypro-Minoan signs. The signs on both kinds of vases also have in common that they were generally incised after firing and that they were intended to be seen (as evidenced by their large scale and prominent positioning on handles). All this suggests that the reason(s) for marking Mycenaean imports was somehow closely linked with the reason(s) for marking local wares.

The signs incised into amphora handles exhibit the same features of application described above: they are also incised after firing and are highly visible because of their large size and prominent locations (fig. 3). The repertoire of signs incised on amphoras differs significantly from those on the local and Mycenaean vases, however, and therefore, at this point, the amphoras cannot be included in the same marking system.

Finally, the painted marks that appear on Mycenaean pottery constitute another marking system (fig. 2). The repertoire of painted marks overlaps extensively with that of the incised local/Mycenaean marks, and the painted marks were added similarly after firing. However, their application is very different in two important respects: they are painted rather than incised, and immediate visibility (on a properly stanced pot) was not the primary criterion in the positioning of the painted signs. Painted marks, although large-scale and therefore quite obvious if looked for, generally appear under the base, occasionally on the interior wall of the vase, and only exceptionally on the exterior lower body.

Thus, four different marking systems are exhibited on the vases found at Enkomi: (1) prefiring marks on RLWM spindle bottles; (2) postfiring incised marks on the handles of local plain wares, mainly jugs and jars, and

Mycenaean pottery; (3) postfiring incised marks on amphoras; and (4) post-firing painted marks on Mycenaean pottery. Only two of these marking sys-tems—the incised marks on local and Mycenaean vases and the painted marks on Mycenaean pottery—exhibit any connection with the signs in Cypro-Minoan script.

The use of different systems may reflect different people making the marks or different functions for the marks. Because the signs, isolated and with undeciphered values, cannot be read, the clues to their meaning must be sought in the differing patterns of occurrence of the marks on vases and the marked vases in the archaeological record. The fact that the incised marks, except for those on RLWM spindle bottles, were cut after firing sug-gests that they were not made by the potter, who had the much easier option of incising into unfired malleable clay. The blatant positioning of the post-firing marks on the handles of vases indicates that they were intended to be highly visible. Beyond this, there are almost no other patterns to indicate any particular function for the marks: there are no consistent correspondences between any particular mark and specific vase shapes or decoration, con-tainer sizes, or general or specific archaeological contexts. Thus, the incised marks on these vases do not seem to be related to workshop, volume, own-ership, or the function of any area in which they were found. The few con-sistencies among these incised marks (postfiring, highly visible) and the variability with respect to all other features of the vases and their depositional contexts are the only clues to the meaning(s) of the marks. One explanation that satisfies all these observations is that the marks were made by individ-uals handling these vases, in the process of trade, exchange, or deposit.[61] There is no reason to think that the Cypro-Minoan-based marks on local plain ware vases were made by anyone but Cypriots. Since the incised marks on Mycenaean vases fit into this same system, the inference is that those marks were also made by Cypriots.

The marks on amphoras belong to a system that differs from the local/Mycenaean system in terms of the repertoire of signs but shares the other features of application (postfiring, highly visible) and the lack of any discernible patterns of depositional contexts. It is not yet clear whether the differences in sign types reflect different reasons for marking or different people making the marks. The shared characteristics of the two marking sys-tems suggest that the function of the marks may have been the same. The simplest explanation for the difference in repertoires is that different people were marking the amphoras.[62] The only sure statement that can be made is that the marking of some Mycenaean imports was closely linked with local Cypriot marking practices, while the marking of amphoras differed somewhat. The significance of those differences cannot yet be pinpointed.

The fourth marking system in evidence at LBA Enkomi is the painted marks. The application of the painted marks is limited and consistent: the marks are painted after firing, on the bases, lower bodies, and interiors of Mycenaean vases.[63] Several of the marks are definitely Cypro-Minoan signs, and many others may be. In general, the painted marks fall into the same sign repertoire as the local/Mycenaean incised signs. Thus the painted marks share the features of repertoire and postfiring application with the marks incised on local and Mycenaean vases. Other features, however, are different, including the use of paint, the positioning of the signs in less obvious places on the vase,[64] and the restriction to Mycenaean vases only. Again, while these characteristics distinguish the vases with painted marks from the groups of vases with incised marks, they do not provide enough evidence to indicate whether the differences in marking are due to different people making the marks or to different functions for these marks. In this case archaeological context does provide an important clue. Almost all vases with postfiring painted marks whose depositional context can be determined were found in tombs. This holds true not only for Enkomi, but also for the rest of Cyprus. It seems, therefore, that the painted marks somehow are connected specifically with the deposit of Mycenaean vases in burials.

Marks appear on vases on Cyprus throughout, before, and after the LBA period at Enkomi. As with ceramic features such as shape, fabric, and manner of decoration, the way in which a pot was marked varied through time and space. It is possible, in many cases, to ascertain the date and orbit of a vase from the form and application of its mark. LBA potmarks found at Enkomi exhibit a distinctive shift from the simple, mostly prefiring, dots and slashes marking Early and Middle Cypriot pottery[65] to more complex signs. This change coincides roughly with the first appearances of writing on Cyprus in the LC I period, and it may be that these two events are related.[66]

Potmarks at Enkomi are most numerous and diverse in LC IIC–IIIA, which are also the periods corresponding to the floruit of formal writing at the site. Thus, the connection between writing and the appearance of complex potmarking systems holds true. But there are marked changes in other aspects of life at Enkomi during the course of these two eras, including substantial changes in the town planning, architecture, and material assemblages, and the arrival of significant numbers of Aegean immigrants. A fall-off of trade with the now-devastated mainland centers is also apparent. The cessation of Aegean imports means, of course, the disappearance of the marks painted and incised on this pottery. The vacuum in Aegean luxury wares is filled by local production of vases in the tradition of the earlier imports (White Painted Wheelmade III, i.e., so-called Mycenaean IIIC, Rude/Pastoral style, Late Mycenaean IIIB, decorated LC III, etc.). The change does not, of course, happen suddenly or cleanly, and it is often difficult to determine whether a vase is a local production or import, especially in the LC IIC period, when both are present. This complicates the very important question of how the new production venues affected the way in which Mycenaean vases were marked. Without doubt, there is a change: marks on identifiable local Mycenaean are extremely rare, and those few exceptions are very different in form and nature from the marks boldly painted and incised on the Late Helladic/Late Minoan (Mycenean) IIIA–B imports. Clearly, therefore, the reasons for marking the Aegean imports did not apply to (most of) the local imitative productions. This supports the hypothesis that the prominently incised marks on Aegean vases were somehow connected with their import into the island, since local production and circulation marked the demise of this marking system. It also indicates that the association of painted marks and funerary contexts seems to have been specific to Mycenaean vases. Clearly, the changes associated with the local manufacture of Mycenaean pottery are very significant to understanding the reasons for marking pottery both before and after the LC IIC/IIIA transition. Partially due to the inadequate publication of the much of the material, partially due to the author's initial lack of expertise in examining the rest, this question has not here been given the thorough treatment that it merits. But efforts are under way to redress this fault by means of extensive investigation of the evidence yielded at Hala Sultan Tekke, another major LBA site on the southern coast of Cyprus. Here, both potmarks and the distinction between Aegean imports and locally made pottery of Aegean type have been subjects of keen interest to the excavators; thus the evidence relevant to this line of questioning is accessible.

The changes observed in the marking of Aegean and Aegean-type vases do not occur among the amphoras and traditional local vases. These both continue to be marked with no substantive changes detectable between LC IIC and IIIA and are found in plenty throughout the later period. If the suggestion that marks were connected with trade of the vases is valid, the fact that the same marking practices continue on amphoras and local plain wares suggests that IIC/IIIA disruption did not alter organization/administration of trade within Cyprus, and, if amphoras were marked in the importing process, between Cyprus and its eastern neighbors.

The absence of marked vases from funerary contexts is the one universal change detectable in the transition from LC II to III. The disappearance of marked Mycenaean pottery in funerary contexts is due to external circumstances—the halt in production and import of the traditionally marked vase types. But the disappearance of marked local pottery in tombs cannot be similarly explained. The number of marked local vessels deposited in tombs was always relatively small, and so this drop-off seems a subtle change. The large number of LC IIIA and IIIB tombs—all without marked vases—makes clear that this change is not a matter of archaeological happenstance (table 4). Whether and in what way the absence of marked local pottery in tombs is related to the disappearance of marked Aegean vases is unknown.

The floruit of potmarks (LC IIC–IIIA) coincides with that of formal writing—at least as far as can be ascertained from the numbers of inscriptions preserved in the archaeological record. Traces of writing continue to be found in later (LC IIIB) contexts, though in much smaller numbers, many of these perhaps misplaced holdovers from the previous period. Potmarks, too, continue to appear, also in decreased numbers. Dikaios points to the number of potmarks as evidence of continued literacy, but, as we have seen, marks cannot be indiscriminately equated with script signs. In fact, the majority of marks found in LC IIIB contexts occur on amphora handles—the ceramic type whose associated marking system(s) has no demonstrable connections with formal writing on Cyprus or anywhere else. If one discounts the potmarks, the evidence for writing in LC IIIB is very meager. The fall-off of the knowledge/use of formal writing on Cyprus may have been much more sudden than Dikaios's tally suggests.

All of these hypotheses can be and are being tested with the examination of potmarking practices at other LBA sites on and outside of Cyprus. Whether or not all the patterns observed at Enkomi hold true elsewhere, I can already state with confidence that one does, and that is the generosity with which excavators have shared material and knowledge. I continue to bump into the spirit of Olivier Masson and Jacques-Claude Courtois.[i]

NOTES

[1] Among the earliest reports: A.S. Murray, "Excavations at Enkomi," in A.S. Murray, A.H. Smith, and H.B. Walters, *Excavations in Cyprus* (London 1900; reprint 1969) 1–54; M. Markides, *Cyprus: Annual Report of the Curator of Antiquities, 1916* (Nicosia 1917) 16–20.

[2] S. Casson, "The Cypriot Script," *Ancient Cyprus: Its Art and Archaeology* (London 1937) 72–109; J.F. Daniel, "Prolegomena to the Cypro-Minoan Script," *AJA* 45 (1941) 249–82; O. Masson, "Répertoire des inscriptions chypro-minoennes," *Minos* 5 (1957) 19–27. E. Masson includes potmarks in her sign lists, which currently serve as the standard reference, published in *Cyprominoica: Répertoires, documents de Ras Shamra, essais d'interprétation* (*SIMA* 31:2, Göteborg 1974) 12–15 figs. 1–4, but does not discuss the potmarks per se.

[3] O. Masson (supra n. 2).

[4] My gratitude also to Jacques-Claude and Elisabeth Lagarce, who have allowed me to continue unhindered the work begun with J.-C. Courtois, and to the officials in the Cyprus Museum: Dr. Demos Christou, past director; Dr. Pavlos Flourentzos, curator of antiquities; and Mr. Gregoris Christou. My work in the Enkomi storerooms of the Cyprus Museum in Nicosia was generously funded by the Mellon 1984 Foundation and Fulbright Commission. Finally, I am tremendously grateful to Joanna S. Smith and Susan Sherratt for taking time to read my thoughts carefully and comment extensively and perceptively. The shortcomings of this paper can only be attributed to me.

[5] Murray (supra n. 1) 9, 27.

[6] A.W. Persson, "Appendix I: More Cypro-Minoan Inscriptions," in E. Gjerstad, J. Lindros, E. Sjöqvist, and A. Westholm, *SwCyprusExp* III, 601–618.

[7] P. Dikaios, "Appendix V: The Cypro-Minoan Inscriptions," in P. Dikaios, *Enkomi: Excavations 1948–1958,* volume II (Mainz am Rhein 1971) 881–91.

[8] C. F.-A. Schaeffer, *Missions en Chypre, 1932–1935* (Paris 1936) 76.

[9] Schaeffer (supra n. 8) 76–79, Appendice I, 119–21.

[10] Schaeffer's argument is based in large part on his supposition that the painted marks were applied *before* firing and, therefore, that they were indicators of where the vases were made. But I believe it is more likely that the painted marks were applied *after* firing, and so could have been applied at any point after a vase's firing until its final deposition. My assessment is based on the following observations: The paint of the marks is always obviously different in hue, luster, and density from the paint used to decorate the vases. There are a few vases where the painted mark and the painted decoration overlap; in these cases, it is apparent that the mark extends over the decoration. This at least shows that the mark was painted after the decoration had dried, and that the two did not meld, as might be expected if the pot was fired after the mark had been applied. Finally, the painted signs are generally faint or even fugitive—as if the paint was never truly fixed and therefore relatively easily rubbed off. These are admittedly subjective arguments; until one or some of the painted marks can be scientifically analyzed, the important question of whether the painted marks were applied before or after firing cannot be answered definitively.

[11] In 1941 J.F. Daniel (supra n. 2) 252 laid out systematic criteria by which to evaluate

whether a potmark might be identified as Cypro-Minoan. Very few subsequent publications have heeded those suggestions or explicitly established alternative guidelines.

[12] Estimates for the size of Enkomi appear in R.S. Merrillees, "The Government of Cyprus in the Late Bronze Age," in P. Åström ed., *Acta Cypria: Acts of an International Congress on Cypriote Archaeology Held in Göteborg on 22–24 August 1991, pt. 3* (*SIMA-PB* 120, Jonsered 1992) 328 and O. Negbi, "The Climax of Urban Development in Bronze Age Cyprus," *RDAC* 1986, 101.

Illustrations (drawings and photographs) and catalogue entries for every potmark known from Enkomi will soon be available on an electronic database, reached via a link with the Program in Aegean Scripts and Prehistory of the Department of Classics at the University of Texas at Austin (http://www.utexas.edu/research/pasp).

[13] Murray (supra n. 1) esp. 51–54; H.B. Walters, *Catalogue of the Greek and Etruscan Vases in the British Museum, volume I, pt. II: Cypriote, Italian, and Etruscan Pottery* (London 1912) passim; J.L. Myres and M. Ohnefalsch-Richter, *A Catalogue of the Cyprus Museum* (Oxford 1899) 183–86.

[14] Indication that the potmarks listed in Myres and Ohnefalsch-Richter (supra n. 13) are an incomplete corpus is found in the many potmarks, previously unnoted, among the Enkomi material published by V. Karageorghis in *CVA Cyprus 1 Cyprus Museum 1* (Nicosia 1963) fig. 3 and passim.

[15] "Mycenaean" here refers to any vase made in the tradition of the fine, decorated wares characteristic of the Late Helladic IIIA–B period in the Argolid.

[16] *SwCyprusExp* I, 467–575, pls. LXXVI–XCII.

[17] V. Karageorghis, "Supplementary Notes on the Mycenaean Vases from the Swedish Tombs at Enkomi," *OpAth* 3 (1960) 135–53; P. Åström, "Supplementary Material from Ayios Iakovos Tomb 8, with a Note on the Terminal Date of Mycenaean IIIA:2 late," *OpAth* 4 (1962) 207–224; E. Mossberg, "Sherds from Enkomi Tomb 5 and Ayios Iakovos Tombs 3 and 5," *OpAth* 11 (1975) 119–28; K. Andersson, "Supplementary Material from Enkomi Tombs 3, 7, 11 and 18 s.c.," *MedMusB* 15 (1980) 25–40; E.T. Skage, "Supplementary Sherds from Ayios Jakovos Tomb 9, Dromos," *OpAth* 20 (1994) 211–20.

[18] Bibliography collected in J.-C. Courtois, J. Lagarce, and E. Lagarce, *Enkomi et le Bronze Récent à Chypre* (Nicosia 1986) xiii–xvi, to which should be added J.-C. Courtois and J.M. Webb, *Les cylindres-sceaux d'Enkomi* (Nicosia 1987); A. Caubet, J.-C. Courtois, and V. Karageorghis, "Enkomi (Fouilles Schaeffer 1934–1966): Inventaire Complémentaire," *RDAC* 1987, 23–48; J.-C. Courtois, "Enkomi (Fouilles Schaeffer 1934–1966): Inventaire Complémentaire (Suite): Les Objets en terre cuite et en pierre," *RDAC* 1988 pt. 1, 307–318; J.-C. Courtois, "La Céramique de la tombe 501 d'Enkomi 1950 du Chypriote Récent IIIA," *RDAC* 1988 pt. 1, 301–305; V. Karageorghis, "Kypriaka XI: A. Late Bronze Age Material from Enkomi," *RDAC* 1988 pt. 1, 331–32.

[19] Many of these had already been noted in an unpublished manuscript compiled and shared with me by Courtois, titled "Corpus céramique d'Enkomi" (n.d.).

[20] Schaeffer (supra n. 8); "Sur un cratère mycénien de Ras Shamra," *BSA* 37 (1936–1937) 212–35. Relevant to this point, Joanna Smith reminded me that Schaeffer's personal library, particularly strong in reference to scripts and seals, especially of the Bronze Age, is

indicative of the original owner's interest in these subjects. Schaeffer's library is now incorporated into and available for use in the holdings of the Cyprus American Archaeological Research Institute (CAARI).

[21] Dikaios (supra n. 7).

[22] For example, Rochester Memorial Art Gallery 51.204; most recently published in E. Rystedt, "New Light on a Mycenaean Pictorial Vase Painter," *MedMusB* 23 (1988) 21–32 passim, fig. 8.

[23] This impression of the relative scarcity of marked vases is further confirmed by recent excavations at numerous other LBA Cypriot sites, where there has been both careful control and an interest in identifying writing and marks on vases.

[24] "A group of at least two signs" is an accepted definition of an "inscription" among some scholars of Aegean scripts; see, for example, J.-C. Poursat, L. Godart, and J.-P. Olivier, *Fouilles exécutées à Mallia: Le Quartier Mu I: Introduction générale, écriture hiéroglyphique crétoise* (*EtCret* 23, Paris 1978) 34. Almost all the inscriptions were incised *before firing* on plain jars of *local* manufacture and can therefore provisionally be classified as examples of the local script, Cypro-Minoan.

[25] Dikaios 2389/16, published in P. Dikaios, *Enkomi: Excavations 1948–1958*, volume IIIa (Mainz am Rhein 1969) 627, pl. 126:53; Schaeffer 1958/216 and Schaeffer 1961/13 are unpublished amphora handles with impressed marks.

[26] Other contemporary LBA marking systems include, for example, those on ingots, masonry, and metal tools. Systematic study of marks in these media, especially the ingot marks [P. Sibella, "The Copper Oxhide and Bun Ingots," *INA Quarterly* 23.1 (Spring 1996) 9–11] is in various stages of completion, and so the far left column in table 1 in future publications could eventually include more parallels. Also still in progress is the full identification of comparanda from other writing systems—Minoan Linear A, Old Canaanite, and other Proto-alphabetic scripts. Preliminary (extensive, but not exhaustive) examinations of these scripts provide no contradictions to the conclusions mentioned in this essay.

[27] See the comments in the text above, in the introductory remarks.

[28] The potmarks that I regard as certainly Cypro-Minoan are those corresponding to CM no. 26, 27, 31, and 87. The potmarks identified with CM no. 25 and with $\mathcal{N}$ should also probably be added to this list.

[29] The repertoire of Cypro-Minoan signs is as yet poorly understood. At present, "Cypro-Minoan" is essentially a catchall phrase used to refer to any trace of LBA writing on Cyprus, including potmarks. The sign lists generally cited (E. Masson, supra n. 2) represent a substantial beginning but are neither accurate nor complete. No Cypriot archives have yet been uncovered; our understanding of the LBA script(s) used on Cyprus is based on sporadic finds of inscriptions on a variety of media on an assortment of objects found in all parts of the island. The sign lists represent a somewhat indiscriminate and largely undocumented compilation of signs from all of these sources. Inaccurate and scattered publication of the inscriptions and objects prevents independent evaluation of the repertoire(s) of Cypro-Minoan signs and writing practices. Each new discovery adds to the repertoire. (See, for example the recent discoveries at Kalavasos-*Ayios Dhimitrios*, first published by E. Masson, "Premiers documents chypro-minoens du site Kalavasos-*Ayios*

Dhimitrios," *RDAC* 1983, 131–41, and "Vestiges écrits trouvés sur le site de Kalavasos-*Ayios Dhimitrios,*" in A. South, P. Russell, and P.S. Keswani, *Kalavasos-*Ayios Dhimitrios II: *Ceramics, Objects, Tombs, Specialist Studies* [*SIMA* 71:3, Göteborg 1989] 38–40, figs. 60–63, pl. XIII, and now being restudied by J.S. Smith, "Cypro-Minoan Inscriptions," in A. South, *Vasilikos Valley Project* 5: *Kalavasos-*Ayios Dhimitrios IV: *The North-East Area* [*SIMA* 71:5, Jonsered forthcoming]). Several unpublished local handles among Schaeffer's finds from Enkomi include multiple sign inscriptions; many of these were incised before firing on local LBA vases and presumably should be incorporated into the Cypro-Minoan corpus. The author and J.S. Smith are presently studying Cypro-Minoan inscriptions to facilitate meaningful study of the script(s) in use on LBA Cyprus.

For the purposes of this paper the existing sign lists are used. In spite of the problems discussed above, because Masson's lists have been derived mainly from a few long inscriptions found at Enkomi and contemporary with the bulk of the potmarks from the site, they are appropriate sources from which to establish at least a provisory impression of the relation between potmarks and script in use at LBA Enkomi. Signs not included in these lists, but attested on multisign inscriptions on local pottery and therefore presumably Cypro-Minoan, are marked with an asterisk(*) in table 1.

[30] The relative complexity of a mark is, of course, a subjective judgment. In my opinion, the only potmark that is both identified with a Linear B sign and is relatively complex is the one associated with LB "ke" or "de" as well as CM 107. The fact that two different Linear B equations are proposed underscores the tenuous nature of this identification. There are three potmarks for which Linear B—but not Cypro-Minoan—equivalents can be suggested: the marks identified with Linear B "ka," "e," and "je." I do not think that any of these equations are compelling. All three are simple signs and so resemblances may easily be attributed to coincidence. The identification of the latter two are particularly questionable because of difference in form between potmark and proposed equivalent. In fact, the tang added to one leg of the X of the last-mentioned sign is more likely to be indicative of Cypro-Minoan.

[31] Murray (supra n. 1), Walters (supra n. 13).

[32] Schaeffer (supra n. 8) 119–21, and Karageorghis (supra n. 14).

[33] N.B.: This table includes only those tombs whose locations could be determined. The work of P.F.S. Keswani (*Mortuary Ritual and Social Hierarchy in Bronze Age Cyprus* [(Diss. Univ. of Michigan 1989]) was of tremendous help in sorting out data pertaining to the locations, contents, and dating of the Enkomi tombs.

[34] Ashlar tombs with marked vases: BM T.66: Murray (supra n. 1) 5, fig. 5 (plan and sections), 18, fig. 34, 22–24 passim, 35, fig. 63, 36, fig. 64, 43, pls. IV and IX, tomb location identified on map, 30; Courtois, Lagarce, and Lagarce (supra n. 18) 42; P. Åström, "Some Pot-marks from the Late Bronze Age found in Cyprus and Egypt," *SMEA* 4 (1967) 9, no. 4; and Walters (supra n. 13) 122; Fr. T.1409 (in dromos, possibly not from within tomb): Courtois, Lagarce, and Lagarce (supra n. 18) 42, marked vase, unpublished; tholoi: BM T.48 (or rubble-lined?): Murray (supra n. 1) 8, fig. 14, 45, fig. 71, no. 927, 47, 48, fig. 73, 52, tomb location indicated on map, 30; Courtois, Lagarce, and Lagarce (supra n. 18) 45, marked vases from BM T. 48: O. Masson (supra n. 2) 20, no. 202; Persson (supra

n. 6) 607; Casson (supra n. 2) 99 (10b), 102 (27); A.H. Smith in *CVA Great Britain* 1 *British Museum (Department of Greek and Roman Antiquities)* 1 (London 1925) 5, 7, Group IIcb, pls. 3.35, 6.10; Walters (supra n. 13) 103, 107; Murray (supra n. 1) 48, fig. 73, nos. 967, 970; P. Åström, "Some Pot-marks from the Late Bronze Age found in Cyprus and Egypt," *SMEA* 4 (1967) 9, no. 5, fig. 7; A. Furumark, *The Mycenaean Pottery: Analysis and Classification* (Stockholm 1941) 615 (FS 185:12); ?Fr. T.1336 (in dromos): W. Johnstone, "A Late Bronze Age Tholos Tomb at Enkomi," in C. F.-A. Shaeffer, *Alasia I* (1971) 80, fig. 18, 111 (D32). A handle with a multisign inscription comes from shaft grave *SwCyprusExp* I, T.7A.

[35] Inadequate documentation of finds and bone counts, looting, and confusion caused by multiple interments makes it difficult to evaluate relative wealth among the burials and tombs, but cf. P.S. Keswani, "Dimensions of Social Hierarchy in Late Bronze Age Cyprus: an Analysis of the Mortuary Data from Enkomi," *JMA* 2/1 (1989) 49–86.

[36] Cypriot T.2 and T.10 in P. Dikaios, *Enkomi: Excavations 1948–1958,* volume I (Mainz am Rhein 1969) 336–47, 357–94.

[37] Out of a total of 75 marked vases found in tombs at Enkomi, 56 are Aegean.

[38] 12 amphoroid and 7 (including one "Rude Style") ring-based.

[39] 13, including one example where the existence of a painted mark is disputable.

[40] Eight small (various types, including one possibly Minoan, and two examples where the existence of painted marks is disputable), five large fine ware, and one large coarseware (Minoan?).

[41] The exceptions are a White Slip bowl (*SwCyprusExp* T.19/146) and an unpublished white shaved juglet handle (Schaeffer 1958/IV-241).

[42] I do not regard the context of handle fragment Dikaios 2199 (Dikaios (supra n. 25) 654, 889, pl. 315:26) found "in debris filling tomb 19" as secure.

[43] With one exception (amphora Dikaios 718/7, see Dikaios (supra n. 25) 596, pls. 77:23, 125:4), painted marks at Enkomi are associated exclusively with Aegean vases. The amphora was found in a nonfunerary context. Perhaps only 2 of the 38 Aegean vases with postfiring painted signs were found deposited in nonfunerary contexts at Enkomi: (1) Schaeffer 1960/C646, an unpublished Mycenaean krater base, was definitely found in a nonfunerary context; its topographical findspot has been noted, but further details about its context are lost; (2) a small Mycenaean closed vessel (Schaeffer 1959/ C334, also unpublished) with a mark painted on its base was recovered from a building which housed industrial, ritual, and domestic spaces; (3) Dikaios 2661/11 (Dikaios (supra n. 25) 580, pl. 69:8) also definitely comes from occupational debris, but its mark is prefiring and therefore probably related to the vessel's manufacture rather than its place of deposition. The findspots of (4) an amphoroid krater handle (H. Catling, "Unpublished Finds from Cyprus (I) Graffiti in the Late Cypriot Linear Script (II) Imported Greek Pottery at Chytroi," *RDAC* 1988 pt. 1, 326 no. 5, 327 fig. 1:5, pl. XLIV:5) picked up by the Cyprus Survey and (5) a vase recorded by S. Casson ([supra n. 25] 102 [27e]) are unknown. Finally, (6) a fairly complete vessel now in the Rochester Art Gallery (51.204, supra n. 22) may or may not have come from Enkomi—its condition suggests that it was probably looted from a tomb.

[44] Persson (supra n. 6).

[45] Persson (supra n. 6) 613.

[46] The starting point for Persson's interpretation of the marks on the vases in Tomb 18 is a general argument that the signs on handles and bases of vases refer to the owner. He arrives at the generalization that the marks refer to names by eliminating other possibilities (potters' marks, marks of dedication, references to contents); the hypothesis that they refer to the owner in particular is grounded in analogy to a Cypriot Syllabic example but is also based on the pattern of finds from Tomb 18 (pp. 611–12). It is, therefore, somewhat circular reasoning to then use this hypothesis to explain the function of the marks in Tomb 18.

Persson postulates that the inscriptions on 12 of the 14 marked vases found in Tomb 18 may all be related to a long inscription on the base of krater no. 47. Persson sees four signs on the ring of this base: three grouped together separated by a punctuation point from a fourth (p. 602 no. 12a); he also notes a fifth sign in the base's central portion (p. 602 no. 12b). Persson's discussion is accompanied by an excellent photograph of this base (p. 614 fig. 318), but it is difficult to see anything beyond the first and last signs of his sequence. Looking for traces to confirm the author's reading, it is perhaps possible to interpret some very vague marks or scratches close to the first sign as representing the middle signs of Persson's sequence. If so, the spacing is very strange, with the first three signs closely packed together and then big blank spaces between those and the isolated sign. I can see no trace in the photograph of the separation marker that Persson transcribed. The inscription would also be unique in that it consists of more than two signs, which is the maximum on all other bases with incised or painted signs. Unfortunately, it is now impossible to confirm Persson's transcription firsthand, because the supporting surface of the base has deteriorated badly in the intervening years.

In accordance with his general theory that marks on handles and bases refer to the owner, Persson suggests that the three signs spell out some form of a name, with the single fourth sign perhaps an abbreviated patronymic (p. 613). (The single sign in the center of the base is a puzzle to Persson and is ignored in his interpretive discussion). It is striking that 11 other vases from Tomb 18 repeat certain combinations of the signs Persson sees on krater no. 47, and the author argues that these are alternative references to the individual most fully identified on the krater base.

In a similar fashion, two other inscriptions on separate vases (p. 603 nos. 13 and 14 = Tomb 18 nos. 74 and 57), both with (according to Persson) the same initial sign, must refer to a single individual, the second of the three bodies known to have been buried in this chamber. However, Persson evidently forgot that one of these inscriptions is found on the base of a jug whose handle also carries inscribed signs that fit the pattern of the vases associated with krater no. 47, i.e., two different inscriptions on a single vase are taken to refer to two separate individuals! In this case, for Persson's ownership theory to hold true, he would have to assume that this vase had been transferred from one individual to another without the original owner's mark having been erased. In fact, my examination of the vase leads me to interpret the marks on the base of no. 74 as accidental scratches, which would eliminate the entire problem of two different sets of marks on the same vase. But it also denies Persson a second pattern (i.e. consisting of more than one example) of marking in the tomb.

In sum, although I agree with Persson that the consistency of marks on the vases found in the side chamber of Tomb 18 is remarkable, I question his argumentation and some of his observations. He uses the same assemblage both to formulate and to confirm the hypothesis that the marks refer to owners' names. The single external piece of evidence cited as evidence that inscriptions on vases can refer to owners is not a convincing analogy—it consists of a true inscription rather than one or two isolated marks. Two centerpieces of Persson's argument are suspect. His reading of the base of krater no. 47 is not visible in the accompanying photograph and cannot be confirmed today; and its uniqueness in regard to both format and nature calls that reading into question. The scratches on the base of no. 74 are still clearly preserved and, in my judgment, are not deliberate. Persson has not satisfactorily demonstrated that the marks are abbreviated names or that those names refer to the vases' owners, buried in the tomb.

[47] Gjerstad et al. (supra n. 16) 546–58, pl. XC. In discussing pottery from this tomb I refer to Furumark shapes (FS) of Mycenaean pottery as classified in Furumark (supra n. 34) and A. Furumark *Mycenaean Pottery III: Plates* (Stockholm 1992).

[48] Only two of FS 36 piriform jar no. 77's handles are preserved: one carries a ⧧ , one is blank. The pattern of marking on all the other incised vases from this tomb makes it likely that the missing handle also bore an incised sign, either a ⊢ or a ⅂ .

[49] Supra n. 47.

[50] The argument against viewing no. 59 as fitting the pattern of the incised signs is further strengthened by consideration of the two additional signs painted on the lower body of this vase. (Persson apparently did not notice them.) At first glance these signs seem actually to further Persson's hypothesis, since one of them, if taken in conjunction with the sign on the base, builds one of the patterns observed among the incised marks. But the apparent fit of the marks painted on no. 59 with the incised sign-groups may well be apparent rather than real. First and most important, there is no certainty whether the signs on the body and that on the base were intended to be read together. It is fairly unusual for the FS 36 shape to carry painted signs, and it is even more unusual for the signs to be distributed on the lower body as well as the base. Only four other vases with painted signs similarly distributed are known. Two FS 36 piriform jars (unpublished) from Kalavasos-*Ayios Dhimitrios* Tomb 13 both bear the same painted sign, in both cases repeated once on the base and once on the body. In this case it may be that the sign on the lower body was intended to reduplicate in a more visible space, rather than supplement, the information provided by the sign on the base. The sign on base of a small stirrup jar (A. Peridiou, "A Tomb-Group from Lapithos 'Ayia Anastasia'," *RDAC* 1966, 9 no. 98b, pl. I:3–4) found in Tomb 2 at Lapithos *Ayia Anastasia* is only partially preserved, and it is difficult to say whether it repeats the sign on the body; based on what is there, it is possible but unlikely. A cup (Åström [supra n. 34] 9 no. 4) found in Enkomi British Tomb 66 has one sign painted on its base and clearly a different one on its lower body. None of these examples give a certain answer as to whether the signs on piriform jar no. 59 from Enkomi Tomb 18 ought to be read in conjunction; common sense dictates that in all these examples, there was plenty of space to display a complete inscription, at least on the body, and that the appearance of a different sign on the base probably pertained to a separate message.

Second, it is also not certain that the ⱶ on the lower body of piriform jar no. 59 is intended to be the same as the incised ⱶ. The painted sign has curvilinear arms of equal length rather than the straight longer vertical and shorter horizontal characteristic of most of the incised marks. Are these significant differences, or incidental features stemming from (careless) painting (on a curved surface)? There is no way to tell. Third, there is a second mark painted on the body of the piriform jar; although it is only partially preserved, the bit which remains shows a form unrelated to any of the signs in the incised groups, and this argues against associating the painted signs on the body and base of jar no. 59 with either of the incised sign groups.

[51] The identification of hands and the hope of associating a particular sign combination with a single inscriber are problematic. In general, the vases carrying the combination ≢ 푸 seem to have been cut with a tool that left a deeper and wider groove; the tool(s) that cut the other sign combination seems to have been sharper and narrower. But it is difficult to carry the argument further. If manner of inscribing, exact form of sign, and order of strokes are all considered essential to characterizing a hand, then only in the case of the amphoroid krater (no. 6) and one of the large stirrup jars (no. 53) can it be hypothesized that the same individual incised these marks. If some leeway is given to the criterion of sign form, and it is allowed that the difficulty of scratching into baked clay may cause an individual to vary the extensions of his strokes somewhat, then it may also be hypothesized that the signs on the jugs (no. 5 and 74) may have been incised by a single hand. However, because of the varied order of strokes—something that presumably is a habit not affected by what medium is being inscribed —it doesn't appear that the same hand inscribed the other vases with this sign combination (nos. 54 and 55). In sum, neither sign combination can be associated with a single hand. (Illustrations can be viewed on the Internet site, supra n. 12.)

[52] If indeed Persson is correct and each sign group corresponds to an individual, it is interesting that neither sign combination can be associated with a single hand, i.e., no one person was making the owner's mark.

[53] Contexts can be established for approximately 80 of the ca. 115 Mycenaean vases marked by means of painted signs found on Cyprus. At least 74 were found in tombs. Of the remaining ca. 40 unprovenanced examples, most were purchased early in this century and, along with the circumstances of acquisition, their relatively intact state suggests that they were also probably looted from tombs. Thus, the proportion of Mycenaean vases with painted marks found in tombs is very high.

[54] See, for example, M. Hadjicosti, "Appendix IV. Part 1: 'Canaanite' Jars from Maa-*Palaeokastro*," and R.E. Jones and S.J. Vaughan, "Appendix IV. Part 2: A Study of Some 'Canaanite' Jar Fragments from Maa-*Palaeokastro* by Petrographic and Chemical Analysis," in V. Karageorghis and M. Demas, *Excavations at Maa-Palaeokastro. 1979–1986* (Nicosia 1988) 340–85 and 386–98. Also, Michael Sugerman, in the context of larger research project, is examining (by means of petrographic analysis) the fabric of some of the marked amphora handles found on Cyprus. Cf. M.O. Sugerman, *Webs of Commerce: The Archaeology of Ordinary Things in Late Bronze Age Israel and Palestine* (Diss. Harvard Univ. 2000); also M.O. Sugerman, "The Production and Distribution of

'Canaanite' Jars in the Late Bronze Age East Mediterranean," in the session "Ancient Mediterranean Trade," organized by A. Leonard Jr. for the annual meeting of ASOR 1995; M.O. Sugerman, "Investigating Contact and Carriage through Petrographic Analysis," presented at the Albright Institute of Archaeological Research, Jerusalem 1996.

[55] The Mycenaean jars with painted marks are typically fine ware and decorated, i.e., fancy. The range of shapes is large, but most often small containers (especially stirrup jars), small open shapes, or, if large, pictorial kraters—i.e., very different shapes (and presumably functions) from those found in the local or amphora categories. Incised marks are indeed found on shapes that overlap somewhat with the amphoras in function: large stirrup jars and large piriform jars. The large coarseware stirrup jars found throughout the eastern Mediterranean certainly functioned as transport jars; their shape, however, suggests specialized commodities, perhaps not carried in amphoras. There were also large stirrup jars made of fine fabric, and large piriform jars, both decorated. Although they, like amphoras, certainly stored and carried commodities, surely this fancy packaging indicates some special use, distinctive from the all-purpose amphoras. Thus, separating amphoras from Mycenaean pottery does reflect real differences in use of the jars.

[56] It could be argued that the category of Mycenaean vases, which is composed of a wide range of shapes and fabrics, should be further subdivided. This is avoided here for reasons of clarity; the table as it stands provides enough information to see clearly where marks overlap categories. Those overlaps are few and can be easily researched (by searching the database available on the Internet, supra n. 12).

[57] The local/Mycenaean and amphora mark repertoires are not completely distinctive. The overlaps are all simple signs, and one explanation is that their appearance in both marking systems is coincidental. A second possibility is that some of the amphoras were locally made and also marked (supra n. 55). There is one complex mark possibly identified with CM no. 25 (without tang) which has been noted on one amphora handle as well as local vases. Two possible explanations may be proposed: First, this design is not terribly complex and may well have been developed independently in the different marking and script systems. Second, it may be that this amphora was one produced (and traded) locally (supra n. 54).

[58] K.O. Eriksson, *Red Lustrous Wheel-made Ware* (*SIMA* 103, Jonsered 1993) 146, figs. 41–42.

[59] For example, C.B. Donnan, "Ancient Peruvian Potters' Marks and Their Interpretation through Ethnographic Analogy," *AmerAnt* 36 (1971) 460–66; B. Wood, "Potters' Marks," *Journal for the Study of the Old Testament* 103 (1990) 45–48; and especially A.S. Bailey, *The Potters' Marks of Phylakopi* (Diss. Univ. of Edinburgh 1996); all with further bibliography.

[60] The place of manufacture of RLWM vases is debated; see Eriksson (supra n. 58) 149–53, who argues that these vases were made on Cyprus.

[61] Further discussion of LBA potmarks (on Mycenaean vases) as marks of handlers in N. Hirschfeld, "Cypriots in the Mycenaean Aegean," in E. De Miro, L. Godart, and A. Sacconi eds., *Atti e Memorie del Secondo Congresso Internazionale di Micenologia I: Filologia* (Rome 1996) 289–97, and "Incised Marks (Post-Firing) on Aegean Wares," in C. Zerner ed., *Wace and Blegen: Pottery as Evidence for Trade in the Aegean Bronze 1939–1989* (Amsterdam 1993) 311–18.

[62] While there is nothing implicit in the amphoras' marking system(s) to require a specific connection with Cyprus, the very few marked amphoras outside Cyprus and the similarity in general character and placement of these marks to those incised on local pottery suggest that incised marks on amphoras may somehow be connected with the island. No comprehensive study of marked Canaanite jars exists, although some commentaries on individual finds from sites scattered throughout the eastern Mediterranean have been published (for example, from mainland Greece, E. Cline, *Sailing the Wine-Dark Sea: International Trade and the Late Bronze Age Aegean [BAR International Series* 591, Oxford 1994] 168–72 passim, with references; from Crete, J. Bennet, "Marks on Bronze Age Pottery from Kommos," in J.W. Shaw and M.C. Shaw, eds., *Kommos* I:2, *The Kommos Region and Houses of the Minoan Town* [Princeton 1996] 316 no. 7 and 317 no. 13; from Thera, C. Doumas, "Aegeans in the Levant: Myth and Reality," in S. Gitin, A. Mazar, and E. Stern eds., *Mediterranean Peoples in Transition: Thirteenth to Early Tenth Centuries BCE* ([Jerusalem 1998] 133–35; from Israel, A. Raban, *The Commercial Jar in the Ancient Near East: Its Evidence for Interconnections amongst the Biblical Lands* [Diss. Hebrew Univ., 1980], esp. 229–41). This author and Michael Sugerman are currently undertaking a comprehensive study of marked Canaanite jars.

[63] The single example of a painted mark on a non-Mycenaean vase from Enkomi—the cross-within-a-circle painted onto the shoulder of amphora 718/7 (Dikaios (supra n. 7) 596, pls. 77:23, 125:4)—can at present only be regarded as an anomaly. There are very few other examples of LBA amphoras with painted marks: another example from Hala Sultan Tekke on Cyprus (G. Hult, *Hala Sultan Tekke 7: Excavations in Area 8 in 1977 (SIMA* 45:7, Göteborg 1981), one from Mycenae (Cline (supra n. 62) 171, no. 308), and perhaps three from Hazor in Canaan (Y. Yadin, Y. Aharoni, R. Amiran, T. Dothan, I. Dunayevsky, and J. Perrot, *Hazor* I [Jerusalem 1958] C11083, pls. LXXXIX.7, CLVIII.8 and D2338, pls. XCIX.20, CLX.2; Y. Yadin, Y. Aharoni, R. Amiran, T. Dothan, I. Dunayevsky, and J. Perrot, *Hazor* II (Jerusalem 1960) C1140/12, pl. CXXVII.6).

[64] Less obvious, if proper stancing is assumed. It is possible that certain shapes were stored upside down or leaning strongly; changing the orientation would affect the visibility of the signs. The large scale of the painted marks does suggest that they were intended to be readily visible, despite their location on bases, lower bodies, and interiors.

[65] V.R. Grace, "A Cypriote Tomb and Minoan Evidence for its Date," *AJA* 44 (1940) 32, 40–43; E. Stewart and J. Stewart, "Appendix 12: Potters' Marks," in *Vounous 1937–38: Field-report on the Excavations Sponsored by the British School of Archaeology at Athens* (Lund 1950) 390–94; P. Åström, "A Corpus of Pot-Marks," *Excavations at Kalopsidha and Ayios Iakovos in Cyprus (SIMA* 2, Lund 1966) 149–92; E. Herscher, *The Bronze Age Cemetery at Lapithos, Vrysi tou Barba, Cyprus: Results of the University of Pennsylvania Museum Excavation, 1931* (Diss. Univ. of Pennsylvania 1978) 732–34.

[66] Similarly, A.H. Bikaki, *Keos,* volume IV, *Ayia Irini: The Potters' Marks* (Mainz am Rhein 1984) demonstrates the effect the introduction of formal accounting and writing systems had on the pottery of Bronze Age Keos. On Cyprus, E. Herscher continues work on defining the changes in potmarks on vases in the transition from the Middle to Late Cypriot periods.

Device, Image, and Coercion: The Role of Glyptic in the Political Economy of Late Bronze Age Cyprus*

Jennifer M. Webb

The Late Bronze Age (LBA) in Cyprus (ca. 1650–1050 B.C.) was a period of major socioeconomic change characterized by the emergence of polit- ically centralized urban polities operating within well-integrated regional networks of alliance and exchange.[1] Intensification of the copper industry and extensive involvement in long-distance trade required enhanced levels of specialized labor and managerial control and led to increased cultural and economic interaction with the more complex state-organized polities of the eastern Mediterranean. These developments were accompanied by signifi- cant transformations in sociopolitical organization, giving rise to institu- tionalized inequalities. Keswani's analysis of mortuary data from Enkomi has demonstrated the presence of a stratified social order with symbolically dif- ferentiated elites at this site by Late Cypriot (LC) IB/IIA (later 16th to 15th centuries).[2] Contemporary tomb groups differ markedly in quantities of wealth and access to sociotechnic and symbolic goods, with highest-order burials marked by distinctive complements of prestige items (gold and silver jewelry, faiences, ivories, and bronzes) and politicoreligious symbolism (imported and locally engraved seals, signet rings, scarabs, Mycenaean pic- torial kraters). Redundancies of wealth in some tombs over generations sug- gest descent group affiliations founded on hereditary wealth and rank, while differences in status paraphernalia and an absence of structured relationships in the locational, architectural, and artifactual dimensions of mortuary variability suggest significant distinctions within the elite and ongoing competition for political dominance.[3]

The development of sociopolitical inequality is likely to have involved newly formed elites in processes of political legitimation as they sought to establish their position and maintain control over localized wealth production and valuables acquired through long-distance exchange.[4] The key role of status legitimation in politicoeconomic relations in LBA Cyprus has recently been examined by Knapp with particular reference to public and ceremonial architecture and the production of elite ritual paraphernalia in "sanctuary" workshops.[5] Other material markers of ideological authority include labor specialization, elite craft technology, and the restricted circulation of unique, exotic or/and symbolic artifacts.[6] In this paper it is argued that seals, as durable symbolic markers of high intrinsic and ideological value, were important instruments of legitimation. Produced in state- or elite-controlled workshops and distributed within a restricted sphere of exchange, they appear to have served both as operational mechanisms (i.e., sphragistic devices) and as bearers of a coercive imagery designed to validate and promote existing socioeconomic structures and negotiate institutionalized inequalities.

Seal Use in Cyprus Prior to the Late Bronze Age

Cypriot seal use began in the mid third millennium B.C. Two conical limestone stamps, incised with abstract linear designs, have been found in Late Chalcolithic Period 4 at Kissonerga-*Mosphilia* and Period 3 at Lemba-*Lakkous*, and a third unprovenanced stamp in Amsterdam may be of similar date.[7] Other innovations in Period 4 at Mosphilia include supra-household storage, metalworking, small conical stones perhaps used as tokens or calculi, chamber tombs, and artifacts diagnostic of the Philia facies.[8] The latter leave little doubt that Period 4 at Mosphilia and Period 3 at Lemba-*Lakkous* were partly contemporaneous with Philia settlement in the northwest of the island.[9] Period 4 innovations may thus be viewed in the context of an early acculturative phase of interaction between indigenous Late Chalcolithic and incursive Philia communities prior to the establishment of a Philia presence at *Mosphilia* in Period 5.

If the origin of the Philia facies lies in a mid third-millennium migration from southwestern Anatolia, as recently argued, the initial adoption of sealing practices in Cyprus may be attributed to the exposure of local communities to more complex organizational structures derived from the mainland.[10] Period 4 at Mosphilia suggests an increasing degree of socioeconomic inequality at this site, with some occupants engaged in the storage and management of surplus agricultural produce.[11] The use of seals within an incipient redistributive economy, marked also by greater social differentiation in mortuary practices and the adoption of new status markers, is in keeping with the introduction of direct object sealing systems elsewhere.[12] Such systems operated to secure and guarantee the contents of sealed containers (jars, baskets, bags, and boxes), providing a mechanism of administrative control.

Continuity of seal use through the Early and Middle Cypriot periods appears unlikely. Neither tomb deposits nor recently excavated settlement levels have produced seals. A steatite object with convex rectangular face and stumplike projection from Ambelikou is unengraved and unlikely to have been a sphragistic device.[13] Limited Middle Cypriot II/III seal use, however, is indicated by the recovery of a steatite stamp decorated with an incised cross and chevrons from Alassa-*Palialona* Tomb 1.[14] Despite attempts by Kenna to attribute a number of stamps from Iron Age contexts to the Early and Middle Cypriot periods on stylistic grounds, this remains the only secure evidence for seal use in the earlier Bronze Age.[15]

Late Bronze Age Glyptic: Distribution and Chronology

The cylinder seal was introduced to Cyprus from the Near East in the late 17th century B.C., in the form of isolated imports circulating well beyond their original area of use and date of engraving. The earliest examples are associated with LC I burials of the early 16th century B.C. at Nicosia-*Ayia Paraskevi*, Enkomi, Dromolaxia-*Trypes,* and a tomb in the vicinity of Ayia Irini-*Paleokastro* (table 1).[16] A Syrian seal from Plot 333 at Enkomi, attributed to a LC I level by Schaeffer, has the earliest depositional context recorded from a settlement.[17] Merrillees has convincingly rejected a Cypriot recutting of an Old Babylonian cylinder from *Ayia Paraskevi* Tomb 1884.1 on chronological and stylistic grounds.[18] The partial reworking of imported cylinders is, however, widely seen as characterizing the beginning of seal carving in Cyprus.[19] This occasional re-engraving of Old Babylonian, Syrian, and Syro-Mitannian cylinders is unlikely to have been accompanied by the development of a concomitant sealing system.

Table 1. Provenanced imported cylinders. Number per site with chronological range of depositional contexts.

Site	No of Seals	Deposition Date	Site	No of Seals	Deposition Date
Enkomi	38	LC IA–LC IIIB	Dromolaxia	1	LC IA
Nicosia-*Ayia Paraskevi*	4	LCIA	Akhera	1	LC IIC
Hala Sultan Tekke	3	LC IB–IIB	Maa-*Paleokastro*	1	LC IIC
Ayia Irini	3	LC IA–IB	Kition	1	LC IIIA
Ayios Iakovos	2	LC IA	Ayios Sozomenos	1	?
Idalion	2	?–LC IIIC	Kourion	1	?
Klavdia	2	?			

Note. This list is not exhaustive and may include cylinders that are copies rather than imports. Foreign cylinders of LC date from Iron Age contexts are not shown. At least 25 additional imports are without reliable provenance.

Local seal manufacture appears to have begun no earlier than the late 16th or early 15th century B.C., by which time the seal corpus is already characterized by a recognizably indigenous iconography. The earliest Cypriot cylinders from securely dated contexts come from the northwest of the island. These are associated with LC IB burials at Morphou-*Toumba tou Skourou*, Myrtou-*Stephania*, and Ayia Irini-*Paleokastro* and may be assumed to have been in use for some time prior to deposition.[20] Other cylinders from tombs in use from LC IB onward at Enkomi, Hala Sultan Tekke, Dromolaxia, Maroni, and Kalavasos may also belong to the 15th or early 14th century B.C.[21] At least one cylinder comes from a late 15th-century settlement level at Enkomi,[22] and other examples from industrial, domestic, and sanctuary deposits of LC IIA (Ayios Iakovos-*Dhima*, Phlamoudhi-*Melissa*), LC IIB (Enkomi, Sanida-*Moutti tou Ayiou Serkou*) and LC IIC (Myrtou-*Pigadhes*, Athienou-*Bamboulari tis Koukounninas*, Kalavasos-*Ayios Dhimitrios*, Maroni-*Tsaroukkas* and *Vournes*, Kourion-*Bamboula*, Kition-*Kathari*).[23] The great majority of seals from nonfunerary contexts, however, were lost or discarded in LC III.[24]

A register of Bronze Age seals published by Kenna in 1972 lists some 661 cylinders and 128 stamps, including imports and Cypriot seals found outside the island.[25] An updating of this register would bring the total close to 1,000, making seals the most common surviving pictorial medium from the LBA. Fewer than 400 cylinders, however, have a recorded findspot, and detailed contextual data is lacking for almost all except the most recently excavated examples. Even these must be treated with caution. Seals were typically in use for long periods of time or abraded and reworked with new designs. They were also subject to considerable intercontextual movement, creating problems for establishing dates of engraving and, at best, providing information only on the location of final use, loss, or discard. The high curation of seals, further, suggests that they are likely to be rare in residual assemblages of earlier phases of use at the beginning of the LC period, with a more concentrated accumulation in late or final LC deposits, coincident with a decline in their manufacture and use.[26] The limitations of mortuary data are also well known. With most Cypriot Bronze Age burials disturbed by looters, flooding, or subsequent interments, seals can rarely be attributed to individual burials, and for the most part tomb groups must be treated as collectivities.[27]

Despite inherent biases of deposition and discovery, raw counts of provenanced cylinders by site are instructive (tables 1–2, figs. 1–2). Over

Table 2. Provenanced local cylinders. Number per site.

Site	No. of Seals	Site	No. of Seals
Enkomi	200+	Maa-*Paleokastro*	3
Nicosia-*Ayia Paraskevi*	43	Alassa-*Pano Mandilaris*	2
Ayia Irini including *Paleokastro*	14	Ayios Sozomenos and Dhali-*Kafkallia*	2
Kourion-*Bamboula*	12	Athienou-*Bamboulari tis Koukounninas*	2
Hala Sultan Tekke-*Visaja*	12	Pyla	2
Maroni-*Tsaroukkas* and *Vournes*	11	Alyki (Larnaca District)	1
Idalion	10	Apliki-*Karamallos*	1
Ayios Iakovos-*Milia* and *Dhima*	7	Arpera	1
Klavdia	7	Phlamoudhi-*Melissa*	1
Palaepaphos-*Evreti* and *Skales*	7	Sha-*Lymbouris*	1
Kition	6	Kythrea	1
Kalavasos-*Ayios Dhimitrios* and *Mangia*	5	Kalokhorio	1
Angastina	5	Kantara	1
Myrtou-*Pigadhes* and *Stephania*	5	Akaki	1
Dromolaxia	4	Sanidha-*Moutti tou Ayiou Serkou*	1
Morphou-*Toumba tou Skourou*	4	Yeroskipou-*Asproyi*	1
Akhera	3	Sinda	1
Kazaphani	3	Ayios Theodoros	1
Kephalonisi	3		

Note. This list is not exhaustive. The number of seals from Enkomi is a minimum estimate. See *Webb* 1987, 25 and n. 1.

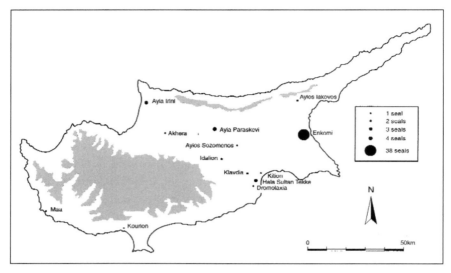

Fig. 1. Map of Cyprus showing distribution of provenanced imported cylinders

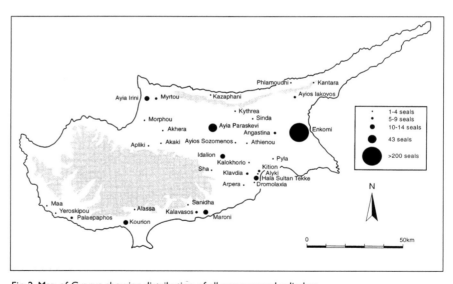

Fig. 2. Map of Cyprus showing distribution of all provenanced cylinders

60% of imported cylinders and well over half of all cylinders provenanced to site level have been recovered from settlement, burial, or surface deposits at Enkomi, in both cases including examples from some of the earliest recorded contexts.[28] While this undoubtedly reflects the longevity of this site (in use from Middle Cypriot III–Cypro-Geometric I) and the fact that it remains the most extensively excavated of all LC urban centers, these figures leave no doubt that Enkomi played a major role in the early development of indigenous glyptic and in seal production throughout the LC period. The only other site to have produced a significant number of cylinders is Nicosia-*Ayia Paraskevi*, an inland center possibly closely linked with Enkomi. The recovery of both imported and locally engraved cylinders in LC IA–IB burials at Ayia Irini-*Paleokastro*, Morphou-*Toumba tou Skourou,* and Myrtou-*Stephania* may indicate a second locus of glyptic development in the northwest of the island. From the 14th century B.C., however, seal use was widespread, suggesting an increase in the number of production units or/and in the distribution of seals from primary centers. Cylinders did not survive the end of the Bronze Age, except as occasional heirlooms in tombs and sanctuaries of the Cypro-Geometric and Cypro-Archaic periods.[29]

Raw Materials, Style, and Iconography

In 1948 Porada classified the indigenous Cypriot cylinders into three broad groups on the basis of their material, iconography, and quality and style of engraving.[30] These were identified respectively as the Elaborate Style, Derivative Style, and Common Style, following an essentially similar classification established for Mitannian glyptic. This basic tripartite division continues to serve a useful purpose and is used here in broad outline to distinguish between the finest, most complex engraving on hematite and less skilled, more schematic work that appears predominantly on softer stones. These were collateral developments evident already from the 15th century B.C., although fine engraving of the Elaborate Style appears at all times to have been less common than either the Derivative or Common Styles. Little work has been done on the identification and source of raw materials. While hematite appears to be present in Cyprus, the stone used for Elaborate Style engraving may have been imported. Other materials occasionally carved in the Elaborate Style, such as lapis lazuli, carnelian, and amethyst, do not occur in Cyprus. The stone most commonly used for other seal types, conventionally identified as steatite or serpentine, appears to be chlorite, a relatively soft stone available in the Troodos mountains.[31]

The main characteristics of Porada's stylistic groupings are as follows:

- *Elaborate Style* cylinders depict complex narrative scenes drawn from mythological sequences and the supra-human realm (see examples on plate I). They show winged and/or double-headed deities with horned crowns and embroidered gowns; sphinxes, griffins, and lions; bull-, lion-, and griffin-headed ministrants; demons and monsters. Presentation scenes, in which ministrants offer inverted animals to major deities, are common and often incorporate elements derived from Near Eastern and Aegean glyptic and other media (e.g., winged sun-disks, Minoan genii, chariot hunts, leonine demons). Designs are formal, often heraldic and highly individualized, and were carved by skilled engravers using hand-held gravers, tubular and snub-nosed drills, and cutting wheels. Cypro-Minoan inscriptions or isolated signs are occasionally included, usually as part of the original design. In most cases engraving is on hematite. Elaborate Style seals were also frequently fitted with gold caps and occasionally mounted as beads or pendants. They occur more often outside Cyprus than other seal groups, most notably at Ugarit.[32]

- *Derivative Style* seals also have a distinctive iconography. Motifs, which occur frequently, show a robed, bareheaded figure with a lion, griffin, or caprid (50+ extant examples; see plate II) and a kilted male figure in similar attitude.[33] Other seals typically depict ritual performances and adoration of a tree by griffins, lions, or/and caprids and occasional script signs. Engraving is predominantly on chlorite with some examples in hematite. Stylistically this group is derivative of the Elaborate Style, but less skillfully carved. Derivative Style seals are also sometimes fitted with gold caps and occasionally found outside Cyprus.

- *Common Style* seals are characterized by schematic engraving and recurrent compositions. The most common show a seated figure

Plate I. Elaborate style cylinders. *1*, unprovenanced (after E. Porada in collaboration with B. Buchanan, *Corpus of Ancient Near Eastern Seals in North American Collections*. Vol. I, *The Collection of the Pierpont Morgan Library* [Bollingen Series XIV, Washington 1948] pl. CLXIII, no. 1073). *2*, Ayios Iakovos-*Dhima* Inv. 12 (after E. Gjerstad, J. Lindros, E. Sjöqvist, and A. Westholm, *SwCyprusExp* vol. I, pl. CL.8). *3*, Enkomi 1934, Trial Trench 37, no. 2 (after H.-G. Buchholz and V. Karageorghis, *Prehistoric Greece and Cyprus. An Archaeological Handbook* [London 1973] no. 1753). *4*, unprovenanced (after A. Moortgat, *Vorderasiatische Rollsiegel, ein Beitrag zur Geschichte der Steinschneidekunst* [Berlin 1940] pl. 69, no. 584). *5*, Ras Shamra 21.014 (after *Schaeffer Corpus 46*). *6*, Ras Shamra 7.081 (after *Schaeffer Corpus 23*). *7*, Kition Tomb 9, no. 16 (after E. Porada, "Appendix V: Two Cylinder Seals from Tomb 9 at Kition," in V. Karageorghis, *Excavations at Kition I. The Tombs* [Nicosia 1974] fig. 2). *8*, Enkomi inv. 1437 (after P. Dikaios, *Enkomi Excavations 1948–1958*. Vol. IIIa, *Plates 1–239* [Mainz am Rhein 1969] pl. 180/4).

Plate II. Derivative style cylinders showing robed figure with animal(s). *1*, unprovenanced (after E. Porada in collaboration with B. Buchanan, *Corpus of Ancient Near Eastern Seals in North American Collections*. Vol. I, *The Collection of the Pierpont Morgan Library* [Bollingen Series XIV, Washington 1948] pl. CLXIII, no. 1074). *2*, Akhera Tomb 2, no. 35 (after H.-G. Buchholz and V. Karageorghis, *Prehistoric Greece and Cyprus: An Archaeological Handbook* [London 1973] no. 1756). *3*, unprovenanced (after M.-L. Vollenweider, *Musée d'art et d'histoire de Genève. Catalogue raisonné des sceaux cylindres et intailles*, vol. I [Genève 1967] pl. 69.9, no. 173). *4*, Enkomi inv. 1694 (after P. Dikaios, *Enkomi Excavations 1948–1958*. Vol. IIIa, *Plates 1–239* [Mainz am Rhein 1969] pl. 182A/4b). *5*, Kourion B1624 (after E. Porada, "Glyptics," in J.L. Benson, *Bamboula at Kourion. The Necropolis and the Finds* [Philadelphia 1972] pl. 38). *6*, Kourion B1623 (after E. Porada, "Glyptics," in J.L. Benson, *Bamboula at Kourion. The Necropolis and the Finds* [Philadelphia 1972] pl. 38). *7*, Ayia Irini-*Paleokastro* Tomb 11, no. 107 (after P.E. Pecorella, *Le Tombe dell'eta' del Bronzo Tardo della necropoli a mare di Ayia Irini "Paleokastro"* [Rome 1977] fig. 211). *8*, Ayia Irini-*Paleokastro* Tomb 3, no. 17 (after P.E. Pecorella, *Le Tombe dell'eta' del Bronzo Tardo della necropoli a mare di Ayia Irini "Paleokastro"* [Rome 1977] fig. 32).

Plate III. Common Style cylinders. *1–4*, seated figure with spear, attendant, bucranium, and snake; *5–8*, standing figure with tree, bucranium, and ingots. *1*, unprovenanced (after E. Porada in collaboration with B. Buchanan, *Corpus of Ancient Near Eastern Seals in North American Collections*. Vol. I, *The Collection of the Pierpont Morgan Library* [The Bollingen Series XIV, Washington 1948] pl. CLXIII, no. 1076). *2*, unprovenanced (after B. Buchanan, *Catalogue of Ancient Near Eastern Seals in the Ashmolean Museum*. Vol. I, *Cylinder Seals* [Oxford 1966] pl. 60, no. 981). *3*, Dromolaxia 1897 Tomb 3 (after N. Witzel, "Finds from the Area of Dromolaxia," *RDAC* 1979, pl. XXII.11). *4*, unprovenanced (after M.-L. Vollenweider, *Musée d'art et d'histoire de Genève. Catalogue raisonné des sceaux cylindres et intailles*, vol. I [Genève 1967] pl. 71.2, no. 178). *5*, unprovenanced (after B. Buchanan, *Catalogue of Ancient Near Eastern Seals in the Ashmolean Museum*, Vol. I, *Cylinder Seals* [Oxford 1966] pl. 60, no. 975). *6*, unprovenanced (after B. Buchanan, *Catalogue of Ancient Near Eastern Seals in the Ashmolean Museum*. Vol. I, *Cylinder Seals* [Oxford 1966] pl. 60, no. 974). *7*, Hala Sultan Tekke Tomb 1, no. 41 (after E. Porada, "Appendix IV: Three Cylinder Seals from Tombs 1 and 2 of Hala Sultan Tekke," in P. Åström, D.M. Bailey, and V. Karageorghis, *Hala Sultan Tekke I. Excavations 1897–1971* [SIMA XLV:1, Göteborg 1976] fig. 77). *8*, unprovenanced (after M.-L. Vollenweider, *Musée d'art et d'histoire de Genève. Catalogue raisonné des sceaux cylindres et intailles*, vol. I [Genève 1967] pl. 71.6, no. 180).

Plate I.

1.

2.

3.

4.

5.

6.

7.

8.

Plate II.   *1.*

2.

3.

4.

5.

6.

7.

8.

Plate III.

1.

2.

3.

4.

5.

6.

7.

8.

with spear, attendant, tree, snake, and bucranium (17+ examples; see plate III.1–4), and a standing male figure with concentric circles, ingots, tree, and bucranium (22+ examples; see plate 3.5–8).[34] These are often difficult to distinguish on individual cylinders. Other seals depict stylized human and animal figures and abbreviated symbols or script signs, carved almost exclusively on chlorite using mechanical tools. They are occasionally fitted with gold caps but rarely found outside the island.

Cypriot glyptic is thus marked by a degree of iconographic, stylistic, and technological exclusivity within the three major groups defined by Porada. Given the size of the database, this is unlikely to be an analytical construct or the result of accidents of discovery. Seals of all classes are also widely dispersed in space and time, and there is little to suggest that these groupings were determined solely by chronological or spatial variables. An alternative explanation, in which seal types are correlated with seal function, is offered below.

Seals as Sphragistic Devices

Establishing normative seal function in LBA Cyprus is surprisingly difficult. Both Kenna and Porada adopted an essentially art historical methodology, primarily concerned with compilation, description, and classification. This approach was encouraged by the lack of provenance for much of the glyptic data and by a marked absence of sealings, the material correlates of seal function in virtually all ancient administrative systems. Kenna nevertheless assumed a functionally distinct class of sphragistic cylinders from the inception of indigenous glyptic.[35] These comprised the finer products of the Cypriot engravers, in contrast to a subsidiary but more common class of less competently engraved seals identified as talismanic. Porada presumed amuletic or talismanic use for most if not all Cypriot seals.[36] More recently, Smith has convincingly argued that Cypriot seals had both sphragistic and votive or amuletic importance, being used for direct administrative control of production and storage in LC IIC and LC IIIA.[37]

The evidence for sphragistic seal function in Cyprus is problematic. Sealings are more likely than seals to have been retained in their context of use, and elsewhere it is the location of sealings that is most helpful in establishing the administrative context of seal use.[38] With the exception, however, of a single clay impression from Enkomi, sealings are missing from the Cypriot record.[39] The Enkomi sealing, recovered in secondary deposition within floor construction in Room 24 of the Ashlar Building (LC IIC/early LC IIIA), was believed by Porada to be an import.[40] Smith, however, has identified a Cypro-Minoan sign added after completion of the original design and suggests that the impression was made in Cyprus, perhaps at Enkomi itself.[41] A second clay sealing bearing the impression of a Cypriot Elaborate Style seal from the Archives Deposit in the Palace at Knossos (ca. 1425–1350 B.C.), another with a cuneiform inscription from Ugarit, and Cypriot seal impressions on two clay tablets bearing Akkadian legal texts from the archive of Rasap'abu at Ugarit tell us nothing about seal use in Cyprus itself.[42]

The only other evidence for object sealing in Cyprus takes the form of rolled impressions on the shoulder, rim, or handle of storage jars or, less frequently, on the rims of basins. Over 40 fragmentary impressions have been published, representing at least 27 vessels from eight coastal and inland sites of the 13th century B.C.[43] A small number were impressed by cylinders similar in size but different in iconography and depth of carving to the extant stone seals, while the majority were produced by examples of significantly greater height and diameter. Motifs are for the most part strongly Aegeanizing, depicting chariot hunts, fighting bulls, and other animal compositions. In all instances the cylinders used appear to have been of wood.[44] While these do not directly inform us of the function of the stone cylinders, they indicate the existence of a well-developed sealing system using finely carved wooden rollers in LC IIC.

The significance of this meager evidence is difficult to assess. Sealings in the Near East and Aegean, typically made of unbaked clay, are less readily preserved than seals, although they must in reality have been more common, and the two classes of object are rarely found together (only three seal/sealing combinations are reported among over 4,000 seals and some 500 sealings from the LBA Aegean).[45] While the lack of sealings in Cyprus may result from accidents of recovery, extensive investigations at Enkomi, Toumba tou Skourou, Kition, and Hala Sultan Tekke and the excavation of administrative and industrial installations and storage facilities at Kalavasos-*Ayios Dhimitrios*, Maroni-*Vournes*, Maa-*Palaeokastro*, and Alassa-*Paliotaverna* render this explanation increasingly unlikely. Both the Kalavasos and Maa complexes were abruptly destroyed by fire—a phenomenon that elsewhere led to the accidental preservation of large numbers of clay sealings. In these circumstances it is difficult to escape the conclusion that economic and administrative records in Cyprus were kept in different, nondurable materials. A similar view is put forward by Smith, who notes evidence, albeit also limited, for the use of papyrus, leather, and wax-filled writing boards and suggests that Cypro-Minoan documents may have been inscribed on wooden cylinders, similar to extant examples in baked clay.[46]

Without sealings we have no way of establishing the socioeconomic setting in which seals served as sealing devices.[47] The contextual associations of the seals themselves therefore gain added importance. These have recently been examined by Smith, who notes their recovery in metalworking, in textile and olive oil production areas, and in association with weights and balances, as well as in cult buildings and burials.[48] Such contexts, however, relate primarily to seal ownership and distribution rather than sphragistic seal function, as seals are likely to have moved independently of the objects they were used to seal, and seals and sealings may be expected to conform to different depositional parameters. If the contextual associations of sphragistic seal use are inaccessible, however, those of seal production, ownership, and distribution may be less so. These allow an alternative point of entry into the role of seals and seal images within LC society.

Seals as Wealth Objects and Prestige Goods

The geopolitical configuration of Cyprus in the LBA has only recently become the focus of explicit debate. There is general agreement that by the 13th century B.C. the island was divided among a series of regionally based peer polities (perhaps as many as eight), administered by local elites whose authority rested largely on the control of regional copper industries and other material and symbolic resources.[49] Keswani has proposed that these polities operated within a highly regulated hierarchical system of primary and secondary centers, mining communities, transshipment points, and agricultural support villages, linked by a complex network of tributary and exchange relations.[50]

The political organization of the island in the earlier phases of the LC period is less well understood. Most recently Peltenburg has proposed the emergence of an archaic state during the 16th century, founded and dominated by a paramount center at Enkomi.[51] Although this fledgling state may

not have been able to establish island-wide authority, it appears to have dominated the island's foreign relations and to have maintained appreciable control over the mining, distribution, and export of Cypriot copper. Since
copper had to be obtained from inland sources, a secure regional infrastruc-
ture must have been in place to ensure the consignment of partly smelted
ores from the mines to refinery and transshipment points. This, Peltenburg
suggests, was achieved by a hinterland strategy of direct procurement, under-
pinned by a network of specialized forts established at critical junctures of
the system to ensure the cooperation of local populations and the safety of
the east–west routes from the mines to Enkomi. Some 21 forts have been
recorded, built during the period in which Enkomi was establishing control
of wealth production and distribution. At the same time Enkomi may also
have been mobilizing agricultural surpluses collected as tribute for distribution to specialists engaged at the mines, along transportation routes and at
Enkomi. The proposed hierarchy of coastal export center/fortified out-
posts/agricultural villages/mines and primary smelting stations correlates
well with what is known of archaic secondary state formation elsewhere.[52]

The organizational strategies that governed the production, consumption,
and exchange of resources in these extensive regional systems remain uncertain. Peltenburg suggests that during the early stages of its formation the
archaic state at Enkomi used staple finance as a means of socioeconomic
integration, in conjunction with the coercive underpinning of the fortified
outposts.[53] The latter, however, do not appear to have been a long-term solu-
tion to the problems of security, and most were out of use by the end of the
16th century B.C. Subsequently, a more complex disbursement system based
on both staple and wealth finance may have come into use. A similar redistribution model has been convincingly applied to the political economy of
the autonomous polities of the 13th and 12th centuries by Keswani.[54] New
mechanisms must also have been developed for instilling compliance among
local elites and those engaged in the extraction, smelting, and transport of
copper. Although these are not well understood, Peltenburg and others suggest that physical coercion was replaced by more covert ideological sanctions,
expressed through monumental architecture, official ritual paraphernalia
and the circulation of symbolically charged goods.[55]

The twofold redistribution model of staple and wealth finance was developed by D'Altroy and Earle in 1985.[56] *Staple finance* is an exchange principle
in which surplus subsistence commodities and other utilitarian goods are

collected, stored, and distributed to non-food-producing members of society (administrators, craft specialists, members of religious hierarchies, military personnel, and specialized labor forces). Collection mechanisms involve obligatory payments in kind to the state of subsistence goods and raw materials in the form of centralized taxation, tribute, or/and administered exchange. In polities with dispersed activities, mobilization of subsistence resources may be highly localized, as these commodities are typically heavy and difficult to transport. Staple finance mechanisms are therefore likely to have remained decentralized, with production, storage, and administration facilities and personnel located close to points of collection and distribution. This mapping of state activities in accordance with the distribution of staple production creates difficulties for the central administration, which in Cyprus are likely to have been exacerbated by the demands of the copper industry.

These difficulties may have been in large part offset by a collateral system of wealth finance in which prestige goods were used as a form of payment and political integration. *Wealth finance* involves the procurement and/or manufacture by the state of special products used to reward or remunerate political officials and other managerial personnel who work or provide services for the state. These may be local or imported raw materials (copper, gold, and ivory) or manufactured goods produced by craft specialists attached to central authorities. The latter function as personal adornment, symbols of status and position, or/and as repositories of esoteric knowledge and stored value, and are normally easily transportable items that can be widely dispersed through regional networks. They can, if necessary, also be converted into food or other utilitarian goods, serving as a form of negotiable wealth in a premarket economy.

Staple and wealth finance typically operate alongside each other to underwrite the political economy in a wide range of small-scale complex societies.[57] They allow the state to fund its own activities and act as a conversion mechanism in a nonmonetary system, linking the local subsistence economy and centralized political elites. Both may be expected to have direct correlates in the archaeological record. In the case of a staple finance system these may take the form of administrative and manufacturing centers with supralocal storage facilities, such as those excavated at Kalavasos-*Ayios Dhimitrios*, Maroni-*Vournes,* and Alassa-*Paliotaverna*, and agricultural support villages, examples of which may have been located at Analiondas-*Palioklichia* and

Arediou-*Vouppes*.[58] In the case of wealth finance we should expect to find evidence for the procurement or specialized production and restricted circulation of elite goods, and a down-the-line movement of prestige items from center to periphery within and perhaps between regional polities.

What role did seals and sealing systems play within such polities? We have already seen that a sealing system, based on carved wooden cylinders and associated primarily with large storage jars, was in use in most if not all regional polities in the 13th century B.C. This system coincides with the appearance of centralized regional administration and large-scale storage facilities, and most impressed pithoi may be linked with supra-household or ritual storage of staple foodstuffs.[59] I have suggested elsewhere that seal impressions were used to identify particular vessels at each site, the contents of which were reserved for certain individuals or groups.[60] These may have been managerial elites or/and members of a specialized labor force. The exaction of a portion of surplus produce (stored in marked pithoi) may have taken the form of a tithe imposed by a local elite for its own use, or by a regional authority operating within a wider political network of tributary alliance. In any case, the evidence for large-scale regionally dispersed storage facilities suggests that a tributary system was the principal means by which resources were mobilized and distributed in the 13th century. Impressed pithoi, the only direct vestiges of sphragistic seal use from Bronze Age Cyprus, further suggest that sealing systems played a significant role in the establishment of socioeconomic institutions designed to channel surplus resources from local production and ensure efficient disbursement mechanisms.

The operational role of seals within a concomitant system of wealth finance is likely to have been more complex. One of the defining characteristics of a wealth finance system is the specialist production of low bulk/high value goods and their controlled distribution within a restricted sphere of exchange. Characteristically such goods involve the use of rare or foreign materials, intensive labor, or/and exceptional manufacturing skills and production by attached specialists. The latter term was proposed by Earle to refer to full-time artisans "attached" to elite households or institutions for which wealth objects were exclusively manufactured.[61] By sponsoring and monopolizing the production and distribution of both raw materials and finished sumptuary goods, elite groups were able to monitor and control the status system, at the same time conferring political rights and privileges legitimized through ownership and display of prestige goods and symbols.

In Cypriot archaeology relatively little attention has been paid to the organization and context of either specialist or subsistence production. Where such issues have been addressed, they have, as elsewhere, been primarily concerned with the manufacture of ceramics.[62] By the LBA pottery production had evolved into a specialized economic pursuit carried out at specific locations by skilled craftspeople engaged full- or part-time. The discovery of a White Slip Ware production center at Sanida–*Moutti tou Ayiou Serkou* suggests decentralized control of at least some major producers of low-value/high consumption utilitarian goods by LC IIB.[63] This may reflect the differential distribution of raw materials as well as regional management of these resources, with finished products probably dispersed through a variety of forms of exchange for both local and foreign consumption. Specialized manufacture is likely, however, to have taken place first in the production of elite or special-purpose goods.[64] The distribution of status-reinforcing goods of this type, as noted above, is likely to have been through a system of circulation distinct from that of subsistence or utilitarian products, further augmenting social distance and ranking distinctions and ensuring control of privileges conferred through their ownership and use. Although independent specialist manufacture of utilitarian goods, such as domestic pottery, is likely to have been driven by considerations of market demand and cost control (resulting in mass production, standardization, and dispersed manufacture), attached production of high-value/low-consumption prestige goods will have been influenced by different factors more likely to have led to increased elaboration and elite-sponsored production in nucleated workshops associated with urban centers.[65]

The degree of elite or administrative management in the production, distribution, and consumption of engraved cylinders is not directly visible in the archaeological record. The only evidence for a possible seal production locus comes from Enkomi Area III in LC IIIA, where a cylinder engraved in the Common Style and two unfinished examples were found in Room 34, together with stone spindle whorls and finished and unfinished ivory plaques and rods.[66] This suggests that cylinders of softer stones and less competent workmanship were carved by artisans who also worked in ivory and on stone objects of other types. The location of Room 34, to the east of Megaron 2 in Sector A of the reconstructed building of Level IIB, may also indicate attached manufacture within an elite residence.[67] The absence, however, of tools and production debris and the occasional recovery of blank or partially engraved cylinders in other rooms at Enkomi make the identification of Room 34 as a seal carver's workshop uncertain.[68]

Indirect data yield further important evidence about the organization of seal production without implicating its exact location. One of the key indicators of specialist production is a differential distribution of relevant artifacts. If cylinders were high-value goods carved under elite sponsorship and subject to restricted disbursement, their recovery in contexts of deliberate deposition (i.e., in burials) should correlate with other material measures of socioeconomic status. This does appear to be the case at Enkomi, the only site with a statistically significant mortuary sample. Despite limitations imposed by multiple burial, past excavation deficiencies, and postdepositional disturbance, the socioeconomic dimensions of mortuary variability are broadly visible for 54 intact or relatively intact tombs (containing a minimum of 281 burials) analyzed by Keswani.[69] In table 3 presence/absence data and raw numbers of seals (cylinders, stamps, and signet rings) in each tomb are correlated with the total estimated weight of gold (following Keswani). All types (including imported, Elaborate Style, Derivative Style, and Common Style cylinders) occur most often in tombs with greater amounts of gold, suggesting a significant connection between seal deposition and the allocation of sumptuary goods for burial.[70]

The operational role of seals is likely, however, to have imposed significant constraints on their removal to closed burial deposits.[71] Seal ownership

Table 3 Distribution of gold (by estimated weight in grams after *Keswani* 1989) and seals and signet rings in intact or near intact tombs at Enkomi (LC IA/IB–IIIB).

Estimated weight of gold	No. of tombs	No. of tombs with seals and signets	% of tombs with seals and signets	No. of seals and signets	No. of seals and signets per tomb
0	18	2	11	3 cylinders	0.2
<50	16	5	31	5 cylinders 1 stamp	0.4
50–100	9	7	78	8 cylinders 6 stamps 1 signet	1.7
100–150	4	3	75	2 cylinders 7 signets	2.3
150–200	2	2	100	1 cylinder 7 signets	4.0
200–500	4	4	100	4 cylinders 5 signets	2.3
>200	5	5	100	6 cylinders 1 stamp 9 signets	3.2

may frequently have been institutional rather than personal, and the rights and privileges attached to the use of particular seals may also have been hereditary (as suggested by the often lengthy period of time between engraving and deposition). It is conceivable, also, that seals were deposited only when they ceased to be operational within a given system (i.e., when canceled, replaced, or worn out). In any case the criteria governing seal deposition are unlikely to have been the same as those that determined the selection of other wealth objects, and simple presence/absence correlations in the burial data should be treated with caution.

Additional evidence for the production context of Cypriot glyptic may be derived from the seals themselves. Elaborate Style cylinders, in particular, show all the hallmarks of attached specialization. They are engraved on rare materials, possibly acquired through long-distance exchange, by skilled engravers using specialized tools. Their iconographic content is complex and involves a high level of esoteric knowledge and frequent evidence of literacy. Elaborate Style sealcutters are likely to have been permanent retainers working within a structured system of production that ensured a supply of raw materials, supported the training of apprentices, and managed and distributed the finished products, as well as providing engravers and other personnel with subsistence commodities (food, clothing, etc.) and other forms of security. Derivative and Common Style seals, less skillfully engraved on more readily available materials, are unlikely to have been carved in the same workshops and were perhaps subject to different disbursement mechanisms. Their restricted distribution, however, suggests that they were also produced under elite sponsorship, perhaps by attached but less highly specialized artisans also working in related media (as may be indicated in Enkomi Area III, Room 34).

Seals of all classes, but particularly those of the Elaborate Style, would also have operated effectively within a wealth finance system. They were mobile objects of high intrinsic value, produced in limited numbers and circulated within a restricted sphere of exchange. If dispersed by the state or institutionalized elites, ownership or use of seals is likely to have indicated a special relationship between sealowner and state. Because seals were items of negotiable wealth, ownership may have automatically entitled a person to goods and services (i.e., ownership of an official or corporate seal may have identified a person's role within the system and authorized his/her right to state-supplied subsistence goods and services). By managing the distribution of seals, the state would in turn have been able to set their value within the system, to control the access of subordinate elites to wealth and other privileges, and to maintain and integrate the managerial sector and promote loyalty.

The operative role of seals of the Derivative and Common Style may have been somewhat different. These classes frequently show recurring motifs and are less likely to have been used in ways that were dependent on the identification of individual seal users or transactions. They may have been corporate or institutional seals, used to signify group affiliation, or indicative of specific types of transactions rather than individual liability. In any case it is difficult to escape the conclusion that Derivative and Common Style seals represent a deliberate production of lesser-quality, less highly-differentiated seals, either for controlled distribution to lesser elites or corporate groups or for use in negotiating particular types of transactions. It is possible, also, that some seal groups were not used for sphragistic purposes.

Seals as Coercive Images of Authority and Integration

These operational aspects of seal ownership and use cannot be divorced from seal content. Seals (assuming sphragistic use) served to authorize and control official transactions and keep records of individual and corporate accountability, and as wealth-generating mechanisms of exchange. In addition, they carry an associated imagery, which may also have been determined and controlled by the state or/and regional elites.

As noted above, the motifs and stylistic conventions associated with Cypriot glyptic suggest a significant divergence between seals of the Elaborate and Common Styles, with a large intermediary group of the Derivative Style. This hierarchical ordering is reflected in raw materials, technology, style, production context, and ideological content. Formal presentation scenes in which mythical animals are offered to major deities are engraved exclusively in the Elaborate Style. Heroic or semidivine figures (in particular a kilted male and robed female[?] figure with dependent animals) are depicted predominantly in the Derivative Style; and human authority figures (a seated man with spear, robed huntsmen, etc.), real world animals, symbols of cult observance (bucrania, ingots), and apotropaic or talismanic motifs occur primarily in the Common Style. High-status images, that is, images that derive their authority from the suprahuman world, appear on finely carved hematite cylinders, while those embedded in a fully human world, associated with subservience to human authority and the appropriate observance of ritual performance, appear in cursorily engraved compositions on softer materials. While there is clearly a danger of overstating these distinctions, and not all seals readily lend themselves to this tripartite division, the use of mutually exclusive, category-specific imagery is apparent and requires explanation.

Recent research has stimulated considerable interest in ways in which the stylistic dimensions of material culture enter into definitions of boundaries.[72] Artifacts may come to stand as markers of ethnic identity, social status, or political alliance, and the distribution of such artifacts may exhibit fall-off behavior at the boundaries of spatially or hierarchically defined groups. Material culture may play a role in reinforcing either interaction or separation among such groups, with corporate emblems distinguished by unique motifs or specific configurations of elements that overtly signify personal identity or group affiliation. Small, durable, and highly mobile image-bearing objects circulating within a controlled exchange environment, such as cylinder and stamp seals, readily lend themselves to use as symbolic markers—their added function as sphragistic devices, items of personal adornment, and tokens of negotiable wealth serving to further reinforce social distance and status distinctions. Elite control over the production and disposition of such ideologically charged goods, moreover, is easily translated into control of the symbolism of power and its legitimation by direct reference to religious authority.

Ownership of Elaborate Style seals, in particular, may have served to link high-level elites with service to the gods, legitimizing their claim to divinely sanctioned authority and promoting a privileged relationship with the supernatural realm. As well as serving as official and personal sphragistic devices, they may have marked and reinforced ascribed privilege, standing as claims to aristocratic ancestry and bearing an ideology formally grounded in a system of social ranking and economic privilege based on principles of inheritance. Both their production and distribution may be expected to be nucleated in paramount civic centers, that is, in Enkomi during the earlier years of the LBA and subsequently within urban centers serving as heads of major polities. As hereditary emblems symbolizing divinely sanctioned authority, they are likely to have been minimally dispersed, retained for long periods of time, and more frequently subject to embellishment (gold caps) or use as items of personal adornment. Elaborate Style seals may also have been used in formal gift exchange, serving to establish horizontal alliances at the intra- and interregional and perhaps extraisland level.

Elaborate Style seals frequently carry Cypro-Minoan script signs, further reinforcing the power of seal and seal image and the identity of the seal owner.[73] Elaborate Style iconography also remained more dependent on its Near Eastern models and more open to external iconographic influences than other glyptic classes, the latter no doubt channeled through the same lines of elite alliances as other prestige goods. The borrowing of foreign symbols may reflect a spatially extensive social identity shared by elites from different polities. This would have strengthened elite monopolies over the acquisition and distribution of foreign items and may be symptomatic of political alliances linking ruling families within and beyond the island.[74] It is possible also that foreign models of political centralization and the ideology that legitimated them provided Cypriot elites with a blueprint for domination lacking in their own iconographic tradition. This need not imply that Cypriots were passive recipients of foreign symbolic referents. Rather, the choice of core symbols may have been determined by their relevance to indigenous political and religious constructs as well as a desire to adopt foreign power styles for ostentatious display. The use of predominantly Aegeanizing designs on impressed pithoi, for the most part depicting high status secular images, may also be seen as an act of self-definition, well suited to the needs of emergent regional elites intent on consolidating their organizational preeminence within the stratified polities of the 13th century B.C.[75]

The iconography of Derivative and Common Style seals is predominantly if not exclusively concerned with ideology, ritual enactments, and the observance of human authority. Such seals may have been used within middle- or lower-level managerial sectors, for straightforward transactional purposes, in reward for services administered to the state, and as a means of communicating state ideology to commoners and secondary elites. As such they may be expected to have moved widely through regional networks, establishing and reinforcing vertical ties with subordinate elites in a down-the-line movement from primary to secondary and tertiary centers. Common Style iconography, in particular, is concerned with the correct observance of ritual performances, the repeated depiction of human authority, and designs of talismanic or amuletic significance. These motifs also frequently include abbreviated representations of copper ingots, suggesting that seals of this type were operationally and ideologically linked with the management of the copper industry.[76] This association of certain seal types and images with particular groups within a centralized, stratified society may have been designed to maintain the organizational and economic requirements of existing elites and ensure the cooperation and cohesion of all social groups. Seals may thus have played a vital role within the broader context of information exchange, marking, maintaining, and furthering social and wealth differentiation and identifying individual and corporate affiliation.

Conclusion

This analysis of Cypriot glyptic is largely drawn from analogous studies of the symbolic and wealth systems of more recent or better documented small-scale complex societies.[77] Studies of seals from other areas, however, frequently suggest a similar correlation among style, iconography, distribution, and function. Nissen, for example, has convincingly linked different groups of seals to different levels of responsibility within the stratified socioeconomic systems of the Late Uruk period.[78] Finely engraved cylinders with detailed individual designs are believed to have been authorized for use within the higher levels of the decision-making hierarchy, while simple-design seals, carved with mechanical tools and a limited range of motifs, are identified as lower-rank, collective, or/and institutional seals. The use of Early Dynastic III seal subjects as overt markers of socioeconomic and occupational status at Ur has also been demonstrated by Rathje and Winter.[79] Similarly, at Hasanlu in northwest Iran a distinction has been made between "local style" seals, which served as administrative devices in a local storage system, and "foreign style" cylinders that appear from contextual data to have been neck and dress ornaments worn by elites.[80] The latter differ in size, material, style, the use of Neo-Assyrian imperial iconography, and the addition of metal caps and have been identified as prestige items marking social differentiation. A connection between high-quality seals and sociopolitical status is evident also in Syrian glyptic inscriptions from the beginning of the second millennium,[81] and close links between the identity of seal owners and seal use are indicated in archival texts from Mari.[82] More generally, the role of Near Eastern cylinders as social emblems and bearers of implicit ideological messages that enhanced social cohesiveness through image and legend has been examined by Winter, Nissen, and, most recently, Gorelick and Gwinnett.[83]

Given the paucity of textual evidence and lack of sealings from LBA Cyprus, it is unlikely that we will ever understand Cypriot sealing structures to the extent that these are now visible in the Aegean and the Near East. It is, nevertheless, the central premise of this paper that seals and related sealing systems, which for the most part remain inaccessible, played an important role in the complex societal and economic structures of LBA Cyprus, as they did elsewhere. It is suggested that seals served as functional mechanisms within a redistributive system of wealth and staple finance—operating as identifying and validating *devices* in regional networks of alliance and resource extraction and exchange and as bearers of *images*, which served to establish social position and legitimate political authority. Seals, both as *devices* and as *images*, helped regulate the mobilization of labor and provided authority for the allocation and redistribution of surplus production. Ideology, expressed through glyptic imagery, also served to sanction central and regionalized elites and to stabilize and integrate other groups within polities characterized by marked sociopolitical and economic inequalities. In the latter context glyptic imagery played or was intended to play a *coercive* role, to perpetuate existing social and economic structures and negotiate inequalities within polities no longer subject to direct physical coercion.

This assumes a structured, covertly manipulated ideology of authority, worked out through objects, which were operative tools and prestige goods symbolic of personal affiliation and status. In reality, however, the politicoeconomic systems in place in LBA Cyprus were probably more opportunistic. We cannot assume that all members of society followed the dominant ideology, or that symbols were always read in the way intended.[84] The relationship between symbolic expression and meaning can be imprecise or even deliberately ambiguous and will almost certainly signal different things to different people at different times. This does not, however, undermine the broader premise that seals and sealings operated as tools of organizational control and that seal imagery was ideologically coercive in intent, if not always in practice. Coherent links between LC systems of authority and the working out of those systems through glyptic imagery *can* be identified. As mobile devices engraved by attached specialists and distributed by central authorities or elite households, seals may have been powerful mechanisms of organizational and ideological control in the dispersed regional systems that characterize Peltenburg's archaic state model and Keswani's multiple autonomous polities.

Although monumental architecture (temples, palaces, and elite tombs) and public ceremony represent highly visible demonstrations of authority within large urban centers,[85] more mobile displays of status and power were required to transport that authority inland to the mines and agricultural villages and to foster vertical alliances critical to the maintenance of systems dependent on geographically widespread activities. At the same time seals and other image-bearing items are likely to have encouraged the spread of a common symbolic system, especially as this related to centralized expressions of power and prestige. Although a degree of ideological diffusion is visible in the glyptic data from its inception, by the late 14th century B.C. the distribution of seals with a relatively homogeneous imagery across the island suggests that the regional polities of LC IIC and LC III were sustained by a complex system of political, economic, and ideological interactions.

The current and predicted archaeological correlates of seal use in Cyprus are summarized in table 4. The verification or otherwise of much of this awaits the discovery of sealings, seal production units, and analyses of the distribution of the output of particular workshops and seal types. In the meantime it is difficult to avoid the conclusion, already expressed by Merrillees, that an exhaustive illustrated corpus of Cypriot glyptic with detailed information on context and petrology is essential if this complex body of data is to be better understood.[86] At present only Enkomi, which has produced over 200 cylinders and many more stamps and signet rings, has a substantial claim to have been a major center of glyptic production throughout the LBA. Given the number of seals of particular stylistic or/and content groups from this site (e.g., so-called Egyptianizing Linear Style cylinders) it would also appear that Enkomi was home to a number of workshops whose products have been found across the eastern half of the island.[87] Smaller-scale research projects might usefully focus on contextual data relating to individual seal types. Much work also needs to be done on raw material provenience, engraving technologies, and the establishment of a methodology for identifying products of individual workshops and engravers.

This paper is an initial inquiry into a complex subject. The propositions raised are intended to stimulate discussion and move the study of Cypriot glyptic beyond the confines of a traditional art historical methodology. The need to match the seal data more closely to the overarching framework suggested is fully recognized. Similarly, it is acknowledged that the significance

Table 4. Indigenous glyptic. Actual (in italics) and predicted correlates.

	Elaborate Style	Derivative Style	Common Style
Raw materials	*Hard stones/exotics. Imported*(?) *or controlled.*	*Local. Relatively soft stones*	*Local. Relatively soft stones*
Location of production	Numerically restricted state-controlled workshops	Workshops linked with elite households	Workshops linked with elite households
Context of production	Attached full-time specialists	Attached specialists, also working in other media	Attached specialists, also working in other media
Function	Sphragistic/*ideological*	Sphragistic/*ideological*	Sphragistic/*ideological*
Technical investment	*High. Hand-held and mechanical tools. Long apprenticeships*	*Medium. Primarily mechanical tools*	*Low. Exclusively(?) mechanical tools*
Stylistic investment	*High*	*Medium*	*Low*
Knowledge investment	*High esoteric. Evidence of literacy and exposure to non-local iconographies*	*Medium esoteric. Some evidence of literacy*	*Medium esoteric*
Iconographic content	*Suprahuman/mythical/ seminarrative*	*Semidivine/heroic/ semi-narrative/ritual*	*Generic human/ritual/ talismanic/aniconic*
Internal variability	*High*	*Medium. Some recurrent motifs*	*Medium/low. Recurrent motifs and look-alikes*
Output	*Highly restricted*	*Restricted*	*Restricted*
Distribution	Nucleated. Owned/used by upper level elites in civic centers. *Found outside Cyprus*	Regionally dispersed to middle level elites and corporate groups. *Occasionally found outside Cyprus*	Regionally dispersed to middle/lower level elites and corporate groups. *Rarely found outside Cyprus*
Intrinsic value	Very high. *Frequently fitted with gold mounts or as beads or pendants.*	High. *Occasionally fitted with gold mounts or in jewelry*	High. *Occasionally fitted with gold mounts or in jewelry*
Curation rate	*Very high*	*High*	*High*
Deposition context	*Elite burials, votive deposits, storage and industrial facilities*	*Elite/middle level burials, votive deposits, storage and industrial facilities*	*Elite/middle level burials, votive deposits, storage and industrial facilities*

of seal designs will remain in large part veiled and that the value of an object or image is culturally defined and hence not wholly reducible to economic or political explanations. This is particularly true in the case of Elaborate Style cylinders, which as individual works of art are likely to have been subject to anomalous or higher-order criteria. The use of skilled artisans, nonetheless, to encode artistic products with symbolic messages is one way in which elites attempt to resolve ambiguity and smooth over contradictions in polities characterized by socioeconomic inequities.[88] Such reorganization

of elite relationships was a key task in building centralized regional states and
the role of glyptic in establishing and legitimating administrative, social, economic, and political structures as well as signaling political transformations
cannot be ignored.

NOTES

* David Frankel, A. Bernard Knapp, and Joanna S. Smith contributed valuable comments
on an earlier version of this paper. Thanks are due to Joanna S. Smith and Ellen
Herscher for organizing the session on "Scripts and Seal Use in Bronze and Iron Age
Cyprus" at the 99th Annual Meeting of the Archaeological Institute of America, and to
the Archaeological Institute of America and in particular the Samuel Kress Foundation
for funding my visit to Chicago. The following abbreviations have been used.

   LC   Late Cypriot

Gibson and Biggs   M. Gibson and R.D. Biggs eds., *Seals and Sealing in the
Ancient Near East* (*Bibliotheca Mesopotamica* 6, Malibu 1977).

Kenna 1967   V.E.G. Kenna, "The Seal Use of Cyprus in the Bronze Age,"
BCH 91 (1967) 255–68; "The Seal Use of Cyprus in the Bronze Age, II,"
BCH 91 (1967) 552–77.

Kenna 1971   V.E.G. Kenna, *Corpus of Cypriote Antiquities 3. Catalogue of the
Cypriote Seals of the Bronze Age in the British Museum* (*SIMA* 20:3,
Göteborg 1971).

Kenna 1972   V.E.G. Kenna, "Glyptic," in L. Åström and P. Åström,
SwCyprusExp IV.1D, 623–74.

Keswani 1989   P.S. Keswani, "Dimensions of Social Hierarchy in Late
Bronze Age Cyprus: An Analysis of the Mortuary Data from Enkomi,"
JMA 2 (1989) 49–86.

Keswani 1993   P.S. Keswani, "Models of Local Exchange in Late Bronze Age
Cyprus," *BASOR* 292 (1993) 73–83.

Keswani 1996   P.S. Keswani, "Hierarchies, Heterarchies, and Urbanization
Processes: The View from Bronze Age Cyprus," *JMA* 9 (1996) 211–50.

Knapp 1996   A.B. Knapp, "The Bronze Age Economy of Cyprus: Ritual,
Ideology, and the Sacred Landscape," in V. Karageorghis and D.
Michaelides eds., *The Development of the Cypriot Economy: From the
Prehistoric Period to the Present Day* (Nicosia 1996) 71–106.

Palaima   T.G. Palaima ed., *Aegean Seals, Sealings and Administration.
Proceedings of the NEH-Dickson Conference of the Program in Aegean Scripts
and Prehistory of the Department of Classics, University of Texas at Austin
January 11–13, 1989* (*Aegaeum* 5, Liège 1990).

Porada Enkomi   E. Porada, "Appendix I. Seals," in P. Dikaios, *Enkomi.
Excavations 1948–1958.* Volume II. *Chronology, Summary and Conclusions,*

Catalogue, Appendices (Mainz am Rhein 1971) 783–810.

Schaeffer Corpus   C. F.-A. Schaeffer-Forrer, *Corpus des Cylindres-Sceaux de Ras Shamra-Ugarit et d'Enkomi-Alasia* I (Paris 1983).

Smith   J.S. Smith, *Seals for Sealing in the Late Cypriot Period* (Diss. Bryn Mawr College 1994).

Webb 1987   J.M. Webb, "The Cylinder Seals," in J.-C. Courtois and J.M. Webb, *Les Cylindres-Sceaux d'Enkomi (Fouilles Françaises 1957–1970)* (Nicosia 1987) 25–91.

Webb 1992   J.M. Webb, "Cypriote Bronze Age Glyptic: Style, Function and Social Context," in R. Laffineur and J.L. Crowley eds., *EIKΩN: Aegean Bronze Age Iconography: Shaping a Methodology. Proceedings of the 4th International Aegean Conference, University of Tasmania, Hobart, Australia 6–9 April 1992* (*Aegaeum* 8, Liège 1992) 113–21.

Webb and Frankel   J.M. Webb and D. Frankel, "Making an Impression: Storage and Surplus Finance in Late Bronze Age Cyprus," *JMA* 7 (1994) 5–26.

[1] See in particular A.B. Knapp, "Production, Exchange and Socio-Political Complexity on Bronze Age Cyprus," *OJA* 5 (1986) 35–60; A.B. Knapp, "Production, Location and Integration in Bronze Age Cyprus," *CurrAnthr* 31 (1990) 147–76; A.B. Knapp, "Social Complexity: Incipience, Emergence, and Development on Prehistoric Cyprus," *BASOR* 292 (1993) 85–106; A.B. Knapp, "Emergence, Development and Decline on Bronze Age Cyprus," in C. Mathers and S. Stoddart eds., *Development and Decline in the Mediterranean Bronze Age* (*Sheffield Archaeological Monographs* 8, Sheffield 1994) 271–304; A.B. Knapp, "Settlement and Society on Late Bronze Age Cyprus: Dynamics and Development," in P. Åström and E. Herscher eds., *Late Bronze Age Settlement in Cyprus: Function and Relationship* (*SIMA-PB* 126, Jonsered 1996) 54–80; A.B. Knapp, *The Archaeology of Late Bronze Age Cypriot Society: The Study of Settlement, Survey and Landscape* (*University of Glasgow, Department of Archaeology, Occasional Paper* 4, Glasgow 1997); *Keswani* 1993; *Keswani* 1996; E. Peltenburg, "From Isolation to State Formation in Cyprus, c. 3500–1500 B.C.," in V. Karageorghis and D. Michaelides eds., *The Development of the Cypriot Economy. From the Prehistoric Period to the Present Day* (Nicosia 1996) 17–44.

[2] *Keswani* 1989. Also P.F.S. Keswani, *Mortuary Ritual and Social Hierarchy in Bronze Age Cyprus* (Diss. Univ. of Michigan 1989).

[3] *Keswani* 1989, 68–69.

[4] Material referents may be regarded as ideological when they contribute to the legitimation or sanctification of special interest groups. Ideology also plays a key role in establishing social position and political authority and validating modes of production, persuasion, and coercion, and serves to stabilize power structures characterized by social inequities. See A. Giddens, *Central Problems in Social Theory: Action, Structure and Contradiction in Social Analysis* (London 1979) 188, 195; M. Bloch, "From Cognition to Ideology," in R. Fardon ed., *Power and Knowledge: Anthropological and Sociological*

Approaches (Edinburgh 1985) 21–48; A.L. Kolata, "Economy, Ideology, and Imperialism in the South-Central Andes," in A.A. Demarest and G.W. Conrad eds., *Ideology and Pre-Columbian Civilizations* (Santa Fe 1992) 65–85; D. Miller, "Structures and Strategies: An Aspect of the Relationship between Social Hierarchy and Cultural Change," in I. Hodder ed., *Symbolic and Structural Archaeology* (Cambridge 1982) 89–98; M. Shanks and C. Tilley, "Ideology, Symbolic Power and Ritual Communication: A Reinterpretation of Neolithic Mortuary Practices," in I. Hodder ed., *Symbolic and Structural Archaeology* (Cambridge 1982) 129–54; T. Earle ed., *Chiefdoms: Power, Economy and Ideology* (Cambridge 1991); *Knapp* 1996.

[5] *Knapp* 1996. See also A.B. Knapp, "Power and Ideology on Prehistoric Cyprus," in *Religion and Power in the Ancient Greek World* (*Boreas* 24, Uppsala 1996) 9–25; and J.M. Webb, *Ritual Architecture, Iconography and Practice in the Late Cypriot Bronze Age* (*SIMA-PB* 75, Jonsered 1999) 284–308.

[6] See, e.g., R.M. Adams, "Ideologies: Unity and Diversity," in Demarest and Conrad (supra n. 4) 205–221; M. Braithwaite, "Ritual and Prestige in the Prehistory of Wessex c. 2200–1400 B.C.: A New Dimension to the Archaeological Evidence," in D. Miller and C. Tilley eds., *Ideology, Power and Prehistory* (Cambridge 1984) 93–110; P. Peregrine, "Some Political Aspects of Craft Specialization," *WorldArch* 23 (1991) 1–11.

[7] E. Peltenburg, "Lemba Archaeological Project, Cyprus, 1986," *Levant* 20 (1988) 234–35, fig. 3; E. Peltenburg, "Kissonerga-Mosphilia: A Major Chalcolithic Site in Cyprus," *BASOR* 282/283 (1991) 29, fig. 9; E. Peltenburg, *Lemba Archaeological Project,* volume I: *Excavations at Lemba-Lakkous, 1976–1983* (*SIMA* 70:1, Göteborg 1985) 198, 289, fig. 85.5, pl. 47.11, found in disturbed plow soil; Peltenburg et al., *Lemba Archaeological Project II:1A. Excavations at Kissonerga-Mosphilia 1979–1992* (*SIMA* 70:2, Jonsered 1998) 196–97, 200–201, 253, fig. 102.6–7, pl. 37.12–13; S.M. Lubsen-Admiraal and J. Crouwel, *Cyprus & Aphrodite* (Gravenhage 1989) 147, no. 21. Note the suggestion, however, in Peltenburg et al., *Lemba Archaeological Project II:1A*, 201, n. 1, that the Amsterdam example is in fact a Christian bread stamp. Reyes has also suggested the use of conical stones and engraved pebbles of the fourth millennium from Khirokitia and elsewhere as seals in A.T. Reyes, "The Stamp Seals in the Pierides Collection, Larnaca," *RDAC* 1991, 118, n. 5.

[8] Peltenburg et al. (supra n. 7) 249–58, Tables 14.7–8. See also Peltenburg et al., "Excavations at Kissonerga-Mosphilia 1985," *RDAC* 1986, 29, pl. VI.3; E. Peltenburg, "Kissonerga-Mosphilia: A Major Chalcolithic Site in Cyprus," *BASOR* 282/283 (1991) 27–30, figs. 8, 10.

[9] E. Peltenburg (supra n. 8) 31–32, fig. 11, M1; Peltenburg et al. (supra n. 7) 256–58. See also J.M. Webb and D. Frankel, "Characterising the Philia Facies: Material Culture, Chronology and the Origin of the Bronze Age," *AJA* 103 (1999) 3–44.

[10] D. Frankel, J.M. Webb, and C. Eslick, "Anatolia and Cyprus in the Third Millennium B.C.E.: A Speculative Model of Interaction," in G. Bunnens ed., *Cultural Interaction in the Ancient Near East. Papers Read at a Symposium held at the University of Melbourne, Department of Classics and Archaeology (29–30 September 1994)* (*Abr-Nahrain Suppl. Series* volume 5, Louvain 1996) 37–50. See also Peltenburg in Karageorghis and Michaelides

(supra n. 1) 17–44. For comparable seal types from the Anatolian mainland see C. Mora, "I Sigilli Anatolici del Bronzo Antico," *Orientalia* 51 (1982) 204–226.

[11] See E. Peltenburg (supra n. 8) 28–29; Peltenburg et al. (supra n. 7) 249–58.

[12] Recent research has considerably advanced our understanding of early seal use. See, e.g., D.J. Pullen, "A Lead Seal from Tsoungiza, Ancient Nemea, and Early Bronze Age Aegean Sealing Systems," *AJA* 98 (1994) 35–52; A. Alizadeh, "Socio-economic Complexity in Southwestern Iran During the Fifth and Fourth Millennia B.C: The Evidence from Tall-i Bakun A," *Iran* 26 (1988) 17–34; G. Van driel, "Seals and Sealings from Jebel Aruda 1974–1978," *Akkadica* 33 (1983) 34–62; P. Ferioli and F.E. Fiandra, "Clay-Sealings from Arslantepe VIA: Administration and Bureaucracy," *Origini* 12 (1983) 455–509; R. Zettler, "Sealings as Artifacts of Institutional Administration in Ancient Mesopotamia," *JCS* 39 (1987) 197–240.

[13] R.S. Merrillees, "Ambelikou-*Aletri*: A Preliminary Report," *RDAC* 1984, 3–4, fig. 4, where the object is identified as a seal or pendant (see also *Smith* 48). It may be compared with rounded objects with similar projections in terracotta and stone from Lemba-*Lakkous* and Marki-*Alonia*. See E. Peltenburg et al., *Lemba Archaeological Project,* volume I: *Excavations at Lemba-Lakkous, 1976–1983* (*SIMA* 70:1, Göteborg 1985) 90–91, 96, 192, 198, figs. 68.1,3, 86.4; and D. Frankel and J.M. Webb, "Excavations at Marki-*Alonia*, 1996–7," *RDAC* 1997, 96, P8948 and S260, fig. 9. They appear to be lids or stoppers.

[14] P. Flourentzos, *Excavations in the Kouris Valley I. The Tombs* (Nicosia 1991) 7, 15, pl. XIV.1.

[15] *Kenna* 1967. In publishing the Alassa seal Flourentzos (supra n. 14) 15, fig. 5, draws attention to a conical limestone stamp in the Larnaca Museum (inv. 1939/X-3/1), also attributed to the Middle Cypriot period by *Kenna* 1967, 262–64, no. 6, figs. 1, 4. Kenna's attribution of unprovenanced seals and seals found in later deposits to the earlier Bronze Age has not been widely accepted. See P. Åström, "Some Aspects of the Late Cypriote I Period," *RDAC* 1972, 46; Reyes (supra n. 7) 117 and n. 5; *Smith* 48, n. 25. It has also been suggested that cylinders with Syrian, Minoan, and Egyptian elements are Cypriot products of the late Middle Bronze Age (E. Porada, "On the Complexity of Style and Iconography in Some Groups of Cylinder Seals from Cyprus," in *Acts of the International Archaeological Symposium "The Mycenaeans in the Eastern Mediterranean," Nicosia 27th March–2nd April 1972* [Nicosia 1973] 268–72; E. Porada, "Cylinder Seals from Enkomi, Cyprus, and a Reappraisal of Early Glyptic Art in Cyprus," *AJA* 73 [1969] 244; *Porada Enkomi* 783–84).

[16] Nicosia-*Ayia Paraskevi* Tomb 1884.1 (R.S. Merrillees, "A 16th Century B.C. Tomb Group from Central Cyprus with Links Both East and West," in V. Karageorghis ed., *Acts of the International Archaeological Symposium "Cyprus Between the Orient and the Occident," Nicosia, 8–14 September 1985* [Nicosia 1986] 114–48); Enkomi British Tomb 57 (*Kenna* 1971, 17, no. 2); Dromolaxia-*Trypes* Tomb 2 (S. Lubsen-Admiraal, "Late Bronze Age Tombs from Dromolaxia," *RDAC* 1982, 53, no. 9, 56, fig. 5, pl. VII:9); L. Quilici, *La Tomba dell'eta' del Bronzo Tardo dall'Abitato di Paleokastro Presso Ayia Irini* (Rome 1990) 125, fig. 326, N.422 from Level VI. Several other imported cylinders, from Ayia Irini-*Paleokastro* Tombs 3 and 11, were associated with deposits spanning LC IA.2–LC IB.2.

See P.E. Pecorella, *Le Tombe dell'eta' del Bronzo Tardo della Necropoli a Mare di Ayia Irini "Paleokastro"* (Rome 1977) 34–35, 79, 263–64, 268, figs. 76, 190. The absolute chronology of the LC period is far from clear with accepted dates for the beginning of LC IA varying by as much as three quarters of a century (from 1650 to 1575 B.C. See *Keswani* 1989, 76, fig. 3). For a more recent discussion, based on a sequence of radio-carbon dates from the earlier Bronze Age, see A.B. Knapp and S.W. Manning, "Terminology and Radiocarbon Time," in A.B. Knapp, "The Prehistory of Cyprus: Problems and Prospects," *Journal of World Prehistory* 8.4 (1994) 379–90, where MC III–LC I (Protohistoric Bronze Age 1) is assigned to 1700–1400 B.C. The following schema is used in this paper but claims only general applicability. LC IA–IB: ca. 1650–1400 B.C.; LC IIA–IIC: ca. 1400–1200 B.C; LC IIIA–IIIC: ca. 1200–1050 B.C.

[17] *Schaeffer Corpus* 164, Enkomi-Alasia 4.108. With a presumed date of engraving of 1550–1450 B.C., this seal must have been lost or discarded soon after its arrival at Enkomi.

[18] Merrillees (supra n. 16) 133–34. See also R.S. Merrillees, "The Glyptics of Bronze Age Cyprus: 'Through a Glass Darkly'," in E. Peltenburg ed., *Early Society in Cyprus* (Edinburgh 1989) 153–59. The recarving of this cylinder has been widely attributed to a Cypriot engraver. See E. Porada, "The Cylinder Seals of the Late Cypriote Bronze Age," *AJA* 52 (1948) 181; E. Porada in discussion of Merrillees (supra n. 16) 140; *Kenna* 1967, 554; *Kenna* 1972, 624–25; D. Collon in Merrillees (supra n. 16) 128–29.

[19] Syrian influence on early Cypriot engraving is suggested by the apparent adaptation of North Syrian motifs on recut seals, their linear execution, and similarities in the use of the drill. See D. Collon in Merrillees (supra n. 16) 128–29. For other imported cylinders with evidence of recarving see P.H. Merrillees in Merrillees (supra n. 16) 129–30, no. 3 from Klavdia-*Tremithios* and *Webb* 1987, 36, no. 1 and n. 44.

[20] E. Porada, "The Cylinder Seals," in E.D.T. Vermeule and F.Z. Wolsky, *Toumba tou Skourou. A Bronze Age Potters' Quarter on Morphou Bay in Cyprus* (Cambridge, MA 1990) 338–42 (Tomb I, nos. 251, 252, 343. Note that Tomb I, no. 251 is identified by Porada as a Cypriot work based on a Syro-Mitannian prototype but may be a genuine import); B. Buchanan in J.B. Hennessy, *Stephania. A Middle and Late Bronze-Age Cemetery in Cyprus* (London 1963) 41, pl. VIIIe (Tomb 14, no. 40); Pecorella (supra n. 16) 22, 57, 61, 101, 182–83, figs. 32, 129, 141, 239, 471 (Tombs 3, no. 17; 10, nos. 6, 31; 17, no. 1; 21, no. 158). Note that Tomb 21, no. 158 is attributed by Pecorella to a LC IA.2 burial stratum.

[21] Enkomi Swedish Tombs 2, 13, and 17; British Tombs 19, 67, 69, 84/84A, and 86 (E. Gjerstad, J. Lindros, E. Sjöqvist, and A. Westholm, *SwCyprusExp* I, 474, 530, 545; *Kenna* 1971, 18, 21, 26, nos. 8, 32, 61); Hala Sultan Tekke Tomb 2, no. 230 (E. Porada, "Appendix IV: Three Cylinder Seals from Tombs 1 and 2 of Hala Sultan Tekke," in P. Åström, D.M. Bailey, and V. Karageorghis, *Hala Sultan Tekke 1: Excavations 1897–1971* (*SIMA* 45:1, Göteborg 1976) 100–101, figs. 75, 78; Dromolaxia-*Trypes* Tomb 1, no. 35 (S. Lubsen-Admiraal (supra n. 16) 43, fig. 5, pl. 3.19); Maroni British Tombs 1, no. 32, 3, no. 45 and 14, nos. 116–117 (J. Johnson, *Maroni de Chypre* (*SIMA* 59, Göteborg 1980) 16, 17, 22, pls. X, XII, XXI–XXII and E. Porada, "Appendice I: Seals from the Tombs of Maroni," in Johnson (supra n. 16) 68–70); Kalavasos-*Ayios Dhimitrios* Tomb 4, K-AD

121 (E. Porada, "Cylinder and Stamp Seals," in A. South, P. Russell, and P.S. Keswani, *Vasilikos Valley Project 3: Kalavasos-Ayios Dhimitrios II. Ceramics, Objects, Tombs, Specialist Studies* (*SIMA* 71:3, Göteborg 1989) 34–35, fig. 36, pl. XVI–XVII). On the dating of the Enkomi tombs see *Keswani* 1989, tables 1–3.

[22] *Porada Enkomi* 799–800, no. 18c, pl. 182 (inv. 2131 from Area I, Room 113 of Level IB—a poorly shaped, unengraved example).

[23] E. Gjerstad, J. Lindros, E. Sjöqvist, and A. Westholm, *SwCyprusExp* I, 357, pl. LXVII.3, 12, 28; S.M.S. Al-Radi, *Phlamoudhi* Vounari: *A Sanctuary Site in Cyprus* (*SIMA* 65, Göteborg 1983) 100; *Webb* 1987, 66–68, no. 16, pls. I, V; J.S. Smith, "The Cylinder Seal and the Inscribed Sherd," in I.A. Todd et al., "Excavations at Sanida 1991," *RDAC* 1992, 104–105, fig. 6a–b, pl. XXX.14 (S-MAS 156); B. Buchanan, "The Seals and an Amulet," in J. du Plat Taylor, *Myrtou-Pigadhes: A Late Bronze Age Sanctuary in Cyprus* (Oxford 1957) 92–93, no. 328, pl. V; E. Porada, "Cylinder Seals," in T. Dothan and A. Ben-Tor, *Excavations at Athienou, Cyprus 1971–1972* (*Qedem* 16, Jerusalem 1983) 120–21, fig. 54.3–4, pl. 38.4–5; E. Porada in South, Russell, and Keswani (supra n. 21) 33–35, K-AD 455, 171, 330, fig. 36, pls. XVI–XVIII; D. Collon, "A Cylinder Seal from Maroni-*Tsaroukkas*," in S.W. Manning et al., "*Tsaroukkas*, Mycenaeans and Trade Project: Preliminary Report on the 1993 Season," *RDAC* 1994, 103–106, fig. 13, pl. XII.4; G. Cadogan, "Maroni and the Late Bronze Age of Cyprus," in V. Karageorghis and J.D. Muhly eds., *Cyprus at the Close of the Late Bronze Age* (Nicosia 1984) 9; E. Porada, "Glyptics," in J.L. Benson, *Bamboula at Kourion: The Necropolis and the Finds* (Philadelphia 1972) 141–44, B1624, pl. 38; E. Porada, "Appendix I: Cylinder and Stamp Seals from Kition," in V. Karageorghis, *Excavations at Kition V: The Pre-Phoenician Levels, Part II* (Nicosia 1985) 251, no. 223/1, pl. A.2 (Area I, Room 44, Floor IV).

[24] E.g., *Porada Enkomi* 785–810, pls. 179–182A, 185–186A; *Webb* 1987, 25–91, pls. 1–11; *Schaeffer Corpus* 56–58, 164; Porada in Karageorghis (supra n. 23) 250–53, pl. A.1, 3–4; A. Hatziantoniou, "Area 6, Southern Sectors," in P. Åström, E. Åström, A. Hatziantoniou, K. Niklasson, and U. Öbrink, *Hala Sultan Tekke 8: Excavations 1971–79* (*SIMA* 45:8, Göteborg 1983) 124, N 2023b, fig. 369; E. Gjerstad, J. Lindros, E. Sjöqvist, and A. Westholm, *SwCyprusExp* II, 545, 555, 564, inv. 482, 877, 892, 1294, pl. CLXXXVI.17, 19, 21, 22; Porada in Benson (supra n. 23) 141–44, pl. 38, B1625, B1627, B1630; S. Hadjisavvas, "A Late Cypriot Community at Alassa," in Peltenburg (supra n. 18) 37–38.

[25] *Kenna* 1972, 646–74.

[26] This is particularly evident at Enkomi where the majority of cylinders were recovered from LC IIC and LC III levels. See *Webb* 1987, 26.

[27] The benefits of such an approach are demonstrated by Keswani in her study of the Enkomi tombs (*Keswani* 1989). Small objects such as seals are also likely to have been redistributed by postdepositional processes (as noted also in *Kenna* 1972, 623).

[28] The estimate (table 2) of 200+ cylinders from Enkomi is a conservative one. For a list of those recovered during well-documented excavations see *Webb* 1987, 25, n. 1. Seals attributed to Kourion by Cesnola, and in particular to the fraudulent "Curium Treasure" (L.P. di Cesnola, *Cyprus: Its Ancient Cities, Tombs and Temples* (London 1877) 302ff), are not included. These seals were probably gathered from a variety of other sources. See O.

Masson, "L. Palma di Cesnola, H. Schliemann et l'éditeur John Murray," *Centre d'Etudes Chypriotes* 21 (1994) 7–14.

[29] V. Karageorghis, "Chronique des fouilles et découvertes archéologiques à Chypre en 1979," *BCH* 104 (1980) 772, fig. 44, from a Cypro-Archaic tomb at Ayios Nicolaos; E. Gjerstad, J. Lindros, E. Sjöqvist, and A. Westholm, *SwCyprusExp* II, 542, 543, 730, 773, pls. CLXXXVI.18, 20, CCXLIII.20–21 (inv. 1550 and 2752 from Period 4 (Cypro-Archaic) of the cult complex at Ayia Irini and inv. 369 and 390 from Period 6 (Cypro-Archaic I–Cypro-Classical I) of the Idalion-*Ambelleri* sanctuary; E. Porada, "Appendix III: Cylinder and Stamp Seals from Palaepaphos-*Skales*," in V. Karageorghis, *Palaepaphos-Skales: An Iron Age Cemetery in Cyprus* (Konstanz 1983) 407–409, pl. CXX (Cypro-Geometric III Tomb 71, nos. 1a, 35, and 46); E. Porada, "A Remarkable Cylinder Seal from Amathus," *RDAC* 1987, 79–80, pl. XXII (a hexagonal cylinder deposited in the seventh century B.C. in Tomb 444).

[30] E. Porada, "The Cylinder Seals of the Late Cypriote Bronze Age," *AJA* 52 (1948) 178–98. Further refined in E. Porada, "The Cylinder Seals Found at Thebes in Boeotia," *AfO* 28 (1981) 9–16, 28–29. On the historiography of Cypriot glyptic research see R.S. Merrillees, "The Glyptic of Late Bronze Age Cyprus: An Historiographical Review," in G. Ioannides and S.A. Hadjistyllis eds., *Proceedings of the Third International Congress of Cypriot Studies, 16–20 April 1996* (Nicosia 2000) 289–300. In that paper Merrillees questions the Cypriot origin of Elaborate Style glyptic, arguing that the iconography of these cylinders is alien to the indigenous artistic repertory and that they are more probably imports.

[31] This identification is based on chemical analyses of several typical Common Style cylinders in the British Museum. See D. Collon, *First Impressions. Cylinder Seals in the Ancient Near East* (Chicago 1987) 73; A. Reyes (supra n. 7) 118 and n. 6.

[32] *Schaeffer Corpus*; P. Amiet, *Corpus des cylindres de Ras Shamra-Ougarit II: Sceaux-cylindres en hématite et pierres diverses* (*Ras Shamra-Ougarit* 9, Paris 1992) 187–200, nos. 451–85.

[33] For a listing of seals with robed figure and lion, griffin, or caprid, see J.M. Webb, "Appendix IV: A Cylinder Seal from Kazaphani-Ayios Andronikos," in I. and K. Nicolaou, *Kazaphani: A Middle/Late Cypriot Tomb at Kazaphani-Ayios Andronikos: T. 2A, B* (Nicosia 1989) 113–14 and ns. 5 and 6, with provenanced examples recorded from Enkomi, Kourion, Nicosia-*Ayia Paraskevi*, Limassol, Ayia Irini, Akhera, Akaki, Maroni, Kazaphani, and Kouklia. For seals depicting a male figure with similar animals, see Webb (supra n. 5) 263–66, fig. 84.

[34] For examples see *Webb* 1987, 68–70 and ns. 205 and 214; Webb (supra n. 5) 272, 276, figs. 16.3, 82.3, 89, 91; A.B. Knapp, *Copper Production and Divine Protection: Archaeology, Ideology and Social Complexity on Bronze Age Cyprus* (*SIMA-PB* 42, Göteborg 1986) 38–40, table 2, nos. 1–12, 14–18, 21, 24.

[35] *Kenna* 1972, 623–36.

[36] On a number of occasions Porada suggested seals were used in the manner of modern "worry beads" (i.e., rubbed between the fingers) in order to account for their extensive surface wear. E.g., Porada in Benson (supra n. 23) 141–42, B 1622; Porada, "A Remarkable Cylinder Seal from Amathus," *RDAC* 1987, 79, n. 3.

[37] *Smith* passim.

[38] In the Aegean and Near East the study of social and administrative structures through seals and sealing practice has been highly productive. See, e.g., articles in Palaima and Gibson and Biggs; I. Pini ed., *Fragen und Probleme der Bronzezeitlichen Ägäischen Glyptik*, (*CMS Beiheft* 3, Berlin 1989); Zettler (supra n. 12).

[39] *Kenna* 1972, 667 lists another sealing, identified as that of an Elaborate Style cylinder, from Ohnefalsch-Richter's excavations at *Ayia Paraskevi* (M. Ohnefalsch-Richter, *Kypros, the Bible and Homer: Oriental Civilization, Art and Religion in Ancient Times* (London 1893) 439, pl. CXXVIII.5). The illustration referred to, however, is a drawing of an impression, not an ancient sealing.

[40] *Porada Enkomi* 790–91, inv. 1905/9, pls. 182/4c, 182A. The seal used to make this impression is also identified as non-Cypriot by *Kenna* 1971, 13.

[41] *Smith* 170–73, fig. 30.

[42] A. Evans, *PM* volume IV, pt. II (London 1935) 598, fig. 593 (Heraklion Museum no. 272). Now see M.R. Popham and M.A.V. Gill, *The Latest Sealings from the Palace and Houses at Knossos* (*British School at Athens Studies* I, Oxford 1995) 20, AECat. no. 20, pls. 12, 29, 42; C.F.A. Schaeffer, "Les Fouilles de Ras-Shamra: Cinquième Campagne (Printemps 1933)," *Syria* 15 (1934) 118, 123, fig. 8 (right); W.H. van Soldt, "Labels from Ugarit," *UgaritF* 21 (1989) 376, no. 4, fig. 8a right (R.S. 5.269); C.F.A. Schaeffer, "Commentaires sur les lettres et documents trouvés dans les bibliothèques privées d'Ugarit," *Ugaritica* 5 (1968), figs. 4, 4A, 7, 8, 8A, R.S. 17.36, R.S. 17.149. I owe the latter two references to the work of *Smith* 176–81.

[43] *Webb* 1992, 114–15; *Smith* 238–313. This number includes a jar fragment from Episkopi-*Bamboula* impressed with an Old Bablylonian seal, of essentially different type from the rest of the group (J.L. Benson, "Aegean and Near Eastern Seal Impressions from Cyprus," in S.S. Weinberg ed., *The Aegean and the Near East. Studies Presented to Hetty Goldman on the Occasion of her Seventy-Fifth Birthday* (Locust Valley, NY 1956) 59–79, pls. VII–VIII). For additional examples see Webb and Frankel 12–14, fig. 5; S. Hadjisavvas, "Alassa Archaeological Project 1991–1993," *RDAC* 1994, 111, pl. XIX; S. Hadjisavvas and I. Hadjisavva, "Aegean Influence at Alassa," in *Proceedings of the International Archaeological Conference: Cyprus and the Aegean in Antiquity from the Prehistoric Period to the 7th Century A.D., Nicosia 8–10 December 1995* (Nicosia 1997) 146, fig. 4.

[44] This was originally suggested by V.E.G. Kenna in H.W. Catling and V. Karageorghis, "Minoika in Cyprus," *BSA* 55 (1960) 123. See now *Smith* 252, who also notes stylistic parallels with Cypriot ivory carving.

[45] Pullen (supra n. 12) 50, n. 65, citing T.G. Palaima in *Palaima* 245, n. 7; D. Collon (supra n. 31) 119 cites four examples of seal/seal impression combinations from the Near East.

[46] *Smith* 61–65, 253.

[47] There is, similarly, little direct evidence for the sphragistic use of stamps in Iron Age Cyprus with only two known sealings from Kition (G. Clerc in G. Clerc, V. Karageorghis, E. Lagarce, and J. Leclant, *Fouilles de Kition II: Objets égyptiens et égyptisants: Scarabées, amulettes et figurines en pâte de verre et en faïence, vase plastique en faïence, sites I et II,*

1959–1975 (Nicosia 1976) 114–16, nos. 516, 1072). Stamps inscribed with names in the genitive, however, suggest common use of seals to safeguard property and authenticate transactions (Reyes [supra n. 7] 127).

[48] *Smith* 106–142.

[49] *Keswani* 1993; *Keswani* 1996; Peltenburg in Karageorghis and Michaelides (supra n. 1); Knapp in Åström and Herscher (supra n. 1); Knapp (supra n. 1); *Smith* 9–44. For a different point of view see R.S. Merrillees, "The Government of Cyprus in the Late Bronze Age," in P. Åström ed., *Acta Cypria. Acts of an International Congress on Cypriote Archaeology Held in Göteborg on 22–24 August 1991* (*SIMA-PB* 120, Jonsered 1992) 310–28.

[50] *Keswani* 1993. See Knapp (supra n. 49) 48–52 for a further discussion and refinement of Keswani's fourfold settlement system.

[51] Peltenburg (supra n. 1). See also Webb (supra n. 5) 305–308. Centralization of political power or/and domination of the copper industry at Enkomi from the beginning of the LC period is also accepted by Knapp (A.B. Knapp, "Social Complexity: Incipience, Emergence, and Development on Prehistoric Cyprus," *BASOR* 292 [1993] 99; *Knapp* 1996, 91) and Muhly (J.D. Muhly, "The Organisation of the Copper Industry in Late Bronze Age Cyprus," in Peltenburg [supra n. 18] 299–330. See, however, *Keswani* 1993, 73–76 and 1996, 234; and Merrillees (supra n. 49).

[52] See, e.g., R. Cohen and E.R. Service eds., *Origins of the State. The Anthropology of Political Evolution* (Philadelphia 1978); J. Haas, *The Evolution of the Prehistoric State* (New York 1982); S. Upham ed., *The Evolution of Political Systems: Sociopolitics in Small-Scale Sedentary Societies* (Cambridge 1990); G. Stein and M.S. Rothman eds., *Chiefdoms and Early States in the Near East: The Organizational Dynamics of Complexity (Monographs in World Archaeology* 18, Madison 1994).

[53] Peltenburg (supra n. 1) 35. For a discussion of staple and wealth finance in the context of the whole of the Bronze Age in Cyprus, see Knapp in Mathers and Stoddart eds. (supra n. 1).

[54] *Keswani* 1993. See also *Webb and Frankel.*

[55] Peltenburg (supra n. 1) 35; Knapp (supra n. 34); A.B. Knapp, "Ideology, Archaeology and Polity," *Man* n.s. 23 (1988) 133–63; *Knapp* 1996, 81–94; *Keswani* 1993, 76.

[56] T.N. D'Altroy and T.K. Earle, "Staple Finance, Wealth Finance, and Storage in the Inka Political Economy," *CurrAnthr* 26 (1985) 187–206. See also T.K. Earle, "Specialization and the Production of Wealth: Hawaiian Chiefdoms and the Inka Empire," in E.M. Brumfiel and T.K. Earle eds., *Specialization, Exchange, and Complex Societies* (Cambridge 1987) 64–75; T.K. Earle and T.N. D'Altroy, "The Political Economy of the Inka Empire: The Archaeology of Power and Finance," in C.C. Lamberg-Karlovsky ed., *Archaeological Thought in America* (Cambridge 1989) 183–204; T. Earle, "Wealth Finance in the Inka Empire: Evidence from the Calchaquí Valley, Argentina," *American Antiquity* 59 (1994) 443–60.

[57] See, e.g., D'Altroy and Earle (supra n. 56); E.M. Brumfiel and T.K. Earle, "Specialization, Exchange and Complex Societies: An Introduction," in Brumfiel and Earle (supra n. 56) 1–9.

[58]See discussion in *Keswani* 1993, *Keswani* 1996, *Webb and Frankel*, and A.B. Knapp, S.O. Held, I. Johnson, and P.S. Keswani, "The Sydney Cyprus Survey Project (SCSP): Second Preliminary Season (1993)," *RDAC* 1994, 337–41.

[59] *Webb and Frankel* 18 with refs.

[60] In *Webb and Frankel* 18–20.

[61] T.K. Earle comment on P. Rice, "Evolution of Specialized Pottery Production: A Trial Model," *CurrAnthr* 22 (1981) 230–31. The same organizational phenomenon is referred to as "administered production" by C. Sinopoli, "The Organization of Craft production at Vijayanagara, South India," *American Anthropologist* 90 (1988) 580–97, and as "tethered production" by R.S. Santley, P.J. Arnold III, and C.A. Pool, "The Ceramics Production System at Matacapan, Veracruz, Mexico," *JFA* 16 (1989) 107–132. For a useful discussion of terminology and related issues see C.L. Costin, "Craft Specialization: Issues in Defining, Documenting, and Explaining the Organization of Production," in M.B. Schiffer ed., *Archaeological Method and Theory* 3 (1991) 1–56, and various papers in B. Wailes ed., *Craft Specialization and Social Evolution: In Memory of V. Gordon Childe* (*University Museum Monograph* 93, Philadelphia 1996).

[62] Especially P.S. Keswani, "A Preliminary Investigation of Systems of Ceramic Production and Distribution in Cyprus During the Late Bronze Age," in J.A. Barlow, D.L. Bolger, and B. Kling eds., *Cypriot Ceramics: Reading the Prehistoric Record* (*University Museum Monograph* 74, Philadelphia 1991) 97–118 and Vermeule and Wolsky (supra n. 20). The organization of copper production has also received attention; most notably in T. Stech, "Copper and Society in Late Bronze Age Cyprus," in A.B. Knapp and T. Stech eds., *Prehistoric Production and Exchange: The Aegean and Eastern Mediterranean* (*Institute of Archaeology, University of California, Monograph* 25, Los Angeles 1985) 100–105; T. Stech, "Urban Metallurgy in Late Bronze Age Cyprus," in J.D. Muhly, R. Maddin, and V. Karageorghis eds., *Early Metallurgy in Cyprus, 4000–500 B.C.* (Nicosia 1982) 105–115; and J.D. Muhly, "The Organization of the Copper Industry in Late Bronze Age Cyprus," in E. Peltenberg (supra n. 18) 298–314. On olive oil production see S. Hadjisavvas, *Olive Oil Processing in Cyprus from the Bronze Age to the Byzantine Period* (*SIMA* 99, Nicosia 1992).

[63] I.A. Todd and M. Hadjicosti, "Excavations at Sanidha 1990," *RDAC* 1991, 37–74; I.A. Todd et al., "Excavations at Sanida 1991," *RDAC* 1992, 75–112; I.A. Todd and D. Pilides, "Excavations at Sanida 1992," *RDAC* 1993, 97–146.

[64] For this argument in regard to elite pottery production see P. Rice, "Evolution of Specialized Pottery Production: A Trial Model," *CurrAnthr* 22 (1981) 223.

[65] See Rice (supra n. 64) 219–27. On the key distinction between attached and independent specialization, geared respectively to elite and general demand, see Costin (supra n. 61) 5–11.

[66] P. Dikaios, *Enkomi, Excavations 1948–1958: Chronology, Summary and Conclusions, Catalogue, Appendices*, volume II (Mainz am Rhein 1971) 811–12; *Porada Enkomi* 796–97, 799, nos. 12, 18, inv. 1484, 1568, pls. 179/12, 18–19. A fourth, copper cylinder was found in the adjoining Room 35 and also attributed by Dikaios to "the cylinder seal carver's rooms" (*Porada Enkomi*, 795, no. 10, inv. 1218, pls. 179/10, 181/10, 186/10).

[67] Dikaios (supra n. 66) 516 and pl. 254.

[68] Preshaped unengraved cylinders were also recovered from Room 113 of Area I (Level IB) and Rooms 67 and 92 of Area III (Level IIIB) (*Porada Enkomi* 799–800, nos. 18a–c, inv. 2131, 1849, and 3288) and during the British excavations at Enkomi (*Kenna* 1971, 19–20, no. 15, 24 (the latter attributed to Enkomi in *Kenna* 1972, 652). For unfinished and abraded examples awaiting re-engraving see also *Webb* 1987, 90–91, nos. 40–43. Other unengraved and abraded cylinders have been found at Hala Sultan Tekke (Hatziantoniou (supra n. 24) 124, fig. 369 (N 2023b), Apliki-*Karamallos* (J. du Plat Taylor, "A Late Bronze Age Settlement at Apliki, Cyprus," *AntJ* 32 [1952] 142, Room 8, no. 11), Ayios Iakovos Tomb 8, third burial period, nos. 39, 77 (E. Gjerstad, J. Lindros, E. Sjöqvist, and A. Westholm, *SwCyprusExp* I, 332, nos. 39, 77, pl. LXIII.1), Ayios Iakovos-*Dhima* (E. Gjerstad, J. Lindros, E. Sjöqvist, and A. Westholm, *SwCyprusExp* I, 358, inv. 41, pl. LXVI.2.), Idalion (E. Gjerstad, J. Lindros, E. Sjöqvist, and A. Westholm, *SwCyprusExp* II, 555, inv. 892, pl. CLXXXVI.22) and Maroni (*Kenna* 1971, 19, nos. 13 [from Tomb 14] and 14).

[69] *Keswani* 1989, esp. tables 1–3. Note that the majority of tombs in the sample appear to have been used by middle- and upper-level elites, with the wider population poorly or unrepresented (*Keswani* 1989, 56–57).

[70] Note, also, a stamp seal and two gold signet rings with Cypro-Minoan inscriptions associated with a high status female burial of LC IIA date in Tomb 11 at Kalavasos, one of the richest intact tombs excavated on the island (A.K. South, "From Copper to Kingship: Aspects of Bronze Age Society Viewed from the Vasilikos Valley," in Peltenburg (supra n. 18) 318–19; E. Goring, "Death in Everyday Life: Aspects of Burial Practice in the Late Bronze Age," in Peltenburg (supra n. 18) 98–104, fig. 13.1.

[71] The deposition of seals in burials is usually seen as indicative of amuletic or votive function or their use as items of personal adornment (*Kenna* 1967, 553; J. Karageorghis, *La Grande Déesse de Chypre et son culte: A travers l'iconographie, de l'Époque Néolithique au VIème s.a. C.* (Lyon 1977) 92–93; *Smith* 106–111). Notably, however, cylinders from settlement deposits at Enkomi outnumber those from tombs by almost three to one (*Webb* 1987, 28, n. 21).

[72] E.g., M. Wobst, "Stylistic Behaviour and Information Exchange," in C.E. Cleland ed., *For the Director: Research Essays in Honor of James B. Griffin* (Ann Arbor 1977) 317–42; A. Appadurai ed., *The Social Life of Things: Commodities in Cultural Perspective* (Cambridge 1986); I. Hodder ed., *Symbolic and Structural Archaeology* (Cambridge 1982); D.D. Davis, "Hereditary Emblems: Material Culture in the Context of Social Change," *JAnthArch* 4 (1985) 149–76.

[73] Inscribed seals have most recently been studied by *Smith* 142–64. Some were designed to be read in the impression, others on the seal itself. In the latter instance signs were usually added after the carving of the design, possibly to enhance votive use. Most signs, however, are symmetrical and could be read in the positive on the seal or the negative on the impression.

[74] Elaborate Style seals, as well as examples of other types, are occasionally found outside the island. See those listed in *Kenna* 1972 and P. Beck, "The Cylinder Seals," in S. Ben-

Arieh and G. Edelstein, "Akko: Tombs near the Persian Garden," *Atiqot* 12 (1977) 63–69; P. Beck, "A Cypriote Cylinder Seal from Lachish," *Tel Aviv* 10 (1983) 178–81; E. Porada, "The Cylinder Seals Found at Thebes in Boeotia," *Archiv für Orientforschung* 28 (1981) 1–78; H. Kantor, "Oriental Institute Museum Notes, No. 9. A 'Syro-Hittite' Treasure in the Oriental Institute Museum," *JNES* 16 (1957) 156–58, pl. XXVA–B; Amiet (supra n. 31).

[75] The function and significance of these impressions is further explored in *Webb and Frankel* 17–20.

[76] The appearance of ingots in glyptic iconography has been most fully discussed by Knapp (supra n. 34) 37–42, who suggests that the repeated Common Style motif with human being, tree, bucranium, and ingot(s) shows a man offering ingots and other objects before a sacred tree. This thematic concept, he argues, served as a symbolic image propagated by the managerial elites of the Cypriot copper industry to encourage copper production and link their desired goals with political, religious, and economic authority. See also Webb 1992, 118–19.

[77] In particular papers in Brumfiel and Earle (supra n. 56); Hodder (supra n. 4); Miller and Tilley (supra n. 6); C. Renfrew and S. Shennan eds., *Ranking, Resource and Exchange: Aspects of the Archaeology of Early European Society* (Cambridge 1982); J. Graham-Campbell ed., *Craft Production and Specialization* (*WorldArch* 23, 1991); K. Kristiansen, "Ideology and Material Culture: An Archaeological Perspective," in M. Spriggs ed., *Marxist Perspectives in Archaeology* (Cambridge 1984) 72–100; Costin (supra n. 61); J.E. Clark and W.J. Parry, "Craft Specialisation and Cultural Complexity," *Research in Economic Anthropology* 12 (1990) 289–346; K.C. Chang, *Art, Myth, and Ritual. The Path to Political Authority in Ancient China* (Cambridge, MA 1983); T.K. Earle, "The Ecology and Politics of Primitive Variables," in J.G. Kennedy and R.B. Edgerton eds., *Culture and Ecology: Eclectic Perspectives* (*American Anthropological Association Special Publication* 15, Washington 1982) 65–83; E.M. Schortman and P.A. Urban, "Living on the Edge: Core/Periphery Relations in Ancient Southeastern Mesoamerica," *CurrAnthr* 35 (1994) 401–413 and others noted supra and infra.

[78] H.J. Nissen, "Aspects of the Development of Early Cylinder Seals," in *Gibson and Biggs* 15–23.

[79] W.J. Rathje, "New Tricks for Old Seals: A Progress Report," in *Gibson and Biggs* 25–32; I.J. Winter, "Legitimation of Authority Through Image and Legend: Seals Belonging to Officials in the Administrative Bureaucracy of the Ur III State," in M. Gibson and R.D. Biggs eds., *The Organization of Power: Aspects of Bureaucracy in the Ancient Near East* (*Studies in Ancient Oriental Civilization* 46, Chicago 1987) 69–116.

[80] M.I. Marcus, "Glyptic Style and Seal Function: The Hasanlu Collection," in *Palaima* 175–93.

[81] B. Magness-Gardiner, "The Function of Cylinder Seals in Syrian Palace Archives," in *Palaima* 61–76; I.J. Gelb, "Typology of Mesopotamian Seal Inscriptions," in *Gibson and Biggs* 107–126; J.-M. Durand, "A propos des légends des empreintes de sceaux des Šakkanakku de Mari," *RAssyr* 75 (1981) 180–181. See also H. Pittman, *Glazed Steatite Glyptic Art: The Structure and Function of an Image System* (Diss. Columbia Univ. 1989).

[82] Magness-Gardiner (supra n. 81) 65 with refs. There is also considerable evidence for the prolonged use of personal seals across generations. See M.T. Larsen, "Seal Use in the Old Assyrian Period," in *Gibson and Biggs* 98–99.

[83] Winter (supra n. 79); H.J. Nissen, "'Sumerian' vs. 'Akkadian' Art: Art and Politics in Babylonia of the Mid-Third Millennium B.C.," in M. Kelly-Buccellati, P. Matthiae, and M. Van Loon eds., *Insight Through Images: Studies in Honor of Edith Porada* (*Bibliotheca Mesopotamica* 21, Malibu 1986) 194–95; L. Gorelick and A.J. Gwinnett, "The Ancient Near Eastern Cylinder Seal as Social Emblem and Status Symbol," *JNES* 49 (1990) 45–56. For an analysis of the relationship between glyptic iconography and status in the Aegean see R. Laffineur, "The Iconography of Mycenaean Seals and the Status of their Owners," *Aegaeum* 6 (1990) 117–60; R. Laffineur, "Iconography as Evidence of Social and Political Status in Mycenaean Greece," in R. Laffineur and J.L. Crowley eds., *EIKΩN: Aegean Bronze Age Iconography: Shaping a Methodology. Proceedings of the 4th International Aegean Conference, University of Tasmania, Hobart, Australia, 6–9 April 1992* (*Aegaeum* 8, Liège 1992) 105–112.

[84] See N. Abercrombie, S. Hill, and B. Turner, *The Dominant Ideology Thesis* (London 1980); Adams (supra n. 6) and *Knapp* 1996, 72 on the dangers of an overly instrumentalist view of ideology.

[85] *Knapp* 1996, 82–85; B.G. Trigger, "Monumental Architecture: A Thermodynamic Explanation of Symbolic Behaviour," *WorldArch* 22 (1990) 119–32; M.J. Kolb, "Monumentality and the Rise of Religious Authority in Precontact Hawai'i," *CurrAnthr* 34 (1994) 521–47.

[86] Merrillees (supra n. 30).

[87] Sixteen cylinders and seven stamps engraved in 'Egyptianizing Linear Style' are extant. Of 20 provenanced examples, 15 have been recovered at Enkomi, with additional examples from Kourion, Hala Sultan Tekke, and Idalion (*Webb* 1987, 74–84 and ns. 237 and 239 with refs). Common Style cylinders depicting a repeated combination of seated figure with spear, attendant, tree, snake, bird, ingot, and/or bucranium also appear to be products of a single workshop. Seven of 11 provenanced seals of this type come from Enkomi, with others recorded at Dromolaxia and Ayia Irini (*Webb* 1987, 68–69 and ns. 205 and 207 with refs). For a discussion of other workshops located at Enkomi see *Webb* 1987, 31.

[88] See, e.g., M. Rowlands, "Power and Moral Order in Precolonial West-Central Africa," in Brumfiel and Earle (supra n. 56) 52–63; E.M. Brumfiel, "Elite and Utilitarian Crafts in the Aztec State," in Brumfiel and Earle (supra n. 56) 102–118.

The Display and Viewing of the Syllabic Inscriptions of Rantidi Sanctuary*

◈

Georgia Bonny Bazemore

Writing in Cyprus during the Iron Age

The epigraphic evidence for writing in Cyprus during the Iron Age is over-whelmingly syllabic. The Cypriot Syllabic writing system was deciphered in 1871, by means of a Phoenician/syllabic, digraphic, bilingual inscrip-tion.[1] The Cypriot syllabary consists of around 60 signs whose phonetic value is recognized, with an as yet undefined number of signs whose stan-dard epigraphic shape and phonetic value have yet to be been determined.[2] Readable inscriptions show that the Cypriot writing system was limited to the phonetic representation of five vowels and syllables only in the form of a consonant followed by a vowel, that is, an open syllable. It is from this syl-labic structure that the writing system gained its name.[3] The syllabic script was used to write both ancient Greek and a language that, although pho-netically largely reconstructed, remains unreadable. This language is believed to have been that of the pre-Greek, native Cypriot population, and thus is termed Eteo-Cypriot.[4]

Eteo-Cypriot is a catchall term applied to those syllabic inscriptions that cannot be plausibly or convincingly translated as Greek.[5] The two acknowl-edged scholars of the Cypriot syllabary, T.B. Mitford, primarily an epigra-pher, and O. Masson, primarily a philologist, disagree on the identification of inscriptions as Eteo-Cypriot. Masson argues that Mitford was often inclined to find Eteo-Cypriot anthroponyms, and that he seems to have been "too bold in these difficult matters."[6] Masson, however, prefers to see most texts as Greek, so much so that he emends texts to achieve readings in the Greek language.[7] The body of syllabic inscriptions in the Eteo-Cypriot language has yet to be identified, specified, and systematically studied. It cannot be said at this time whether syllabic inscriptions identified as Eteo-Cypriot contain one or more languages. Ancient authors identified three distinct linguistic groups on Cyprus: Greek, Phoenician, and autochthonous.[8] Scylax refers to cities in the interior of the island as being barbarian, but it is not known whether these so-called barbarians are to be identified with the autochthonous population or were a distinct cultural and linguistic group or groups.

Most of the Phoenician population of Cyprus was located in the city-kingdom of Kition, an early foundation from the Phoenician homeland on the nearby Syro-Palestinian coast.[9] The rulers and population of this city used the Phoenician writing system, although a few syllabic inscriptions also have been found there.[10] Outside of Kition, a small number of Phoenician inscriptions have been found scattered throughout the island.[11]

Despite the epigraphic and literary evidence for a Greek-speaking population on the island, the Greek alphabet made little impact on Cyprus until a relatively late date. Only six alphabetic inscriptions can be cited for the period before the end of the fifth century B.C., some created by persons identifying themselves as being not native to Cyprus.[12] The small numbers of syllabic/alphabetic digraphs created during the fourth century, as well as the explosion in the number of alphabetic inscriptions seen at the very end of the fourth century, reflect contemporary political realities, culminating in the annexation and rule of the island by the Ptolemies, rather than some type of script change or transfer by the native Cypriots.[13]

I have identified 1,378 published syllabic inscriptions,[14] of which 1,206 were found on the island itself. Of those inscriptions found in Cyprus, 81 have no known or assured provenience, leaving 1,125 syllabic inscriptions whose provenience within Cyprus is (reasonably) assured. One hundred seventy-two syllabic inscriptions have been found outside of Cyprus. A few of these come from the Aegean and the Near East, but the majority of the syllabic inscriptions found outside of the island are found in Egypt, written on temple walls by Cypriot soldiers serving in that area.[15] Within Cyprus, syllabic inscriptions are not found evenly scattered throughout the island but instead occur in large numbers only in certain sanctuaries and necropoleis. By far the largest body of syllabic inscriptions, 268 in number, has been recovered from the siege mound of ancient Paphos.[16] This mound was thrown up against the northeastern gate of the city wall and is associated with the events of 498 B.C., when the Persians laid siege to those Cypriot cities that had joined the Ionian Revolt.[17] The inscriptions are among more than 1,000 pieces of worked limestone, including statues of humans, lions and sphinxes, stelae, freestanding columns, and incense altars, which the Persians used to anchor the soil in their mound of siege. The worked stones of the siege mound represent votive offerings taken from one or more extramural sanctuaries;[18] modern survey has failed to locate any trace of what must once have been rich and thriving cult centers.[19] The stone objects found in the siege mound date from the seventh and sixth centuries B.C., but Masson assigns the bulk of the epigraphic material to the last half of the sixth century.[20] The 268 inscriptions recovered from the siege mound represent 22.22%, or more than one-fifth, of all syllabic inscriptions found on the island, and 23.82% of those syllabic inscriptions found Cyprus whose provenience is known.

Only 6 km to the northeast of Paphos in the Rantidi Forest was situated the sanctuary on the hilltop known today as Lingrin tou Dhiyeni. The 174 inscriptions published as having been discovered at this site[21] constitute 14.43% of the body of syllabic inscriptions found in Cyprus, and 15.47% of those with known provenience. The epigraphic forms displayed in the inscriptions from Rantidi led the perceptive Mitford to note that the sign forms of Rantidi and those of the siege mound "show the closest kinship" and are "palpably monuments of the same society and the same age."[22] Together, these Paphian sanctuaries of the siege mound and Rantidi Forest have produced 442 inscriptions, constituting 36.65%, or more than one-third, of all the syllabic inscriptions found on the island, and 39.29% of inscriptions with known provenience within Cyprus.

To put these numbers in perspective, it should be noted that, after Paphos, the syllabic inscriptions of the city kingdom of ancient Marion are the most numerous in the archaeological record. However, during the complete span of the use of the syllabic writing system, the entire city kingdom of Marion, including its outlying settlements, has produced only 149 inscriptions, less than the single site of Lingrin tou Dhiyeni in the Rantidi

Forest. The inscriptions of Marion are dated to the fifth and fourth centuries B.C. and, unlike the other large groups of syllabic inscriptions, originate primarily from the necropoleis that surrounded the city.[23] In the eastern part of the island, Golgoi has been especially productive in syllabic inscriptions, offering up 72 inscribed objects, most of which originate from the temple of Apollo; these inscriptions date from the sixth to the fourth centuries B.C.[24] The cults of the Paphian lady and of Apollo at Chytroi have produced 29 syllabic inscriptions, which are probably of a similar date.[25] At Kaphizin, 66 syllabic inscriptions were found on dedications made to the cult of the Nymphs there; these inscriptions are dated, through regnal years given in their content, to 225–218 B.C.[26] The latest known use of the syllabic writing system is from neither a sanctuary nor a necropolis, but rather is found on 23 sealings accidentally preserved by a fire in the archives at Nea Paphos; debris from these archives is dated from later second to the end of the first century B.C.[27] These few sites alone have produced 781 syllabic inscriptions, or 64.76% of all syllabic inscriptions found in Cyprus and 69.42% of those syllabic inscriptions having a known provenience within Cyprus. The remaining 30+% of syllabic inscriptions have been found in lesser numbers, scattered throughout various sanctuaries and necropoleis of the island.

The Syllabary and the City-Kingdom of Paphos

It was Sir Arthur Evans who first argued that the similarity of sign forms indicated that the Iron Age writing system of Cyprus had, through the medium of the local Bronze Age script, ultimately descended from the Minoan scripts of Crete.[28] According to this theory, Cyprus did not lose the knowledge of writing at the end of the Bronze Age and Cypriot literacy, and literate practices, continued unbroken. Evans's theory of the derivation and continuity of Cypriot scripts continues to find acceptance today;[29] on the basis of his beliefs about its origins, Evans designated the Bronze Age script of Cyprus as Cypro-Minoan.[30]

Inscriptions in the syllabic script first appear in the archaeological record in ancient Paphos. A bronze obelos from a tomb in the necropolis of Palaepaphos-*Skales* carries five signs representing a Greek name in the Arcado-Cypriot dialectal genitive, Ὀφελταυ. The excavator dates this object to the Cypro-Geometric (CG) I period, specifically the second half of the 11th century B.C.[31] There are difficulties with this dating. CG I is not limited to the 11th century, but runs into the 10th century B.C. as well.[32] Furthermore, this was a large tomb group, containing the offerings from at least three separate burials; even the author admits certain objects as suggestive of the CG II period.[33] Whatever the exact date of this object, the sign forms on this obelos are widely interpreted as representing a transitory phase between Cypro-Minoan and the distinctive sign repertoire used by Paphos in the Archaic period.[34]

The second oldest syllabic inscription is that painted before firing on a White Painted III ware jug dated to the beginning of the CG III period, specifically the second half of the ninth century B.C. This vase is believed to have come from ancient Paphos; unknown variant sign forms prevent the reading of this inscription.[35] The number of inscriptions attributed to the eighth until the sixth century B.C. remains small, but the use of the syllabary is attested throughout the island during those centuries.[36]

Syllabic inscriptions appear in Paphos not only much earlier than elsewhere, but also in far greater numbers than are attested for any other area on the island. Before the end of the sixth century B.C., the temples surrounding the city of Paphos created inscribed objects whose sheer number represent an outpouring of literate activity unparalleled in the archaeological record throughout the (near-) millennium of attested syllabic use. The literate activity first displayed in large numbers in the Paphian sanctuaries was paralleled, but to a lesser degree, in later periods by a few other sanctuaries within the island. As can be seen even in the brief review above, syllabic inscriptions are associated primarily with sanctuary use; outside of Marion, Cypriot necropoleis have produced relatively few inscribed objects. The sanctuaries of Paphos, then, offer the best opportunity to study the archaeologically preserved syllabic inscriptions within their most commonly known social and ritual context. By observing the way in which inscriptions are presented in the Paphian sanctuaries, their medium, method of display, opportunities to be viewed, and content, the scholar can then begin to reconstruct the uses of the syllabic script as reflected by the archaeological record. The multiplicity of examples in the Paphian record may lead to insights into the causes for the creation of durable written documents on stone in ancient Cyprus, and the role of these inscriptions in Cypriot social and religious life.

Much of the Paphian corpus, however, specifically those inscriptions of the siege mound, were *ex situ* at the time of their excavation, and the site of their original deposition remains unknown. If the inscribed objects from the siege mound should originate from more than one sanctuary, then materials associated with the inscriptions are indiscriminately mixed with disassociated material, and inscriptions from individual sites cannot be identified. Other than general observations concerning the physical characteristics of the inscriptions and their content, this large and valuable body of material, ripped out of the context of its deposition, cannot be used to examine the display and viewing of syllabic inscriptions in ancient Cyprus. The evidence for this study then is limited to the inscriptions of the sanctuary at Rantidi-*Lingrin tou Dhiyeni*.[37]

The Sanctuary at Rantidi-*Lingrin tou Dhiyeni* and Its Context in the Paphian Landscape

The city of ancient Paphos sits at the eastern end of a long, narrow coastal plain (fig. 1). North of the city are the mountains of the Troodos massif that dominate western Cyprus. The mountainous nature of this area is alleviated only by the coastal plain, which served as the main route of communication for the western part of the island. Immediately to the east of Paphos, from the wide, deep gorge of the Khapotami to the acropolis of Kourion, the southern coastal plain is interrupted by a finger of the Troodos that juts out

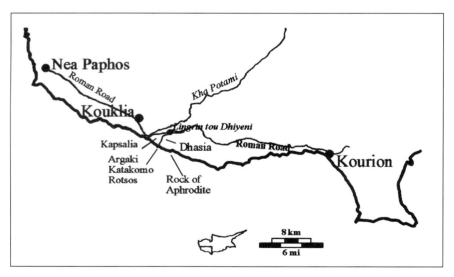

Fig. 1. Map of Rantidi-*Lingrin tou Dhiyeni* and environs

down to the sea. From the eastern lip of the Khapotami rise two elevated plains: Kapsalia to the west overlooking the gorge, and Dhasia to the east. Kapsalia and Dhasia are themselves separated by the narrow, precipitous gorge of the Argaki Katakomo-Rotsos. The Argaki Katakomo-Rotsos, meaning "the stream of the splintered rock" is named after the spectacular rock formation found at the bottom of Lingrin tou Dhiyeni. To the north, these plains end abruptly in mountainous foothills. Together, these elevated plains with their associated foothills are today known as the Rantidi Forest. Upon the large hill that rises at the very head of the Kapsalia plain was a large and rich temple complex of the Archaic period. This hill is today known as Lingrin tou Dhiyeni, or the playing stones of Digenis, after the building stone that litters the area.

The rough geography along the coast east of the Khapotami caused the ancient road leading eastwards from Paphos to turn inland and pass through the Kapsalia plain. Upon reaching Lingrin tou Dhiyeni, the combination of deep gorges and mountainous foothills allow only a single passageway through this area. This road, clearly marked by Roman milestones, was used and maintained well into the 20th century, until the advent of dynamite allowed the construction of the modern coastal road and the ever-increasing use of the automobile diverted traffic from this cobblestone thoroughfare.[38] Today, the ancient road is much deteriorated and, having lost large stretches of its cobbles through neglect and erosion, is little more than a dirt track.

This inland road, humble though it is today, was, until recently, the main road leading from Paphos to Kourion, Amathus, and the city-kingdoms of the east and north. This road runs directly beneath the northern slope of Lingrin tou Dhiyeni and the sanctuary buildings situated there. The position of the sanctuary hill causes the road to skirt the edge of the slope of the Khapotami gorge at a point where the ground falls away steeply. Below the sanctuary the road has been widened by the cutting back of the bedrock of the sanctuary hill, seemingly in ancient times. Northeast of Lingrin tou Dhiyeni, the lower slopes of a high, long hill encroach upon the bottom of the sanctuary, forcing the road to pass through a narrow defile.

The eastern end of the acropolis of the sanctuary hill (fig. 2) offers a fine vantage point from which to observe the progress of travelers on the road leading to the east. Furthermore, the western end of the acropolis offers to the pilgrim visiting the sanctuary buildings there an unfettered and spectacular view of the entire Paphian plain. On a clear day, this vantage point offers

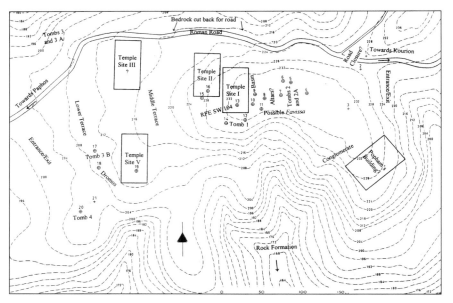

Fig. 2. Rantidi site map, proposed reconstruction of area. Adapted from *Rantidi* Plan I. (Courtesy of the German Archaeological Institute)

a panoramic view of more than 28 km to the sea beyond the western coast of the island.[39] Looking to the west, the Rantidi sanctuary, furthermore, had a commanding view of the Kapsalia and, less so, the Dhasia plains. To date no evidence of habitation has been found on either plain before the Hellenistic period; this area may have been covered in antiquity, as it is today, with trees and shrubs. Rantidi sanctuary then sat atop a narrow bottleneck in the main road, guarding a narrow defile that could be closed and defended easily. From this hilltop, traffic on both the eastern and western approaches to ancient Paphos could be monitored visually; if needed, the traffic flow on the east could be controlled or even stopped. No other hilltop or peak in this area replicates these attributes displayed by Lingrin tou Dhiyeni. Although it was certainly a sanctuary site, its strategic and defensive nature cannot be ignored.

The city of Paphos cannot be understood without reference to the cult of the great goddess housed in that city. The worship of a goddess of fertility in Cyprus seems to have begun as early as the Neolithic period.[40] In Greek mythology, the goddess Aphrodite is said to have been born in Cyprus, with Paphos as the home of her temple and fragrant altar.[41]

Archaeology demonstrates that a great temple existed in this city as early as the Late Bronze Age.[42] In Cyprus sanctuaries of the goddess are found outside of Paphos, where the goddess was referred to as τὰς Παφίας, or the Paphian lady.[43] In Paphos itself, she was referred to as ϝάνασσα, or the Queen; however, inscriptions identifying her as such, when datable, are limited to the late fourth century B.C.[44] Although identified in Greek mythology as Aphrodite, the Cypriot worship of the goddess appeared to the Greeks to be quite different from their own forms of veneration.[45] Today, the site where Aphrodite washed onto Cyprus, self-birthed and fully grown, is identified as a large rock located offshore about 6 km east of Paphos. It is officially known as Petra tou Romiou but often referred to more colloquially as the Rock of Aphrodite. This rock sits just off the southeastern end of the plain of Dhasia. Today the modern road runs past this rock. In antiquity this area was isolated from the main traffic patterns; one of the easier approaches to the Rock of Aphrodite would have been through the Rantidi Forest. If the modern site identified as the birthplace of the goddess is the same as that referred to by Hesiod, then the sanctuary at Lingrin tou Dhiyeni was placed between sites most holy to the great goddess, with the ability to control access to both.

Thus it is seen that the sanctuary on Rantidi Hill was an important part of the ancient Paphian landscape, both strategically and in matters of cult. It is not known whether those officiating the cult here took economic advantage of their control of the main road in any way. Overtly, tolls could have been levied for passage, but other types of extraction are possible, such as obligatory visitation and offerings at the sanctuary.

Excavations at Rantidi

The first formal excavations of the Rantidi sanctuary took place in 1910.[46] In that year Max Ohnefalsch-Richter, a native German who had excavated on Cyprus from 1878 to 1890, made his last sojourn to the island.[47] Informed by a local antiquities dealer of the recent discovery by looters of the sanctuary of Lingrin tou Dhiyeni, he managed a visit to the site. Ohnefalsch-Richter had explored personally more than 72 Cypriot sanctuaries during his time in Cyprus.[48] The sanctuary in the Rantidi Forest was his final discovery and, he believed, his richest.[49] His enthusiastic reports to the Preussische Akademie der Wissenschaften were enough to convince this body to fund exploration of the site. Those responding to his requests were among the luminaries of the academic world, including U. von Wilamowitz-Moelendorff and Eduard Meyer. They appointed Robert Zahn, one of the assistant keepers of the Royal Berlin Museum, to lead the excavation of the Rantidi sanctuary. J.C. Peristianes, an officer of the Cyprus Government Service, was appointed to supervise these excavations, which took place from August 28 until October 7, 1910.[50]

Zahn and Peristianes recovered large numbers of colossal terracotta male and female statues, fragments of phalli, figurines characterized as satyr figures, large storage jars such as amphorae and oinochoae, as well as other types of pottery, statuettes, and syllabic inscriptions. In all, well over 2,000 pieces of statuary and pottery and around 135 syllabic inscriptions are recorded from these excavations.[51] Unfortunately, little information concerning this work survives. As director, Zahn submitted no report or list of his finds to the Cyprus Museum Committee, nor did he publish any report of his excavation results.[52] The documentation for the Rantidi sanctuary was critically depleted with the loss of Peristianes' two diaries, where details of buildings, rock-cut chambers, and the findspots of many objects had been recorded. Equally damaging is the loss of the entire collection of pottery and terracotta statues found during the excavations.[53]

In 1937 T.B. Mitford began the task of identifying and retranslating the inscriptions from the Rantidi sanctuary. It would be a task that would last his lifetime.[54] In 1958 Mitford studied Zahn's excavation notes in Berlin, with the final publication of these inscriptions appearing posthumously.[55] Mitford's study of the inscribed stones showed that Richard Meister's translations of the Rantidi inscriptions, made soon after their discovery, were largely erroneous, and he subsequently rejected Meister's readings, offering new interpretations of his own.[56]

This paper represents part of a larger effort to reconstruct the history of cult and the sanctuary found in the Rantidi Forest. The University of Indianapolis Rantidi Forest Excavations is a multisite, diachronic project, seeking to map, through excavation and survey, the land use, traffic patterns, and evidence for human settlement in the Rantidi Forest, from the earliest evidence of settlement in the Chalcolithic period to the present. Multisite excavation and preservation currently being carried out at sites threatened by development has led to a greater understanding of the potential uses of this area in ancient times. This initial examination of the role of the inscriptions in the Rantidi sanctuary is to be followed by the publication of Zahn's and

Peristianes' excavation notes, as well as an attempt to locate the more than 2,000 pieces of life-sized and over-life-sized terracotta sculpture produced in their excavations. The results of current excavation and survey, including the more than 40 new syllabic inscriptions found and new evidence for erotica in the Paphian cults, is currently being prepared.

The Syllabic Inscriptions of Rantidi Sanctuary: Medium

Of the 173 published inscriptions from the Rantidi sanctuary site, only 103 can be located and identified today.[57] The inscriptions from this sanctuary present a high degree of patterning in both medium and shape. Inscriptions seem to be limited to the medium of stone, with only local Cypriot limestone being used. Not a single example of the well over 2,000 terracotta fragments found in the 1910 excavations was observed to bear an inscription. This observation, however, cannot be confirmed. The inscribed stones come in four shapes. The largest are rectangular slabs of stone with roughly worked sides and a shallow basin covering the entire upper surface.[58] On slabs of the same width as these large stones but smaller in height, the upper basin has been placed to cover only partially the top of the stone, leaving a flat lip to one side.[59] These basins are usually well carved and have sloping sides. Thus there is a correlation between the size of the stone and the shape of the carved basin.[60] Also, inscriptions were placed on rectangular stone slabs with no basin. Of these rectangular slabs only a few are well worked, while the majority have been shaped only roughly, if at all.[61] Finally, only a few examples of stele-shaped stones have been found.[62] Most inscribed stones at Rantidi were sufficiently large and heavy to discourage frequent change in position once they were set up within the sanctuary.[63] The cumbersome nature of these inscribed blocks resulted, early in this century, in several inscriptions being sawn off to ease their transport to the antiquities dealer in Limassol.[64] At Rantidi the preferred face to receive the inscription is a side face that presents a width larger than the height. The inscription could run to more than one side of a stone and, when a basin did not cover the entire upper surface of a stone, the flat lip or edge of the upper surface could be inscribed.[65]

Peristianes suggested that the stones with basins on top, inscribed and uninscribed, could have been used as pedestals for statues.[66] Mitford notes, however, that such shallow depressions with smooth sloping sides are "singularly ill-suited" for the reception of statues, the more so as they are totally devoid of any dowel holes.[67] Mitford argues that these inscribed stones, with or without the basin, were ex-voto offerings to the deity of Rantidi. Stones with basins on top probably served for libations. A lack of traces of burning suggests that these stones were not used as incense altars; Mitford suggests that these libations were of wine.[68] The dedication by Philotimos, the perfumer, led Masson to believe that the libations may have been of some kind of perfume as well, perhaps perfumed oil.[69] Peristianes suggested that these basins could have been used as altars for sacrifices.[70]

Many inscribed stones carry no basin on top and might have been used as statue bases. These stones often show more care in the shaping of the upper surface than that of the inscribed surface.[71] Although the flat-topped stones lack any cuttings for the insertion of a statue, there is a good indication that at least some inscribed stones were used as such. Zahn's photograph of one of the temple buildings clearly shows three large blocks placed in front of a thick wall. On consulting Zahn's plan of this wall, one of these blocks can be identified as *Rantidi* no. 30, a block with a flat upper surface; the other two blocks are uninscribed.[72] The position of these stones next to the wall is highly suggestive of the placement of statues. If this interpretation is correct, then uninscribed stones were used for this purpose as well.

The Syllabic Inscriptions of Rantidi Sanctuary: Their Content

No long texts have been found at the Rantidi sanctuary. Indeed, the inscriptions from this site are so brief that Masson argues that even the word inscription "is often too ambitious for the brief documents of Rantidi."[73] Inscriptions that can be read are limited to proper names, with two exceptions only: a dedication to the deity and a stone that names a maker of perfumes.[74] The addition of a patronym to the personal name is uncommon.[75] Some inscriptions found here are complete and have intelligible sign forms but do not lend themselves to a transliteration into the Greek language. These inscriptions are thought to be in Eteo-Cypriot. Mitford identifies several of the inscriptions from Rantidi as being written in the Eteo-Cypriot language, but Masson is highly critical of such identification.[76] Whether accepted as Eteo-Cypriot or not, these inscriptions today remain unread.

A number of complete inscriptions from Rantidi contain only two characters separated by a punct, a short vertical line, which in longer inscriptions marks the separation of phrases and the end of inscriptions.[77] Short inscriptions of this type are seen also in Bronze Age inscriptions in the Cypro-Minoan script, and this practice at Rantidi is interpreted as indicative of the cultural continuity that existed in southwestern Cyprus between the Bronze and Iron Ages.[78] Mitford first suggested that these inscriptions represented a personal name and a patronym abbreviated simply to the initial sign of each. No other interpretation has been offered for the contents of these inscriptions, and the idea that these might represent abbreviations is widely accepted.[79]

Reading the Syllabic Inscriptions

Reading the syllabic inscriptions found at the Rantidi sanctuary requires close proximity to the inscribed stone. The tallest sign from Rantidi is 15.5 cm in height, while the smallest are only 3 cm tall.[80] Furthermore, signs were shallowly incised, most having an open angle in cross section (fig. 3). Without some contrast in the light upon the inscription, either light raking across the inscription or hitting the signs at an angle to create a shadow effect, even the largest incised sign could be dif-

Fig. 3. Syllabic signs, shallowly inscribed and difficult to discern. From Rantidi Forest Excavations, no. 077, 1998 season. (Photo by G.B. Bazemore)

ficult to distinguish from the medium. There is no evidence to indicate that the syllabic signs at Rantidi were either painted or inlaid to facilitate viewing. Inscriptions of the size and form of those found at Rantidi are viewed most easily when at eye level. If the stone was deposited directly upon the ground, the inscription on the front face would indeed have been difficult to read while standing above and over it. Rather, a squatting stance would be needed. Displaying the inscriptions upon a shelf, thus raising them to eye level, would have increased greatly the visibility and readability of the inscription.

Lapidaries at Rantidi seem to have made little effort to aid the viewer and potential reader of their inscribed signs. Mitford notes that the inscriptions

Fig. 4. Syllabic inscription with deliberate defacement. From *Rantidi* no. 10, pl. 11.10. (Courtesy of the German Archaeological Institute)

of Rantidi "are in general cut with an extreme uncouthness."[81] Examination of the inscribed surface itself, however, reveals that many stones have had multiple uses. Some inscriptions show evidence of the deliberate defacement of the syllabic signs (fig. 4).[82] Others are commonly agreed to be palimpsest, where one inscription has been incompletely erased and a second inscription placed among the debris of the first (fig. 5).[83] Reinscription of stone could also occur on a second, previously uninscribed, face.[84] Also difficult to read are stones where inscriptions have been created upon chipped or broken surfaces, or upon fragments broken off from worked stone.[85] Modern scholars, even when examining these inscriptions with painstaking care, cannot be certain in their distinction between deeply incised tool marks on a stone and erased inscribed signs. Mitford notes that "the difficulty of many of the Rantidi documents [is that] the direction, number and values of its signs are open to serious doubts."[86] Through disagreement on the number of signs or number of lines in an inscription, wildly variant readings can occur.[87] These observations go beyond orthographically sloppy or inelegant lapidary practice. Many of these inscriptions are virtually unreadable by persons who put forth great effort in their attempts. The significance of these observations concerning the appearance of the inscribed stones has obvious ramifications for the ancient viewer. Faced with such sloppy presentation, the casual passer-by had no hope of interpreting many of these inscriptions.

Fig. 5. Palimpsest syllabic inscription. From *Rantidi* no. 21, pl. 15.21b. (Courtesy of the German Archaeological Institute)

Archaeological Evidence for the Display of the Inscriptions

The following discussion is based on the documents of Peristianes, now lodged in the government archives of Cyprus, as well as on the published notes and photographs of Zahn; the evidence from both sources is found in Mitford and Masson's publication of the inscriptions. No master plan or general overview of the site has been recovered. Peristianes' and Zahn's descriptions of the architecture and the layout of the buildings differ both in substance and in detail; Peristianes wrote of six temple sites, while Zahn identified at least two sanctuaries.[88] Zahn also refers to the same building using multiple names. F.G. Maier has discussed thoughtfully and carefully the evidence for the varying terminology used by the excavators. Zahn divides Rantidi into two sections, the Upper and the Lower Temenos. He referred to the Upper Temenos as the Temenos Terrace or the Large Temenos Terrace; the Lower Temenos was known as the West Terrace, the Temenos west of the Terrace Wall, or as the Greek Temenos. In trying to interpret which of Peristianes' temple sites belonged to which of Zahn's Temenoi, Maier noted that the description of Temple Site II as having two huge double lines of foundation seems to correspond to Zahn's plan of the Lower Temenos. This identification seems confirmed by the fact that the inscriptions *Rantidi* nos. 31 and 65 are reported by Zahn as having come from the West Terrace and by Peristianes as from Temple Site II. Maier concludes that Peristianes' Temple Site I could be identified with the Upper Terrace of Zahn, while his Temple Site II belonged to the Lower Terrace.[89] It is upon Maier's equivalences of the varying terminology used by

Table 1. Provenance of inscriptions as numbered in *Rantidi* based on Peristianes' and Zahn's information.

Find Location	*Rantidi* inscription nos.
Temple Site I or Upper Temenos	7
South of Temple Site I	17, 23, 35?, 62?, 63, 70, 84
North of Temple Site I	20, 33
East Wall of Temple Site II or Lower Temenos	30, 59, page 87 nos. 16* and 48*
West Wall of Temple Site II or Lower Temenos	12A, 14, 29, 68, 72, 98?
Surface of Temple Site II (both inside and immediately outside the building)	12, 31, 47?, 50, 60, 65, 79
From the Vicinity of Temples Sites I and II	93, 95, 97, 100
West of Temples Sites I and II	10, 11, 44, 58
Popham's surface finds, probable wash from hilltop	1, 6, 38, 39, 41, 57, 77
Found Between the Upper and Lower Temene	3, 73
Between Temple Sites II and V	5
Temple Site V	55
In the area of Temple Site V	22, 54, 102
Temple Site VI	27
Possible Temple Site found in 1955	2, 19, 25, 28, 43, 67
Tomb 1	16, 34, 42, 71, 75, 80
Tomb 2	9, 13, 15, 24, 36, 45, 52, 53, 56, 89
Tomb 2A	21
Tomb 3	page 87 nos. 55* and 67*
Tomb 3A	76
Tomb 3B	4, 26, 91
In the Walls of the Mandra around Tomb 3B	37, 51
Tomb 4	The two inscriptions reported as coming from this tomb cannot be identified today

*Lost stone.
Note. Numbers not listed have no known find spot at the site

Peristianes and Zahn that current scholarly interpretation of the find spots of inscriptions rests (table 1, fig. 2).[90] Based on the available evidence from Zahn and Peristianes, a reconstruction of the Rantidi sanctuary is offered in figure 2.

The Upper Temenos or Temple Site I

This was the first building to be excavated. From within its foundations hundreds of fragments of terracotta statues and statuettes were recovered. These included figures described as satyrs, two fragments of the beard of a colossal statue, quadrupeds such as dogs, horses, and bulls, as well as phalli. From the same site also came 11 syllabic inscriptions, some built upside down in foundations of the temple walls. One of these inscriptions can be seen in Zahn's photograph of the west wall (fig. 6).[91] The background of this photograph shows a distinctive rock-cut basin that still can be seen at the site today. Thus

Fig. 6. East wall of Temple Site I, with rock-cut basin in the background. From *Rantidi* pl. 4.1. (Courtesy of the German Archaeological Institute)

Temple Site I can actually be located on the western edge of the acropolis of Rantidi sanctuary. The appearance of this basin, labeled as a "pool" in Ohnefalsch-Richter's drawing of the ruins of the site indicates that Ohnefalsch-Richter is referring to the same building (figs. 7–8).[92] Of the 11 inscriptions that Peristianes found here, only one can be identified securely today, *Rantidi* no. 7.[93] Peristianes makes the puzzling remark that "on this site three altars or sanctuaries were laid bare."[94] His use of the terms "altars or sanctuaries" is not defined. If he meant an altar in the sense of a place of slaughter and of burning, one would expect his "altars" to have been placed outside of a building.

The Lower Temenos or Temple Site II

There exists no photographic evidence for the location of Temple Site II, and only its relative position is known. Zahn, when describing the "Erste Mauer westl. der Temenos terrasse" on his wall plan, mentions that "in dieser Line liegt die nördl. Ecke der Quermauer des Temenos" and gives the distance of 14.50, interpreted by Maier as meters.[95] The center of the Lower Temenos then lay 14.5 m northwest of the northern wall of the

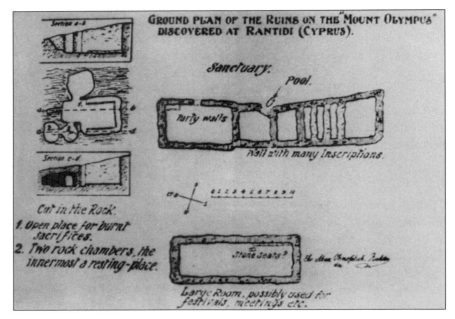

Fig. 7. Drawing of Temple Sites I and II and Tomb I by M. Ohnefalsch-Richter. Note the basin labeled as a "pool" on the plan. From *Rantidi* pl. 1.2. (Courtesy of the German Archaeological Institute)

Fig. 8. Zahn's photograph of Temple Site I, said to be of the northern wall, taken from the southeast. From *Rantidi* pl. 4.3. (Courtesy of the German Archaeological Institute)

Fig. 9. East side of the western wall of Temple Site II from the north. Arrow points to inscription *Rantidi* no. 72. From *Rantidi* pl. 3.3. (Courtesy of the German Archaeological Institute)

Upper Temenos. Maier localizes this Lower Temenos at about 10 m north of Point 13 on his Plan I, in a stone-strewn flat area.[96] Peristianes' description, with the Lower Temenos having lines of foundations running from north to south,[97] places the walls of Temple Site II parallel to those of Temple Site I. This information corresponds well to the Ohnefalsch-Richter drawing.[98]

Peristianes records 19 inscriptions found in association with Temple Site II.[99] Zahn's drawings of these walls show that 10 of the inscribed stones were found in the east and west wall foundations.[100] Photographs of the inside of the west wall show *Rantidi* no. 72 placed with the inscription upside down (fig. 9).[101] No trace is seen in this photograph of *Rantidi* no. 68, noted in Zahn's plan next to no. 72; this is probably because of the stone being placed with its inscribed face inward. The inscribed stone standing in the row of three stones before the east wall of this building can be identified as *Rantidi* no. 30 (figs. 10–11); the suggestion that this may be a statue base has been evaluated above.[102] It seems to be these stones that Ohnefalsch-Richter had referred to in his drawing as possible "stone seats."

Fig. 10. East wall of Temple Site II from the north. Arrow points to inscription *Rantidi* no. 30 From *Rantidi* pl. 3.4. (Courtesy of the German Archaeological Institute)

Fig. 11. *Rantidi* no. 30. From *Rantidi* pl. 17.30. (Courtesy of the German Archaeological Institute)

Temple Sites III and IV

The location of Temple Sites III, IV, and VI are not known.[103] At Temple Site III the excavators discovered 219 fragments of statuettes having simple tubes for bodies and wearing a conical cap; this is the so-called snowman type of figurine. Here also they found statuettes that they described as satyrs as well as quadruped fragments. The single fragment of an inscribed slab found here cannot be identified today.[104] The order of the excavation of Temple Sites I and II and their relative locations indicate that Zahn and Peristianes were working their way down the west slope of the sanctuary hill. If they continued in this fashion, then the next building they encountered, Temple Site III, was probably found to the west of Temple Site II. The syllabic inscriptions found west of Temple Site II[105] indicate that Temple Site III did not lie immediately next to Temple Site II, nor was it located to the southwest of Temple Site II, as the commentary and findspot of *Rantidi* no. 5 shows. Temple Site III could have been further west of Temple Site II, perhaps even to the northwest, near the ancient road.

In comparison with Temple Site III, Temple Site IV was especially poor in finds, producing only 23 terracotta statue fragments.[106]

Temple Site V

Peristianes twice describes this site as being located on a small hill, or alternatively an overhanging hill, about 800 yards southwest of the sanctuary hill. Zahn calls this site the "Polygonalbau" and designates the inscriptions found here as having come from the "Mittlere Terrasse." Maier identifies Temple Site V as probably being located in the stone-strewn area at Point 19 on his Plan I.[107] Peristianes describes the big stone blocks built in the double line of foundations of this building as an "imposing view," and he characterizes these as "very ancient remains." Temple Site V produced 41 fragments of large terracotta statues, fragments of various-sized pots, several uninscribed stone basins, and a single inscribed one, *Rantidi* no. 55.[108] It would be helpful to know what attributes caused Peristianes to attribute great antiquity to this temple site.

Temple Site VI

As its name suggests, this is the last site to have been excavated. As its discovery came at the very end of Zahn's campaign, it is reported as having been only partially explored. The existence of Temple Site VI was signaled by the presence of a large stone basin on the surface. Here Zahn and Peristianes uncovered only a single line of wall foundations, finding only 19 fragments of terracotta statuettes and pottery. Within this building they found two syllabic inscriptions.[109]

A Possible Temple Site

In 1955 M. Popham, then a member of the team excavating the Kouklia siege mound under the direction of Mitford, surveyed the Rantidi sanctuary.

During this survey, 21 syllabic inscriptions were found. Six of these inscriptions are reported to have come from an area about 250 yards to the southeast of the summit of the hill, and Popham believes that this may be the site of a separate building.[110] This area is on a steep incline of Rantidi Hill with no indication of ever having been terraced. In ancient times a monumental piece of stone conglomerate stood on the edge of hilltop above the site of this possible building, impeding access to the top of the hill. It seems to be because of the difficult terrain of all the northern, eastern, and southern sides of the hill that the other buildings uncovered at this site were all found on the long, sloping, southwestern side. Popham's suggestion of a building in this area, if correct, would extend the sanctuary buildings into an area hitherto undocumented.

Surface Finds

Many inscriptions were found simply littering the ground. Ohnefalsch-Richter noted the number of inscribed stones on the surface during his visit on 9 May 1910, before Zahn's excavations began. He declared that "no place has ever been discovered where, as at Rantidi, heaps of [syllabic] inscriptions are simply lying on the surface of the ground."[111] Zahn wrote to the chief secretary of the Cyprus government on September 7 of the same year, "I began my exploration (on) the 30th August. . . . I found at once about 20 to 25 inscriptions scattered over the ground."[112] Ohnefalsch-Richter's narrative does not specify the locations of his "heaps of inscriptions," but Zahn must have been referring to inscriptions visible on the hilltop itself, as that is where his work began. Popham's survey found syllabic inscriptions on the slopes of the hill and in the road, believed all to have been washed down from the summit.[113] Surface finds, when their location is known, were concentrated around Temple Sites I and II. This accords well with the excavation data for the location of inscribed stones.

Conclusions for the Distribution of Inscriptions Within the Temple Sites

Of the 57 inscriptions described by the excavators as having been found in association with the Temple Sites, 43 are identified with Temple Sites I and II on the western side of Rantidi Hill (table 1). The six inscriptions interpreted by Popham as indicative of a hitherto unattested structure may have themselves washed down from the summit above, just as he theorized for those stones found on the north slope of the hill. The steep terrain in this area discourages the interpretation of a building at this site, and these inscriptions could have been pushed off the side during the documented bulldozing and plowing activities. Thus only eight inscriptions are associated with the buildings on the lower slopes. Evidence from the temple sites, then, indicates strongly that most inscriptions were set up within and around the area of Temple Sites I and II, on the western side of Rantidi Hill.

The So-Called Tombs

Two types of rock-cut chambers are found at the Rantidi sanctuary. Cut into the top of the acropolis and burrowed into the sides of its western half are large chambers entered through wide openings. One is documented with a forecourt. To the west, at the bottom of the sanctuary hill, and to the northwest across the road, a different type of rock-cut structure is found. Here, the chambers are approached through rock-cut dromoi, are entered through narrow openings, and often have multiple chambers. Both types of rock-cut chamber were termed by their excavators as "tombs."[114] Peristianes, in his report to the Cyprus Museum Committee, catalogues four tombs, numbered, it seems, in the same way as the temple sites, by the order in which they were found. Those at the bottom of the hill were tombs; however, those on the acropolis are better termed *favissae*, and one may have been an oracular chamber.

Tomb 1

Tomb 1 was cleared out during the first eight days of the excavation (fig. 12).[115] This was the largest of the rock-cut chambers excavated, however its location on Rantidi Hill is only roughly known. Peristianes placed Tomb I in association with Temple Sites I and II saying that "the Temples . . . lie quite close to it." Furthermore, he describes the find spot of *Rantidi* no. 11 as "about 50 feet west of Tomb 1 and Temple Sites I and II."[116] From this information, Maier would like to place Tomb 1 south of Temple Site I,[117] in the southwestern corner at the highest point on Rantidi Hill. Peristianes reports that this tomb consists of three chambers from which were extracted 1,329 statue fragments. These pieces included fragments of colossal terracotta male and female statues as well as statuettes of satyrs, fragments of phalloi, pottery including large storage vessel fragments, and 23 "inscribed stone basins . . . and tablets with Cyprian characters." This seems to be the site described by Zahn in his first letter to the chief secre-

Fig. 12. "Tomb" I after cleaning. From *Rantidi* pl. 4.4. (Courtesy of the German Archaeological Institute)

tary of the Cyprus Museum Committee. He characterizes this deposit as a group of tombs with a forecourt. He says that the terracotta finds were scattered "between the stones which filled the court and barricaded the entrance of the tombs." In a later letter Zahn describes this Tomb I as "the greatest of these interesting tombs."[118] Today, only six of these inscriptions can be identified.[119]

Tombs 2 and 2A

Peristianes locates Tomb 2 "on top of the hill."[120] Ohnefalsch-Richter designates this site as lying about 20 m under the highest point of the hill.[121] The highest point of Rantidi Hill is the eastern side, sloping down towards the west. Tomb 2 then seems to be located in the center of the hilltop of Rantidi. This chamber had been looted by local villagers before the excavations of Zahn and Perisitianes took place.[122] It seems that this chamber had been cleared only partially by the looters, for Peristianes records finding here a further 50 fragments of large and small terracotta statues and pottery, as well as 10 inscribed stones.[123] Ohnefalsch-Richter's visit to the Rantidi sanctuary occurred after this looting had taken place. He seems to believe that some of

the inscribed stones in this chamber were still in situ.[124] Zahn registers no
inscription from this chamber. This seems to be the result of a lack of interest
on Zahn's part rather than a true lack of inscribed materials. Mitford
observes that Zahn carefully noted the inscriptions from Grave I in his daily
notebook. "Thereafter," writes Mitford, "he neither draws them or records
their finding. Thereabouts his interest seems to concentrate on the terracottas, and phalloi."[125]

These rock-cut chambers were explored in localized groupings. A small
chamber was found to the south of the looted tomb, Tomb 2; the excavators
designated this chamber as 2A. Maier would place Tomb 2A in the area
between Points 4 and 7 on his Plan I,[126] at the very center of the acropolis.
Two inscriptions were found either inside or on the surface near this
chamber, *Rantidi* no. 21 and no. 53.[127]

Tombs 3, 3A, and 3B

Peristianes described Tomb 3A as "an open tomb about 250 yards N.W. of
Temple Site V" and as "lying near on a parallel line with tomb nr. 3."[128]
Tomb 3B was located at some distance from Tombs 3 and 3A. Zahn places
Tomb 3B on the "lower Terrace"; Peristianes says that this site is "about 800
yards south west of the hill of Ranti[di], and 50 feet west of Temple site V."[129]
Tombs 1, 2, and 2A, on top of the sanctuary acropolis, are of the first type
of rock-cut chamber with an open mouth and forecourt. By contrast, Tombs
3, 3A, and 3B, located at the foot of the hill, are, however, of the second
type, having chambers that are approached through rock-cut dromoi,
entered through narrow openings, and often with multiple chambers. Zahn
describes Tomb 3B as "a grave with dromos."[130] The recorded findings from
Tombs 3, 3A, and 3B differ from the contents excavated from the rock-cut
chambers on the sanctuary hill. The primary finding in Tomb 3 was pottery,
with only a few fragments of terracotta statues dated by Peristianes to the
Hellenistic period. In addition, there were found only two fragments of
stone "bearing some doubtful Cyprian characters."[131] Nothing is known of
the contents of Tomb 3A; a single syllabic inscription was found on the surface near this rock-cut chamber, *Rantidi* no. 76. Tomb 3B was one of the
larger tombs excavated; it had been made into a sheepfold by local shepherds.[132] Five inscriptions were found, some built into the mandra walls[133]
and others lying on the ground nearby.[134] Again, there is no further information on the contents of this chamber.

Tomb 4

Peristianes describes his Tomb 4 as "this very beautiful rock cut tomb of the Graeco-Phoenician period with an arched entrance and a vaulted roof like a small Byzantine chapel."[135] Tomb 4 can today be identified in the terrain. It is located ca. 300 m southwest of the hilltop, at Maier's Point 20 on his Plan I.[136] Today, this tomb is filled with debris and only the dromos is visible; this dromos is almost 2 m wide. Here again, the majority of finds were pottery, with only bits of terracotta statues reported. Two inscribed stones are said to have been found here, neither of which can be identified today.[137]

Conclusions for the Distribution of Inscriptions
Within the So-Called Tombs

There are 27 inscriptions that can be identified as being found in association with the rock-cut chambers referred to by the excavators as tombs. Of these, 17 inscriptions were found in Tombs 1, 2, and 2A on the hilltop. Tombs 3 and 3A, which seem to be located across the road, produced only three inscriptions, while those of 3B and 4, at the bottom of the hill, produced seven. Of the seven inscriptions found in tomb 3B, two were found built into a modern shepherd's mandra, and thus their original deposition may not have been associated with this structure. The evidence of the tombs then joins that of the buildings themselves, and it is seen that the majority of syllabic inscriptions were deposited on the top of the hill, concentrated in, if not limited to, its western side.

The So-Called Temples and Tombs of Rantidi: A Reassessment

The presence of tombs, especially those on the acropolis, found in connection with the terracotta objects and inscriptions led scholars to question the identification of this site as a sanctuary. Maier concluded that, from the archaeological finds of 1910, the interpretation of these buildings as a sanctuary is "in keinem Falle zwingend."[138] Popham questions whether these are buildings at all. Responding to the fact that inscriptions were built upside-down in the line of foundations of Temple Site I, he remarks, "I cannot help suspecting that Zahn had found a 'mandra,' a sheep-fold, which had been built in more recent times from inscriptions lying on the surface."[139] Maier is also disturbed by the presence of inscribed blocks in the building walls. He concludes that Popham's suggestion that these buildings are relatively late, even postancient, cannot be rejected.[140] The reservations expressed contain two key elements, the nature of the rock-cut chambers, and the dating of the buildings.

The rock-cut chambers uncovered by Zahn at the bottom of Rantidi Hill and to the northwest of the road are certainly tombs, of a type well known in the island at least as early as the Cypro-Classical period.[141] Ohnefalsch-Richter was correct in identifying the area as containing "tombs and . . . whole cemeteries."[142] Future excavations in the area north and northwest of the road will help to establish the chronological range of the tombs in the necropoleis of Rantidi. The chambers on the hilltop, however, are not tombs of any known type. Zahn's photograph of Tomb 1 after cleaning shows only an open, cleared area, more like an excavation trench than a tomb (fig. 12). Masson questions Zahn's identification of these rock-cut chambers as tombs.[143] Maier himself suggests that Tomb I might be a cistern, located in the interior of the settlement to collect rainwater.[144] The obvious drawback to Maier's suggestion is that most of these chambers were cut into the sides under the hilltop, looking outward. Rainwater would not run into these chambers, but rather over their tops and down the hillside.

Recent excavation by the University of Indianapolis Rantidi Forest Expedition has partially explored one of the rock-cut chambers on the top of the acropolis, SW 104 on the current grid system (fig. 13). It cannot be identified with any of the chambers excavated by Zahn. The entrances to four similar chambers can be seen in this area, and one is illustrated in figure 14. SW 104 was created by cutting into the bedrock to a depth of about 1.35 m, then turning inward to excavate a large chamber, roughly semicircular in shape and about 5.35 m in depth. The result is a chamber with a forecourt. On top of the chamber are a series of circular cuttings arranged in a rough line scattered across and carved into the bedrock. These cuttings, in the shape of inverted cones, have smooth sides and are of various widths and depths; their purpose is unknown. The height of this chamber is not known, as bedrock has not yet been reached. The floor level inside the chamber, however, is significantly lower than the level of the forecourt. Although the forecourt is narrow, it easily accommodates the width or girth of a large person. The forecourt is reached through a rock-cut entrance to the west. When this chamber went out of use, this entrance was blocked by a finely made wall upon which a double line of wall foundation had been placed. Only scant traces of this double line of wall foundation survive today. It is believed that these are the remains of one of Peristianes' temple sites, probably the east wall of Temple Site II.

Fig. 13. Rantidi Forest Excavations, Square South West 204, June 1998. Note the cutting in the bedrock to the left and the retaining wall above. (Photo by G.B. Bazemore)

The multiplicity and location of these chambers is puzzling. Could they be *favissae* or pits dug specifically for the disposal of sanctified votive materials? Such pits have been found in the sanctuaries at Polis-*Peristeries* and Kition.[145] Certainly, the sanctuary at Rantidi received a sufficient number of votive offerings to need such depositories for their ritual refuse; indeed this might well be the interpretation of some of these rock-cut chambers on the acropolis. However, current information from surface survey suggests that the plains of Kapsalia and Dhasia were empty of settlement during the period of sanctuary use and so could have been available for such ritual disposal. Furthermore, as our excavations have discovered, the greater soil overburden found on these plains coupled with the substratum of soft chalk make digging in these areas not very difficult. Future geomorphological analysis may clarify whether these findings accurately reflect landscape use and change in antiquity. The chambers on top of Rantidi Hill, however, have been carved into the limestone bedrock. Such considerations suggest that the emplacement of these chambers in the cult area itself was a significant factor in their creation and perhaps is an indication of these chambers' functions. One chamber at least, that found in SW 104, was clearly not created to be

Fig. 14. North side of Rantidi Hill looking south, north of the rock-cut basin, the opening of a *favissa*, July 1998. (Photo by G.B. Bazemore)

used as storehouse for ritual refuse, to be filled and closed. Rather, the careful and labor intensive creation of a forecourt and entranceway suggest the need for repeated access to this chamber. In trying to identify the use and significance of the rock-cut chambers on top of the sanctuary hill at Rantidi, the evidence of other Paphian cults is useful.

At Nea Paphos, the city founded in the late fourth century by the last Paphian king, a late Classical and Hellenistic cult of the oracular Apollo was found at the site of Alonia tou Episkopou just east of the city.[146] Here, in a rock-cut hypogeum with a stepped dromos entrance, two syllabic dedications to Apollo Hylates have been carved into the rock above the entrance into the first chamber and on the wall to the right of the entrance to the second chamber. These inscriptions were created for a person who characterized himself as 'ο(μ)φιϝοχεύσας, or "carrier of the divine voice."[147] This hypogeum was surrounded by a sacred complex, in which the bedrock was carved into five different levels. The carved bedrock structures have been interpreted as courtyards and building platforms; it is presumed that a sacred grove was located nearby.[148] This sacred precinct is situated within a necropolis of rock-cut chamber tombs.[149] Scattered across the carved bedrock surfaces, rectangular basins and inverted cones have been carved. These bedrock cuttings are similar in both shape and dimension to those found in the Rantidi sanctuary.

In attempting to define the type of worship that took place at this Apollo precinct, Młynarczyk turns to the mythological traditions surrounding the great goddess of Cyprus. Although the pairing of Adonis with Aphrodite is often noted, Młynarczyk correctly points out that in Cypriot cult practice, the Paphian goddess is associated with a male deity sometimes appearing under the Greek name of Apollo but found also under other epithets alone, such as Dauchnaphorios, Hylates, and Magirios.[150] In antiquity great religious festivals surrounded the death and resurrection of the young male lover of the Paphian goddess; Młynarczyk interprets the overlap of burial and cult found at Alonia tou Episkopou as part of this worship.[151] The characterization of the person responsible for the creation of the hypogeum as "carrier of the divine voice" is highly suggestive of the oracular functions of Apollo known in other parts of the Greek-speaking world, such as Delphi and Claros. In combing the evidence from inscriptions, the cult of the deity worshipped there, and the physical reconstruction of the hypogeum and its surroundings, Młynarczyk interprets the cult precinct within the necropolis at Alonia tou Episkopou as an oracle of both a chthonic and sepulchral nature. It is suggested that the underground chamber of the oracle itself may have been regarded by the ancients as a tomb of the goddess's slain lover.[152] If this interpretation is correct, then the sanctuary precinct would have been the scene of rituals in connection with the death and rebirth of the goddess's lover.

This Apollo cult could have participated in the burial rites of the surrounding necropolis actively only if the cult precinct and the necropolis were in use at the same time. The syllabic inscriptions there can be dated with certainty. The sign forms used in these inscriptions are clearly contemporary with those found in the inscriptions of King Nikoklewes, the last Kinyrad king of Paphos and the founder of the city outside of which this cult precinct was located.[153] The syllabic inscriptions, then, were cut in the last decades of the fourth century B.C. The date of the surrounding necropolis, however, is less clear. Mitford regards the hypogeum as a reused tomb and bases his interpretation of the syllabic inscriptions found there upon this assumption.[154] Also based on Mitford's assumptions, Młynarczyk concludes that "the fact that a tomb was re-used here signifies the abandonment of at least a part of the necropolis at the time that the hypogeum was dedicated."[155] The abandoned necropolis is interpreted as containing the remains of persons connected with "some settlement or village" at the site where Nikoklewes' new foundation was later to stand.[156] This proposed "settlement or village" is dated to the Classical period, beginning in the late fifth century B.C.[157] If these interpretations are correct, no active interments occurred while this cult was functioning, and, in this necropolis at least, the Apollo cult was not actively involved in funerary ritual.

The available evidence, however, does support other interpretations. First, Mitford's argument that the creation of the hypogeum represents the reuse of a tomb is purely hypothetical. The building improvements documented by the syllabic inscriptions were made to a σπέος a cave or grotto, not to a τάφος, or tomb. The hypogeum may represent then, not the results of the reuse of a tomb, but simply a natural cave that has been widened and shaped. The celebration of cult ritual could well have been the primary, rather than the secondary, function of this chamber. Furthermore, extensive soundings in the area of the purported "settlement or village," whose inhabitants were to have occupied and later abandoned the necropolis, failed to find any evidence of pre-Hellenistic occupation.[158] Other arguments for a settlement in this area earlier than the time of Nikoklewes rests primarily on the analysis of tomb types, with little or no support from the ceramic evidence.[159] Młynarczyk, however, admits that "very meagre information" exists for the dating of the necropolis that surrounds the cult precinct at Alonia tou Episkopou.[160] Furthermore, one is hard put to explain the reason for the abandonment of a useful necropolis area at the very time when a sharp and sudden increase in local population levels would put pressure on such resources.[161] Although modern shepherds use ancient tombs with impunity to house their flocks, it is to be wondered how the inhabitants of the hypothesized "settlement or village" would have reacted to the violation and reuse of the resting place of someone who, at the most, was only three generations removed. For these reasons, I believe it is far better to see the tombs in the necropolis surrounding the cult precinct at Alonia tou Episkopou as having been cut from the rock and used for interments during the time when the cult precinct of Apollo Hylates was in use.

Similarly, an oracular interpretation for some, at least, of the rock-cut chambers on the hilltop of the Rantidi sanctuary is consistent with what is known about Cypriot cult practices. It is documented that ancient Cypriots would consult oracles in times of doubt or need.[162] Diviners stood in the highest places of status and power in the city-kingdom of Paphos. Tacitus records that descendants of the Cilician Tamyras formed a dynasty of diviners in Paphos. The Tamyrads, he notes, played a role in the cult of Aphrodite equal to that of the descendants of the cult's founder, Kinyras.[163] The descendants of Kinyras were the kings of the Paphian kingdom and high priests of the goddess's cult.[164] Other ancient authors refer to the practice of prophecy in Cyprus, but most especially in the Paphian cult.[165] In this regard, the toponym Mantissa, or Prophetess, that exists today in Kouklia village for an area near the temple of Aphrodite may be significant.[166]

There are several close parallels between the cult of the god at Rantidi sanctuary and the oracular cult of Apollo in Nea Paphos: both contain underground rock-cut chambers allowing repeated access; both cult areas bear the evidence of the sculpting of bedrock into groups of rectangular and circular cuttings of unknown use; most significantly, both cult areas are encircled by large necropoleis of rock-cut tombs. The sacred grove believed to have stood near the Apollo cult in Nea Paphos is mirrored by the large groves that seem to have covered the plains of Kapsalia and Dhasia in the Rantidi Forest in ancient times. The oracular nature of the hypogeum at Alonia tou Episkopou is but a part of the strong oracular tradition documented for Cypriot cults, and those of Paphos in particular. Given this evidence, the interpretation of at least some of the chambers on Rantidi Hill as sites of oracular transmissions from the deity seems likely. The parallels with the cult of Apollo in Nea Paphos suggests that the deity worshipped at Rantidi may have had chthonic and sepulchral ritual powers as well.

The Cult of the Deity at Rantidi

Support for oracular cult at Rantidi also finds support in an inscription from the site. Despite the wealth of inscriptions from this site, only a single example, *Rantidi* no. 1, is addressed to a deity; it is assumed that this deity is the patron of the sanctuary.[167] The grammar of this inscription records the definite (or demonstrative) article twice, so that the fact that this deity is male cannot be disputed. Sign 6 of this inscription, however, displays an unusual variant form, the only questionable reading in an otherwise quite legible script. Mitford interprets sign 6 as /ne/, and he reads the deity's name as φωνῆος, a genitive singular form meaning "of the God who speaks." This epithet, Mitford argues, indicates that the deity at the Rantidi sanctuary is oracular.[168] Both Mitford's reading of sign 6 and his interpretation of this word have been rejected by Masson. Masson says that Mitford's reading, "although attractive, seems to be much too optimistic, both in the reading and in the morphology."[169] Masson will only concede that this inscription contains "a possible god's epithet, though unclear."[170] The shape of sign 6 of this inscription is indeed puzzling. However, within the cadre of Paphian sign forms, I find no other that fits the marks on the stone as well as does /ne/; the central vertical line is simply a bit shorter than regularly seen for this sign. Masson's rejection of the reconstructed form on dialectal grounds is weak, for the Cypriot dialect regularly displays grammatical forms unparalleled in other dialects of ancient Greek.[171] Therefore, the fact that Mitford's reconstruction gives φωνε- rather than Masson's expected φωνα- is not particularly disturbing. Mitford's gloss of the name of the deity at Rantidi, if read correctly, is closely related in meaning, if not semantics, to the person described as "the carrier of the divine voice" in the Apollo cult precinct in Nea Paphos. In this connection it is interesting to note also the single inscription from this site that displays sign forms that are certainly not syllabic. These signs have previously been interpreted as Phoenician, and were read as the number 32 and the formula qlj, "His/Her Voice"; recent efforts achieved no reading, and these signs have been labeled "quasi-Phoenician."[172]

The loss of all associated terracotta artifacts and many of the inscriptions found in the 1910 excavations at the Rantidi sanctuary impedes the reconstruction of cult practices there. From the published parts of the remaining excavation notes, it can be observed that the primary offerings appear to have been both male and female life-sized terracotta statues, statuettes, some described as satyr figures, terracotta phalloi, and syllabic inscriptions. Further evidence for erotica at the Rantidi sanctuary has been uncovered by the current excavations. A miniature phallus has been found, obviously broken off from a figurine of a type similar to Zahn's satyr figures. A large stone phallus, measuring almost 80 cm in height, was recovered from an 18th century retaining wall built at the bottom of the sanctuary hill. From the sanctuary itself, an unusual female figurine was found in the surface debris littering the top of the hill. It can seen that the figurine, although now fragmentary, originally showed a person with legs spread open and arms flung over the head; between the legs, a single deep line incised before firing indicates the female sex of the figurine.[173] The arrangement of the limbs of this figurine strongly suggests the act of copulation. The offerings of phalloi, in connection with figurines depicting male and female sexual acts and attributes, indicate that parts of the cult of the deity at Rantidi were concerned with sexual activity and perhaps the accompanying reproduction and childbearing results as well.

Again, the cult at the Rantidi sanctuary must be examined in the context of the other cults in the Paphian kingdom. The cult of the Cypriot goddess, whose main sanctuary was located in the plain below the Rantidi sanctuary, is reported to have practiced sexual and orgiastic ritual.[174] Justinus, a relatively late source writing in the third century A.D., records that it was the custom among the Cypriots to send their young women before marriage for a certain number of days to the seashore to gain money for their dowry by prostitution.[175] This custom is similar to the practices described much earlier by Herodotus for the Babylonian worship of Aphrodite. In these cult rituals, females were required at least once in their lives to have intercourse with a stranger within the temple precinct; no one was exempt from this duty, not even the wealthy elite. Herodotus mentions that there were similar customs in some parts of Cyprus but adds no details.[176] Whether these accounts are accurate or not, orgiastic activity as part of a religious ritual is clearly portrayed on a decorated bowl of the Archaic period from Achna, in eastern Cyprus, depicting a line of dancing women and couples in the act of copulation.[177] Terracotta phalloi, along with an amount of salt, were offered to initiates into the mysteries of the Paphian goddess, after they underwent ceremonies described as "orgies, full of lust."[178] Such representations of phalloi not only may have been indicative of ritual practices, but may also have served as physical reminders of the goddess's birth from the dismembered genitals of her father.[179] The cult at Rantidi sanctuary, then, not only stood in close proximity to the temple of the great goddess of Paphos, but also, in its orgiastic and oracular ritual, seems to have shared important attributes of the cult of goddess on the plain below.

In view of the physical and cultic connections between the sanctuary on Rantidi Hill and temple of the goddess in Paphos, these two sanctuaries may well have shared events in their ritual calendars, such as the appointed days of celebrations and feasts. It is not known whether the male deity at Rantidi sanctuary was associated, either in ancient Cypriot mythology or in cult legend, with the great goddess of Paphos, playing a role such as her consort or child. It has been noted that the death and resurrection of the goddess's male lover played a central part of her cult and worship. Bound up as it is with the Paphian cult of the goddess, the chthonic and sepulchral aspects of the Rantidi cult may well reflect its participation in these death and resurrection rituals as well.

It is interesting to note that the only decorated stone from this site bears on its front face the crescent moon and solar disc, symbols common on Phoenician and Punic votive offerings.[180] The cutting on the top of this stone suggests that it served as a base, or perhaps an altar.

Dating of the Site

The Epigraphic Evidence

The lapidaries incising the signs of the inscriptions found at Rantidi shared an orthographic tradition in which standardized sign forms show little variation over the time of the use of the script here. Admittedly, these lapidaries do create variant sign forms, a few quite confusing, but the agreed general observation is that very little sign variation or development is seen. The quite similar and equally rigid orthographic tradition shared by the siege mound inscriptions has been recognized as a clear indication of the contemporaneity of the two groups of inscriptions; a firm terminus ante quem of 498 B.C. has been assigned to both. When examining and comparing the epigraphic forms displayed by these two groups of inscriptions, it should be borne in mind that individual lapidary hands probably are not limited to a single cult center. Rather it seems more logical to argue that a group of Paphian lapidaries inscribed for all the sanctuaries represented by this material. There are no inscriptions from Rantidi or the siege mound that display the epigraphically distinct sign forms shown in the later inscriptions of Paphos, the so-called Middle and Late Paphian, seen in the fifth century B.C. and later.[181] The complete absence of Middle and Late Paphian sign forms in the inscriptions of Rantidi and of the siege mound led Mitford to conclude that "neither temenos had any later history."[182] As seen above, Masson would limit the inscribing activities at the Rantidi sanctuary to the sixth century B.C. alone.[183]

If the inscribing activities seen in the cult center(s) represented by the Rantidi and the siege mound material came to a sudden halt in 498 B.C., and if the inscribing activity was indeed limited to a single century, some inscriptions among this copious material must date to the very latest years before the Persian reduction of the city and surrounding areas (fig. 15). If this reconstruction is correct, then one must note that Paphian inscriptions of the fifth century B.C., only slightly later than the latest Rantidi and siege

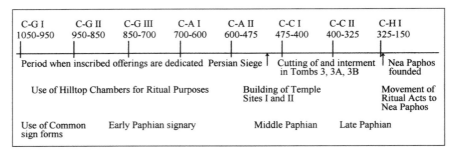

Fig. 15. A proposed chronology for the Rantidi sanctuary. (By G.B. Bazemore)

mound inscriptions, display distinctly different sign forms, representing clear orthographic developments. The inscriptions that display the so-called Middle and Late Paphian sign forms are primarily tomb epitaphs.[184] One explanation for this seemingly sudden development in orthographic forms in Paphos may have been the difference between sanctuary and nonsanctuary deposition. The orthographic tradition in Paphos during the Archaic period is scarcely represented outside of the dedications from the siege mound and Rantidi sanctuary. It is possible that the rigidity of forms seen in these sanctuary inscriptions was not found in inscriptions created for other types of ritual use. Funerary inscriptions may have allowed the influence of a non-lapidary, or cursive, tradition of writing that surely was practiced in the Paphian kingdom during the years when inscribed stone dedications were also offered. Indeed, by the fourth century B.C., the signs of Late Paphian are heavily influenced by a contemporary, but archaeologically invisible, cursive tradition.[185]

There are further epigraphic considerations that bear upon the dating of these inscriptions. In the orthographic tradition seen in the siege mound and Rantidi, only a single development of sign forms indicates the creation of variants over time. This is the rare use of signs not belonging to the peculiar set of forms used in Paphos and Rantidi, the so-called Paphian forms, or signary, but to those found elsewhere in the island, the so-called Common forms, or signary.[186] The use of a Common form, the /o/, is an attribute of the earliest dated syllabic inscription, the inscribed obelos from the necropolis of Skales in ancient Paphos. Of all the inscriptions of the siege mound, only a single example displays the use of the Common /o/;[187] four of the inscriptions from Rantidi sanctuary contain examples of the Common form of the sign /to/.[188] The evolution away from Common forms is seen to have been an attribute of the earliest Paphian writing only.[189] The use of Common forms in these inscriptions suggests that the numerous inscriptions of the siege mound and the Rantidi sanctuary, rather than the result of a single epoch of literate activity, accumulated in these sanctuaries over a period of three to five centuries. If these epigraphical observations and their chronological conclusions are valid, the rigidity of script seen in these inscriptions then becomes more striking. The distinct differences seen between the orthographic tradition of the Rantidi inscriptions and that of the Middle Paphian signary may indicate not a distinction in function but true chronological differences. Although 498 B.C. does provide a firm terminus ante quem, there is no evidence that compels the continuation of inscribed dedications down to that date.

Therefore, a strong case can be made from the evidence of epigraphy that some the inscribed dedications offered at the siege mound and the Rantidi sanctuary are among the earliest written documents known from the city-kingdom of Paphos. It seems quite likely that the offering of inscribed dedications in the Paphian sanctuaries ceased at some point before the end of the sixth century B.C.

The Nonepigraphic Evidence

There is no reason not to believe that the sanctuary was looted and perhaps destroyed by the invading Persian army. However, based upon the epigraphic evidence, Mitford postulated that the destruction by the Persian invasion brought all sanctuary use at Rantidi to an end. Ceramic evidence from the Rantidi sanctuary suggests otherwise. Peristianes records that the archaeological material found in the 1910 excavation was not uniform, and that some pieces could belong to the Hellenistic or later period.[190] Maier's survey of 1980 confirms these observations, recording material ranging from the Archaic period down to the Hellenistic and Roman periods.[191] The results of current excavations bring further support. Among pottery dating as early as the Archaic period are mixed numbers of sherds datable to the fifth and fourth centuries B.C. Some vessels of the later periods have survived nearly intact (fig. 16). These findings suggest that, although the inscribed dedications had ceased, offerings of votive objects and non-inscribed dedications at the Rantidi sanctuary continued into the Hellenistic or early Roman period.[192]

Further evidence for probable post-Persian activity comes from the tombs and the sanctuary building constructions. As seen above, the tombs at the

Fig. 16. An example of fifth/fourth century B.C. pottery fround at Rantidi in 1998. (Photo by G.B. Bazemore)

bottom of the hill and to the northwest across the road from the sanctuary can be dated. The creation of these tombs, the cutting of the dromoi and chambers, as well as one or more interments, took place during the fifth centuries and later, after inscribed dedications had ceased to be offered at the Rantidi sanctuary. The use of these tombs may have been concurrent with the building and use of Temple Sites I and II on the hilltop above. The cutting of tombs and rites of interment in the great necropoleis surrounding the Rantidi sanctuary, however, were probably not limited to a single period only. The dating of the individual tombs, the full extent of these necropoleis, and the chronological range of these necropoleis cannot be determined fully at this time.

Additional evidence for use at a later period comes from the inscribed stones found built upside down in the walls of Temple Sites I and II that led Popham to suggest that these foundations did represented not ancient buildings but sheep folds, or mandras. Mandras are indeed found at the Rantidi sanctuary site, as at many ancient sites, and Peristianes reports that Tomb 3B was used as such. The combination of rock-cut chambers and the building stone to block or enclose them provide the necessary means for the building of quick and easy corrals for grazing animals. Their masonry is usually thrown up for temporary use, typically has no mortar nor any earth filling, and consists simply of loose stones piled one upon the other; they are made of dry stone construction. Mandra walls are usually only one layer of stone in thickness; this lack of mortar and single-thickness construction makes the walls of a mandra subject to easy collapse. These are not the types of walls seen in Zahn's photographs of the temple sites. Temple Site I has well-preserved double lines of wall foundations. Temple Site II shows an even wider wall structure with worked and smoothed stones in both the eastern and western walls (figs. 9–10). Peristianes' description of these walls as "two huge double lines of foundations, consisting of blocks of regularly cut stones,"[193] in no way describes a mandra-type construction.

Rather than mandras, the current excavations in SW 104 suggest that the presence of inscribed stones in the foundations of Temples Sites I and II are examples of chronological phasing at the site, where older material was incorporated into newer structures in antiquity. In SW 104, we can see that the wall blocking the entrance to the rock-cut chamber provided the foundation for the wall of a temple site. The use of this rock-cut chamber seems to have come to an end at the time when, or at some time before, the foundations were laid for the temple buildings. The number of inscriptions reported to have been built into these foundations must have been dedicated at a time when the (probably oracular) chamber was still in use. They were used secondarily in the construction of the temple buildings. Temple Sites I and II, then, were built in an area that had previously been devoid of buildings, effectively closing what must have once been a center of ritual activity. No other building uncovered in the 1910 excavations is described as having numbers of inscriptions built into their foundations.

The Persian pillage and possible destruction of the Rantidi sanctuary would have required rebuilding and reconstruction if the life of the sanctuary was to continue. It is tempting to associate the construction of Temple Sites I and II with such repairs. The rock chamber(s) previously used for oracular ritual could then have found a secondary use as a *bothros* for the disposal of destroyed and damaged ritual objects, with some inscribed stones separated from the debris to be used in the construction of new sanctuary buildings. Such building activities are documented for this period in sanctuaries throughout the island.[194] Oracular activity need not have ceased at the time when these chambers went out of use but was probably shifted to

another location within the sanctuary site. The comparative evidence from
Alonia tou Episkopou shows that, without the evidence of inscriptions, certain oracular chambers were indistinguishable from the architecture of
tombs. It is entirely possible then, that one or more of the rock-cut structures seen at the bottom of the sanctuary hill became the site of the rituals
previously enacted in the chambers on the hilltop above.

This hypothesis is, I believe, likely, based on the extant evidence. It, however, cannot be tested in the absence of detailed excavation notes and in the
loss of the associated terracotta material. Zahn, too, believed that the filling
in of Tomb 1 on top of the acropolis occurred after a destruction of the sanctuary, but he would date this event "in [the] early Roman period according to
the fragments of pottery found between the rubble work."[195] If Zahn's dating
is correct, the chamber he designated as his Tomb 1 must have been open in
order that such late debris could be cast in. Indeed, evidence of destruction at
this site does not need necessarily to be limited to the Persian reduction of
Paphos, or associated with any political event at all. Such destruction could
have been natural, as Cyprus is prone to violent earthquakes. It is recorded
that, by the first century A.D., Paphos had been thrown down several times
by seismic events.[196] Analysis of the evidence of the 1910 excavations is made
more difficult when it is considered that the recorded disturbances at the site
could have been the result of the efforts of looters in more modern times,
rather than an accurate representation of events in ancient times. Therefore,
on the basis of the available evidence, it cannot be established whether, when
sanctuary use ended in the late Hellenistic or early Roman period, the site
was, at the last, abandoned or destroyed.

Conclusions for Literate Practices in Ancient Cyprus

The temple of the goddess in Paphos was one of the preeminent holy places
in the ancient world.[197] Pilgrims would have come from throughout the
ancient world to visit her shrine. Some at least would have visited Rantidi as
well. All pilgrims traveling to Paphos from the east passed directly underneath
the sanctuary, and thus the opportunities to visit this shrine were increased.
These visitors would see inscribed and uninscribed statue bases and stone
offering basins, some having quite distinct sign forms, others quite illegible.
Indeed, for many visitors to the shrines of Paphos, these inscriptions would
have been meaningless, for the use of the syllabic writing system seems to

have been confined to the natives of Cyprus. Even among literate Cypriots, the peculiar sign forms whose use was limited to the Paphian kingdom could well have caused difficulty to persons not native to this city-kingdom. Even for literate Paphians, the viewing of two inscribed signs separated by a single line would have carried little or no information not related to the oral tradition, if known, concerning the object. Ease of reading and independent interpretation of a monument and its contents were not the primary goals of those who created these inscriptions found at the Rantidi sanctuary.

The inscriptions cannot be separated from the objects upon which they have been placed. These stones are all dedications in a sanctuary, and thus they have become consecrated and sacred. The inscription becomes part of the ritual act signified by the dedication of the object. Such consecrated objects, and their texts, are believe to be "invested with some form of numinous power, vessels of coercive forces that may benefit or harm those who come into their sphere."[198] The inscribed object can become the focus of subsequent ceremonies, representing the "event, decision, or individual whose name they record. The document has become "fetishized."[199]

When the powers of the inscribed object are considered to be dangerous or harmful, or if the event commemorated by the inscription is subsequently seen to have been disadvantageous or unpopular, the destruction of the object, or perhaps just the inscription, could take place. Destruction of the inscription or object, such as seen in the Rantidi material, reversed or nullified the events surrounding the dedications and separated the original connection between the object and the dedicator. The erasure of a name seems to be sort of a *damnatio memoriae*.[200] At the Rantidi sanctuary, the sacred object whose inscription had been destroyed was often rededicated, and a second inscription placed upon the stone. The credit for the creation of the stone and its dedication in the sanctuary is now given to another, and the symbolic meaning of this object is redefined.[201] The fact that the second dedication was difficult or impossible to be read was not a major consideration in the creation of such inscriptions, for the texts of many public documents are not complete by themselves, but, as we have seen, are associated with an oral tradition.[202] Even legible inscriptions seem to have been seldom consulted for their texts, but rather the oral tradition is seen to be the primary way in which many ancient monuments were known.[203] To those who were not literate in the syllabic writing system, the visual impact of the inscribed signs may have held an importance not related to the inscription's content.[204]

The content of Cypriot Syllabic inscriptions is far more laconic and regulated than contemporary inscriptions on the Greek mainland. Some of the earliest inscriptions found there in the alphabetic script are sacred laws and
treaties, both of which could be displayed within sanctuary precincts.[205]
Alphabetic writing was used to record treaties, lists of priests, public officials,
and curse tablets; all are attested in Greece in the era contemporary to or
shortly following the creation of the inscriptions at Rantidi.[206] Such documents, if ever created in Cyprus, have not survived in the archaeological
record. It has been noted that most of the inscriptions from Rantidi were limited to a single name, with some inscribed stones containing as few as two
signs. The contemporary inscriptions from the siege mound are equally
brief.[207] Syllabic inscriptions found at other sanctuaries sites can display greater
length or content, but only a handful of inscriptions written in the syllabary
deviate from established ritual formula either in content or length.[208] This
practice is most surprising in those inscriptions created by kings, who, with the
exception of Stasikypros on the Idalion bronze, recorded little more than a
series of names and at most give a verb of dedication and the name of a deity.[209]
R. Thomas points out that reading names and lists of names required a much
lower level of literacy than other types of documents.[210] Furthermore, I have
observed that the repetitive nature of the inscribed monuments allows the easy
recognition of sign groups representing phrases, a recognition enhanced by the
use of puncts, vertical lines used as phrase dividers.

Not only are these inscriptions brief and formulaic, but the archaeological record for syllabic inscriptions is also singularly patchy. The obscure
beginnings of this writing system, represented by two inscriptions only from
the Paphian region, have been discussed above. Syllabic inscriptions then
appear throughout the island until the end of the fourth century B.C. The
Cypriot syllabary disappears from the archaeological record at the time when
Ptolemy has abolished the last of the native city-kingdoms and consolidated
the island under his rule. After a century-long hiatus, the syllabary is attested
at a single sanctuary, Kaphizin, with a burst of inscribing activity dated to
the years 225–218 B.C. This brief glimpse is followed by another long
period of silence, before the conflagration in the Paphian archives preserved
clay sealings with syllabic characters that may be up to a century later than
the inscriptions at Kaphizin.

The plurality of the evidence that has survived in the archaeological record
shows for the Cypriot syllabary a writing system represented by inscribed

objects found in large numbers in certain specified sites only. The content of these inscriptions, largely limited to abbreviated sections of well-established formulae, is the primary evidence of literate practices throughout the island for centuries. The writing system was used by the Cypriots in such a way that it had limited impact upon the archaeological record and, for long periods of time, no impact at all. The view of Cypriot writing presented by the surviving material evidence, however, seems to reflect only a small portion of the full range of Cypriot literate practices. It can be argued that literacy played a much larger role in Cypriot society than has been observed so far.

Cypriots could easily and quickly create long and informative documents, which can be clearly read in the peculiar dialect of Greek used on the island. The small bronze tablet found by local villagers in Idalion sometime before 1852 remains the longest and most easily read of all syllabic documents.[211] This early fifth-century document[212] records an agreement between the king and city of Idalion, on the one hand, and a physician and his brothers, on the other, arranging for the medical care of casualties incurred during the repeated attacks of the Persian armies, allied with the forces of the nearby kingdom of Kition, upon the city and territories of Idalion. The immediacy of the situation described in the text of the bronze, coupled with the fact that Idalion was soon reduced by the Persians and assimilated into the kingdom of Kition, indicates that no long time elapsed before this text was cast in metal.[213]

Other long and easily readable syllabic documents have been found, primarily in Amathus. Scylax characterized Amathus as autochthonous,[214] and indeed the inscriptions found there are not written in the Greek language and cannot yet be understood.[215] Four syllabic inscriptions have been interpreted as recording oaths. Three of these four syllabic inscriptions interpreted as oaths or laws are unfortunately fragmentary.[216] The fourth possible example of an oath text is complete; however, many sign forms are uncertain, and the dialectal and grammatical peculiarities contained in the reconstructed text make the reading so uncertain that no consensus has been reached on its meaning.[217] Notable in its content is a fourth-century B.C. inscription containing a votive epigram.[218] This inscription clearly shows that syllabic writing could be and was used to write Greek verse.

It is theorized for the Greek alphabet that standardized script forms as well as levels of literate ability depended on the development of a school system.[219] An argument can be made for the systematic teaching of syllabic writing in Cyprus. On his funeral stele, one Onasagoras describes himself as τῶ διφθεραλοιφῶν.[220] Hesychius explains this term as γραμματοδιδάσκαλος παρὰ Κυπρίοις, or what the Cypriots call a writing teacher. The grammar of the syllabic form is unclear. This term could be either a genitive singular, indicating a single individual, or plural, indicating a group such as a guild or clan.[221] The fact that Hesychius could write about Onasagoras's profession using its colloquial terminology almost a millennium after the death of the writing teacher suggests the latter.

Literate practices in Iron Age Cyprus must be placed in the context of the literate practices of the cultures by which the island was surrounded. Nearby Egypt, for example, had been practicing the art of writing for millennia. In 709 B.C. Cyprus fell under Assyrian rule, under which it stayed, more or less closely bound, until the end of the seventh century, when the Egyptians gained control of the island.[222] During the last part of sixth century B.C., Cyprus fell under Persian domination, the defiance of which, as the Paphians learned early on, drew swift and severe punishment. These far-flung, literate empires must have used writing, at least to some extent, to communicate with their subject kingdoms. Indeed, Sargon II erected an inscribed stele at Kition to record the Cypriot submission to his rule.[223] For the late Archaic and early Classical periods, the annals of Herodotus depict Egyptian and Persian administrations that were heavily reliant upon written documents.[224] Steiner cogently argues that Herodotus does not approach the topic of writing neutrally, but rather writing is seen as a tool of the Oriental despot by which he commands and claims ownership over lands and persons. In Herodotus's hands, Steiner claims, writing "gathers both sinister and pejorative associations."[225] Despite Herodotus's attitude toward the role of writing in these administrations, his account must, to some extent, reflect actual practice. The Cypriot kings would have received ambassadors and heralds from the kings of the successive empires by which they were ruled; it would be difficult to argue that written documents did not play at least some role in such communications.[226]

The sheer tenacity of the Cypriot script is quite telling. The end of the native city-kingdoms would seem to have heralded the end of the syllabic script if it were not for the evidence of the sanctuary of Kaphizin. Here, in the grotto of the Nymphs, potters from several cities of Cyprus's central plain, Chytroi, Kyreneia, Tamassos, and Idalion, are writing short notes in the Cypriot syllabary to the potential customers of these votive objects by inscribing into the wet clay.[227] Numerous hands are detected, and local script variation is seen.[228] The act of writing is done unself-consciously, freehand, with the expectation that those visiting the grotto would see the pots, read the inducement written there, and buy these potters' wares. Centuries after the grotto at Kaphizin was closed, the syllabary is still recognized and used in the official documents of the island's administration.

The archaeological record, then, does not record the full range of literate activities practiced in Iron Age Cyprus. Despite the limited content and patchy archaeological record of these inscriptions, strong arguments can be made that Cyprus had rates of literacy similar to those found in other parts of the ancient world.[229] It is seen that in our study of writing on Cyprus, the absence of inscriptions does not indicate a loss of literate practices in the ancient society. The archaeological record of Cyprus adds weight to the argument that "we should abandon the idea that literacy is a single definable skill with definite uses and predictable effects. [The] manifestations [of literacy] seem . . . to depend on the society and customs already there."[230]

NOTES

* Many thanks are due to Joanna S. Smith for her continued efforts for the promotion of the study of Cypriot scripts, the most recent being this volume. Her kind suggestions and informative discussion have added much to ideas presented in this paper. Thanks go to the University of Indianapolis, its president, G.B. Lantz, and its trustees, for their generous funding of the Rantidi Forest Excavations. I would like to thank F.G. Maier for his kind permission to publish photographs from his publication of the inscriptions of the Rantidi sanctuary, including Zahn's photographs from the 1910 excavations and the site plan of C. Polycarpou. It is currently planned for the author to study and publish Zahn's notes and drawings housed at the Staatliche Museen in Berlin, and I thank V. Kästner, director of the archives, for his kind permission allowing me access to this material.

Abbreviations:

Evans   A.J. Evans, *Scripta Minoa Volume I* (Oxford 1909).

Kourion   T.B. Mitford, *The Inscriptions of Kourion* (Philadelphia 1971).

Rantidi   T.B. Mitford and O. Masson, *The Syllabic Inscriptions of Rantidi-Paphos* (*Ausgrabungen in Alt-Paphos auf Cypern* 2, Konstanz 1983).

[1] O. Masson, *Les inscriptions chypriotes syllabiques*[2] (*Études chypriotes* I, Paris 1983) 48–51 outlines the history of the decipherment; the bilingual is no. 220 of Masson's collection.

[2] Sign charts displaying the syllabic sign forms, such as those found in Masson (supra n. 1) figs. 1–6, reproduce those forms only for which the phonetic equivalents are known.

Upon inspection, it is seen that certain inscriptions, such as Masson (supra n. 1) nos. 285 and 298, for example, display sign forms for which no phonetic equivalent is known. No systematic study has been undertaken of signs with unknown phonetic value, and their exact number is not known.

[3] See Masson (supra n. 1) 51–57, 68–78.

[4] A discussion of the history of scholarship on the Eteo-Cypriot subject is found in Masson (supra n. 1) 84–87.

[5] Masson in *Rantidi* 27, "only when we are not able to find a Greek interpretation do we turn to the Eteo-Cypriote hypothesis, though this is hardly a satisfactory method."

[6] Masson in *Rantidi* 27, 64 no. 46 and n. 216. Masson's reluctance to accept Eteo-Cypriot interpretations for syllabic inscriptions is long-standing, as is his criticism of Mitford's work in identifying the inscriptions in that language, see Masson (supra n. 1) 86 n. 9 and 120 n. 3.

[7] Masson in O. Masson and T.B. Mitford, *Les inscriptions syllabiques de Kouklia-Paphos* (*Ausgrabungen in Alt-Paphos auf Cypern* 4, Konstanz 1986) 25–27, no. 3, where /ya/ is emended to /mo/; Masson (supra no. 1) nos. 110, 112, 113, 115 passim, where 1–3 syllables have been added to complete inscriptions to achieve Greek anthroponyms.

[8] Scylax 103 is the most complete account; Isoc. *Evag.* 47–56 emphasizes the differences between the Greek and Phoenician populations of the island.

[9] V. Karageorghis, *Kition: Mycenaean and Phoenician Discoveries in Cyprus* (London 1976) 95–96.

[10] O. Masson and M. Sznycer, *Recherches sur les phéniciens à Chypre* (*Centre de recherches d'histoire et de philologie* 2, *Hautes études orientales* 3, Genève 1972) discuss many of the Phoenician inscriptions from Cyprus; to be added to this list are Masson (supra n. 1) nos. 215, 216 and 220. For syllabic inscriptions at Kition, see Masson (supra n. 1) 272–74, nos. 256–259.

[11] Masson and Sznycer (supra n. 10) 79–131.

[12] G.B. Bazemore, *The Role of Writing in Ancient Society: The Cypriote Syllabic Inscriptions* (Diss. Univ. of Chicago 1998) 14–15, 24–27, with references; this number includes the funeral stele of Idagygos from Halikarnassos.

[13] Bazemore (supra n. 12) 29–81. The history of the fourth and third centuries B.C. in Cyprus can be found in Sir G. Hill, *A History of Cyprus,* volume 1, *To the Conquest by Richard Lion Heart* (Cambridge 1940) 143–211, and V. Tatton-Brown, "The Archaic Period, The Classical Period, and The Hellenistic Period," in Sir D. Hunt ed., *Footprints in Cyprus* (London 1982) 98–109.

[14] Bazemore (supra n. 12) 237–38. These inscriptions are listed, with bibliographical references for each, in Bazemore (supra n. 12) vols. 2–3. This listing is the most complete yet complied, and includes those inscriptions rejected by Masson due to brevity of length or difficulty of reading, Masson (supra n. 1) 127 n. 2, 168 n. 1, 175 n. 2, 300 n. 2 passim, as well as those inscriptions published after the appearance of the first edition of Masson's collection.

[15] Bazemore (supra n. 21) 548–81 for a list of syllabic inscriptions found outside of Cyprus. For partial listings of such inscriptions, see Masson (supra n. 1) 353–88 and O. Masson,

"Les graffites chypriotes alphabétiques et syllabiques," in C. Traunecker, F. le Saout, and O. Masson, *La chapelle d'Achôris à Karnak II* (*Recherche sur les grandes civilisations, Synthèse* no. 5, Paris 1981) 253–84.

[16] The city of ancient Paphos today lies under the modern village of Kouklia. Nikoklewes, the last king of Paphos, in the late fourth century B.C. moved the site of his city away from the famed temple of Aphrodite there to a harbor site some 15 km to the west. This city too was named Paphos, and the two cities were distinguished in antiquity as Paphos and Palaepaphos (e.g., Strabo 14.6). In this paper, the name Paphos refers to the ancient city alone, and the later foundation is distinguished as Nea Paphos. For Nikoklewes' foundation of the new city, see J. Młynarczyk, *Nea Paphos III* (Warsaw 1990) 25, 67–105.

[17] The siege of the Cypriot cities is mentioned in Hdt. 5.115; for the siege of Palaepaphos and the construction of the siege mound see T.B. Mitford, *Studies in the Signaries of South-Western Cyprus* (*BICS Suppl.* no. 10, London 1961) 1 and F.G. Maier and V. Karageorghis, *Paphos: History and Archaeology* (Nicosia 1984) 192–203.

[18] V. Wilson, "The Kouklia Sanctuary," *RDAC* 1974, 139–46; Maier and Karageorghis (supra n. 17) 183–92; O. Masson in Masson and Mitford (supra n. 7) 7–8.

[19] Mitford (supra n. 17) 1; Maier and Karageorghis (supra n. 17) 183–92.

[20] Maier and Karageorghis (supra n. 17) 186–87 and Wilson (supra n. 18) 139–46; but see O. Masson in Masson and Mitford (supra n. 7) 7–8.

[21] Many inscriptions from Rantidi today cannot be located and are presumed to be lost. A list of these lost stones is supplied in *Rantidi* 86–88.

[22] Mitford (supra n. 17) 7, followed by Masson in *Rantidi* 26.

[23] Masson (supra n. 1) 45–46, 150–53 for the dating of the objects from Marion.

[24] Masson (supra n. 1) 44–46, 275–81 for the dating of the inscribed objects from Golgoi.

[25] Actually, no attempt has been made to date the inscriptions from Chytroi; see Masson (supra n. 1) 44–46, 258–59.

[26] T.B. Mitford, *The Nymphaeum of Kafizin: The Inscribed Pottery* (*Kadmos Suppl.* 2, Berlin 1980) 251–52, 264–65.

[27] I. Michaelidou-Nikolaou, "Nouveaux documents pour le syllabaire chypriote," *BCH* 117 (1993) 346–47.

[28] First suggested in A.J. Evans, "Primitive Pictographs and a Prae-Phoenician Script from Crete and the Peloponnese," *JHS* 14 (1894) 348–49, table I; developed more fully in Evans 68–77.

[29] O. Masson (supra n. 1) 30–39; J. Chadwick, "The Minoan Origin of the Classical Cypriote Script," in *Acts of the International Archaeological Symposium "The Relations Between Cyprus and Crete, ca. 2000–500 B.C."* (Nicosia 1979) 139–43; J. Karageorghis, "Histoire de l'écriture chypriote," Κυπριακαί Σπουαί (1961) 44–45, 51–52.

[30] *Evans* 69.

[31] V. Karageorghis, *Palaepaphos-Skales: An Iron Age Cemetery in Cyprus* (*Ausgrabungen in Alt-Paphos auf Cypern* 3, Konstanz 1983) 59–76; V. Karageorghis, "Fouilles à l'Ancienne-Paphos de Chypre: Les premiers colons grecs," *CRAI* (1980) 123, 134–35.

[32] E. Gjerstad, *SwCyprusExp* IV.2, 427 dates the CG period to 1050–950 B.C.

[33] Karageorghis (supra n. 31) 76; about the dating of the latest contents of this tomb, he says,

"There are no objects which may be attributed with certainty to the CG II period." The Cypro-Geometric II period is dated by Gjerstad, (supra n. 32) 427, to 950–850 B.C. I thank J.S. Smith for discussing with me the problems surrounding the chronology of this obelos. Further specialist studies are needed to confirm the dating of the obelos and the pottery from the tomb. With a new understanding of the earliest development of the syllabary, the discussion of these sign forms found in T.G. Palaima, "The Advent of the Greek Alphabet on Cyprus: A Competition of Scripts," in C. Baurain, C. Bonnet, and V. Krings eds., *Phoinikeia Grammata: Lire et écrire en Méditerranée (Studia Phoenicia, Collection d'études classiques* 6, Namur 1991) 454–55 needs to be readdressed. A discussion of the continuity of script use in Cyprus from the Bronze to the Iron Ages, as well as the dating of the obelos, will appear in my forthcoming article on the origins of the syllabic script.

[34] E. Masson and O. Masson, in Karageorghis (supra n. 31) 413–14; Palaima (supra n. 33) 451–53; A.-M. Collombier, "Écritures et sociétés à Chypre à l'Âge du fer," in C. Baurain, C. Bonnet, and V. Krings eds. (supra n. 33) 426–27; C. Baurain, "L'Écriture syllabique à Chypre," in C. Baurain, C. Bonnet, and V. Krings eds. (supra n. 33) 406–408. The questions concerning the sign forms raised by E. Bennett in B. Powell, *Homer and the Origin of the Greek Alphabet* (Cambridge 1991) 90 n. 42 have been answered by O. Masson, "La plus ancienne inscription chypriote syllabique," *Centre d'études chypriotes cahier* 22 (1994) 33–36.

[35] Masson (supra n. 1) 187, 408, no. 174 = 18c; V. Karageorghis and J. Karageorghis, "Some Inscribed Iron-Age Vases from Cyprus," *AJA* 60 (1956) 353 no. 4, 357 no. 2.

[36] Masson (supra n. 1) 43–45.

[37] Although the official name of this site is Rantidi-*Lingrin tou Dhiyeni*, in this paper it is often referred to simply as the Rantidi sanctuary.

[38] T.B. Mitford, "Milestones in Western Cyprus," *JRS* 29 (1939) 184, 194; T.B. Mitford, "Roman Cyprus," *ANRW* II.7.2 (1980) 1332–37; T. Bekker-Nielsen, "The Road Network," in J. Fejfer ed., *Ancient Akamas I* (Aarhus 1995) 87–96.

[39] The view of the Paphian plain from the sanctuary hill has often been remarked upon; see M.R. Popham, "Rantidi 1910 and 1955," in *Rantidi* 10; Mitford (supra n. 17) 11; J.C. Peristianes, *A Study on the Ancient Site in the Randi State Forest* (Nicosia 1911) 34.

[40] J. Karageorghis, *La grande déesse de Chypre et son culte (Collection de la Maison de l'Orient Méditerranéen ancien* no. 5, Série archéologique 4, Paris 1977) 7–18.

[41] Homer *Od.* 8.359–366; Hom. *Hym.* 6.1–18, 10.1–6; Hesiod *Theog.* 188–200.

[42] Maier and Karageorghis (supra n. 17) 81–102.

[43] Especially in the region of ancient Chytroi on the eastern part of the island, see Masson (supra n. 1) nos. 234–249a.

[44] Masson (supra n. 1) nos. 1, 4, 6, 7, 16, 17, 90, and 91.

[45] So it appeared to Herodotus 1.199, who compared this Cypriot rite for this goddess with the Babylonian ones. See also Maier and Karageorghis (supra n. 17) 81, 84, 354–72 and J. Karageorghis (supra n. 40) 223–27.

[46] Considering its proximity to the road, the fact that this site was not noticed by archaeologists until 1910 is interesting. G. Jeffery, *A Description of the Historic Monuments of Cyprus* (Nicosia 1918) 385 cites travelers' reports that the ruins of the site were visible

from the Limassol-Paphos road in the 1850s. Peristianes (supra n. 39) 7 and 10 in n. 38 claims that the site "did not escape the attention of the mercenary grave-diggers and sacrilegious labourers of Cesnola" and reports that an ancient site nearby, "just opposite to and below the Randi Hill," was excavated by Cesnola's head laborer. It is doubtful, however, that Cesnola knew about this site. Cesnola often spoke of his interest in inscriptions; see L.P. di Cesnola, *Cyprus, Its Ancient Cities, Tombs, and Temples* (New York 1878) 221, 225, 239, 244, 281, 282, 285, 304 passim. For this reason, it is difficult to believe that, having known about the number of inscriptions littering the ground at Rantidi, he would have not have carried out extensive excavations there.

[47] M. Ohnefalsch-Richter, "The Shrine of Aphrodite-Astarte: An Important Discovery," *The Times* (London) Wednesday July 27, 1910, 10; M. Krpata, "Max Hermann Ohnefalsch-Richter: Bibliography and Biographical Remarks," *RDAC* 1992, 337–41.

[48] M. Ohnefalsch-Richter, *Kypros, the Bible, and Homer* (London 1893) 1–28.

[49] Ohnefalsch-Richter (supra n. 47) 10; M. Ohnefalsch-Richter, "The Dwelling-Place of Divinities? A "Mount Olympus" in Cyprus: The Remarkable Discoveries of Dr. Max Ohnefalsch-Richter at Rantidi," *ILN* Feb. 4, 1911, 162.

[50] Peristianes (supra n. 39) 33; Popham (supra n. 39) 4–5, 12.

[51] The reports and inventory submitted by Peristianes to the Cyprus Museum Committee are reproduced by Popham (supra n. 39) 6–8.

[52] The Cyprus Museum Committee granted Zahn's permit so that his excavations might "enable him to present a preliminary report upon the archaeological characteristics of the said site." Zahn might have intended to make a report of his excavations, as he did express his intention to return to Cyprus to study the terracotta finds; see Popham (supra n. 39) 5–6. The article by R. Zahn, "Der angebliche Räucheraltarplatz der Aphrodite in Paphos," *BPW* Feb. 4, 1911, 155–57, is simply an attack on Ohnefalsch-Richter's continuing series of newspaper articles concerning the site, saying nothing informative about the excavations. A bibliography of the writings of Ohnefalsch-Richter, including those pertaining to the Rantidi sanctuary, can be found in Krpata (supra n. 47) 340–41.

[53] Popham (supra n. 39) 6; T.B. Mitford, "Prolegomena to the Syllabic Inscriptions of Rantidi," *Emerita* 26 (1958) 113.

[54] There is some confusion about the exact date of the beginning of this work. In one source, Mitford (supra n. 53) 115, says that he squeezed, copied, and photographed the Rantidi inscriptions in 1937; elsewhere, Mitford (supra n. 17) 11, this date is 1938.

[55] Masson in *Rantidi* 23–24.

[56] R.d Meister, "Inschriften aus Rantidi in Kypros," *Sitzungsberichte der (Königl.) Preußischen Akademie der Wissenschaften* (1911) 630–50. Zahn had wanted Meister to travel to Cyprus and study the originals; however, his translations were taken from squeezes and photographs of the stone inscriptions, see Popham (supra n. 39) 6. Mitford (supra n. 17) 11 says of Meister's work, "This *corpus* was thereupon published by R. Meister with a speed and an inadequacy which I have found equally astonishing." He (supra n. 53) 113 later added, "Meister himself died in 1912 without (I believe) having offered any hint of dissatisfaction with his services towards Rantidi." Mitford's translations of the Rantidi material, with commentary from O. Masson, are contained in *Rantidi*.

[57] *Rantidi* nos. 1–102, with no. 12 having two entries; *Rantidi* 86–88 lists the lost and presumably lost inscriptions.

[58] Examples of this shape of inscribed stone are *Rantidi* pl. 7 no. 2 (on the right), pl. 11 no. 10, pl. 14 no. 16, and pl. 16 no. 26.

[59] Examples of this shape of inscribed stone are *Rantidi* pl. 7 no. 2 (on the left), pl. 7 no. 3, pl. 10 no. 3, and pl. 18 no. 37b.

[60] Illustrative examples of the relative dimensions of each shape are: for the taller stones with basins covering the entire upper surface, *Rantidi* no. 10 is 30 cm in height, 63 cm in width, and 35 cm in thickness; for the shorter stones with the basin covering only part of the upper surface, *Rantidi* no. 3, for example, is 14 cm in height, 54 cm in width, and 33 cm in thickness.

[61] Examples of this shape are *Rantidi* pl. 17 no. 30, an exceptional example of a well-worked stone; for roughly worked or unworked stones, see pl. 10 no. 5, pl. 12 no. 12a, pl. 14 no. 19, and pl. 15 no. 22, nos. 51 and 82 (no plate) with associated commentaries. The rectangular slabs vary in dimensions.

[62] Examples are *Rantidi* no. 14, 67 cm in height, 56 cm in width, and only 20 cm in thickness; no. 1 is 94 cm in height, 38 cm in width, and 36 cm in thickness. Two large stones found by Zahn and Peristianes, now lost, *Rantidi* 87 nos. 12 and 15, measured 99 cm in height, 46 cm in width, 20 cm in thickness and 96 cm in height, and 25 cm in width respectively.

[63] Peristianes, in Popham (supra n. 39) 7, describes "a very big stone basin . . . which could not have been brought there from a far point." Personal experience has shown that moving inscribed and uninscribed basins from the Rantidi sanctuary often requires the efforts of three large adults.

[64] Ohnefalsch-Richter (supra n. 47) 10; Popham (supra n. 39) 4.

[65] *Rantidi* no. 45 is inscribed both on the top as well as the front face; *Rantidi* no. 37 is inscribed on the basin lip as well as two sides.

[66] Quoted in Popham (supra n. 39) 6–7.

[67] Mitford (supra n. 53) 125–26.

[68] Mitford (supra n. 53) 121, 125–26.

[69] Masson in *Rantidi* 28; see *Rantidi* no. 2.

[70] Peristianes (supra n. 39) 11.

[71] Examples include *Rantidi* nos. 17, 19, 29 32, 33, and 53.

[72] *Rantidi*, pl. 3 no. 4, Plan II.

[73] Masson in *Rantidi* 27.

[74] *Rantidi* nos. 1 and 2 respectively. *Rantidi* 37 is not included here as the end of the inscription is lost and the reading of the dedicatory phrase, σὺ(ν)τύχαι, is a reconstruction.

[75] *Rantidi* nos. 39, 40, 41, and 42; no. 43 contains a patronymic; see Masson in *Rantidi* 29–30.

[76] Masson rejects Mitford's interpretation of *Rantidi* 45 as Eteo-Cypriot but offers no interpretation of his own, saying merely that the text is obscure. Faced with the impossibility of a Greek reading for the inscriptions on *Rantidi* no. 48, Masson accepts that it is written in the Eteo-Cypriot language. See the discussion of Masson and Mitford's relative views of Eteo-Cypriot above and supra n. 6.

[77] *Rantidi* nos. 65–73, 78, 79, 80, 81, 83, 84, 86, 92–95, 97, 98, and 100–102.

[78] *Rantidi* 27, 74–75.

[79] Mitford (supra n. 17) 3–4; *Rantidi* 74–75.

[80] The signs seen on *Rantidi* nos. 1 and 71 are among the largest found at the site, while those seen on nos. 33 and 34 are among the smallest.

[81] Mitford (supra n. 17) 7.

[82] These include *Rantidi* nos. 10, 21, 37 sides a and c, 62, 66, and 99.

[83] Examples are *Rantidi* 3, 14 side a, 21, and 38. *Rantidi* nos. 2 and 13 are possibly palimpsest.

[84] *Rantidi,* no. 14 seems to be palimpsest on the broad face but carries a different, more regular and deeply cut, lapidary hand on the narrow face to the left. The same difference in lapidary hands can be seen on the two inscribed faces of *Rantidi* no. 34. For *Rantidi* no. 37, it is the change in the direction of script from the signs on the upper part of the inscription (sinistrograde) to those on the broad face (dextrograde) that suggests two, rather than one, inscriptions for this object. For *Rantidi* no. 65, the position of the inscription upon the stone as well as the lapidary forms indicate two separate episodes of inscribing. A clear example of reuse and reinscribing is *Rantidi* no. 77, which has a basin both on its upper and lower surfaces; on the back are traces of a defaced inscription to match the basin of the lower surface.

[85] On *Rantidi* no. 12, the first sign to the left was incised after a large curved section was knocked away from the front of the stone. *Rantidi* no. 70 is inscribed on a fragment of limestone shaped as if struck from a cippus or column drum. *Rantidi* no. 37 seems deliberately broken away to the lower right.

[86] *Rantidi* no. 54.

[87] For *Rantidi* no. 9, Peristianes (supra n. 39) 11 no. 3 reads two lines but Mitford only one; see *Rantidi* no.13, where Peristianes (supra n. 39) 20–22 no. 7 reads four lines, but Mitford sees only three signs and *Rantidi* no. 24, where Peristianes (supra n. 39) 10–11 no. 2 reads three lines while the editors see only one partial line; *Rantidi* no. 54 has been read either as two lines on two faces (see Masson [supra n. 1] no. 46) or only four uncertain signs on one face (*Rantidi* no. 54); *Rantidi* no. 65 has been read with either seven signs (see Masson [supra n. 1] no. 43) or four; *Rantidi* no. 68 has been read as the name of Apollo (Masson [supra n. 1] no. 44) although other editors saw only two signs, neither of which were compatible with the earlier reading; *Rantidi* no. 72 once again has been read as the name of Apollo (Masson [supra n. 1] no. 43) where other editors can see only three signs. This is only a sample of such divergent readings.

[88] In Popham (supra n. 39) 6–7.

[89] F.G. Maier, "Rantidi 1910: Dokumente und Kommentare," in *Rantidi* 15–16.

[90] Masson in *Rantidi* believes that, following Maier's discussion, "most of the sites dug by Zahn can, however, be ascertained now with a fair degree of probability. Thus in many cases the find-spots of the inscriptions can be clearly determined."

[91] Popham (supra n. 39) 7. Zahn's photo is here reproduced as fig. 6; note the second stone from the lower left, with the inscribed face in shadow; this block cannot be identified with any of the published inscriptions.

[92] Ohnefalsch-Richter (supra n. 49). Maier (supra n. 89) 16 also accepts that Ohnefalsch-Richter's drawing is that of Peristianes' Temple Site I.

[93] The three inscriptions listed by Masson in *Rantidi* 25 as originating from Temple Site I came from the area of the building, not the building itself.

[94] In Popham (supra n. 39) 7.

[95] Zahn's drawing is reproduced in *Rantidi* Plan II; Maier (supra n. 89) 16.

[96] Maier (supra n. 89) 16, 19, Plan I. This plan shows the results of surveys undertaken during 1979–1980 and is used as the basis for the sanctuary reconstruction given here.

[97] Quoted by Popham (supra n. 39) 7.

[98] Maier (supra n. 89) 16, however, has reservations as to whether "Large Room" drawn by Ohnefalsch-Richter does indeed represent the Lower Temenos and, if so, if this representation is accurate, "Es fragt sich weiterhin, ob der von Ohnefalsch-Richter neben dem 'Sanctuary' skizzierte 'Large Room' den Unteren Temenos wiedergeben soll. . . . Da Zahn jedoch nur eine östliche und ein westliche Mauer des Unteren Temenos beschreibt, ist Ohnefalsch-Richter's Skizze eines langrechteckigen Baus eine mögliche, aber keine gesicherte Wiedergabe des ausgegrabenen Befundes."

[99] In Popham (supra n. 39) 8.

[100] Reproduced in *Rantidi* Plans II and III. Zahn's numbering of these drawings as 6 and 13 indicates that several more such plans once must have existed. The stones found in the wall are *Rantidi* nos. 59, 30, 16, 12A, 14, 29, 68, 72, and *Rantidi* 87 nos. 16 and 48; there is a possible concordance of one of these stones with *Rantidi* no. 98.

[101] *Rantidi* pl. 3 no. 3, *Rantidi* no. 72 is seen in the near wall, third stone from the bottom right.

[102] *Rantidi* Plan II and pl. 3 no. 4. In the photo the inscribed stone is the uppermost of the three; the inscribed face can be seen in pl. 17 no. 30.

[103] See also Maier (supra n. 89) 16, who says, "Für Baubefund und Lage von T.S. III, IV und VI fehlen vorläufig alle Anhaltspunkte." Adding to the confusion is the fact that "Festzuhalten ist zudem, daß Peristianis T.S. II, IV und VI mehrfach nur als mögliche 'Temple Sites' bezeichnet, die auch 'Building Sites' gewesen sein könnten."

[104] In Popham (supra n. 39) 7–8. It was Ohnefalsch-Richter (supra n. 47) 10 who gave the name "snowman" to these figurines.

[105] *Rantidi* nos. 10, 11, 4, and 58.

[106] In Popham (supra n. 39) 7–8.

[107] Maier (supra n. 89) 16–17, 19, Plan I. Maier believes that the term "Middle Terrace" designates the flat spur of the Rantidi hill situated under the 200 m line. See also the commentary for *Rantidi* nos. 22, 37, and 55.

[108] In Popham (supra n. 39) 7–8; *Rantidi* no. 22. It is interesting to note that Peristianes' inventory submitted to the Cyprus Museum Committee lists no inscription as coming from this site.

[109] Peristianes reports *Rantidi* no. 27 as having come from Temple Site VI, but Zahn gives the provenience of this stone as "the great Temenos Terrace" or Temple Site I; no other inscriptions can be assigned to this site. As with Temple Site V, Peristianes, in his inventory submitted to the Cyprus Museum Committee of the finds at Rantidi, contradicts

his own notes and lists no inscription as having been found at this site (see Popham [supra n. 39] 7–8).

[110] Popham (supra n. 39) 9–10. *Rantidi* nos. 28, 43, 67, 25, 2, and 19 come from the possible building site suggested by Popham.

[111] Ohnefalsch-Richter (supra n. 47) 10.

[112] In Popham (supra n. 39) 5–6.

[113] Popham (supra n. 39) 9–10.

[114] In Popham (supra n. 39) 5–6; Zahn (supra n. 52) 156. Ohnefalsch-Richter (supra n. 47) 10 and (supra n. 49) also thought all the rock-cut chambers were tombs.

[115] Excavations began on 30 August, and Zahn was able to make a final plan of this tomb on 8 September; see Popham (supra n. 39) 5–6, 101 (for date of drawing), and Plan IV.

[116] In Popham (supra n. 39) 6; *Rantidi* no. 11.

[117] Maier (supra n. 89) 17.

[118] Popham (supra n. 39) 5–6;

[119] *Rantidi* nos. 16, 34, 42, 71, 75, and 80.

[120] Maier (supra n. 89) 17 and n. 72.

[121] M. Ohnefalsch-Richter, "Entdeckung des bei Homer erwähnten Räucheraltarplatzes der Aphrodite in Paphos auf Cypern," *Globus* (1910) 294–95.

[122] Popham (supra n. 39) 6 and n. 35; Maier (supra n. 89) 17 and n. 71. The looting of Tomb 2 is dated to March 1910.

[123] In Popham (supra n. 39) 6.

[124] Ohnefalsch-Richter (supra n. 121) 294–95, saying, "In welcher acht oder neun von den zehn hergeschenkten Inschrifträucherbecken aufgestellt waren."

[125] Quoted by Maier (supra n. 89) 18 n. 75.

[126] Maier (supra n. 89) 18; *Rantidi* no. 21.

[127] *Rantidi* nos. 21 and 53; Maier (supra n. 89) 18 and n. 76. Stone no. 21 was photographed by Ohnefalsch-Richter (supra n. 121) 295 fig. 4 and (supra n. 49) 162 figs. 1–2 and 2.

[128] *Rantidi* no. 76. Maier (supra n. 89) 18 and n. 78 speaking of Peristianes List no. 50, which is published as *Rantidi* no. 76.

[129] Quoted in *Rantidi* no. 37; see also Maier (supra n. 89) 18.

[130] *Rantidi* no. 37.

[131] Quoted in Popham (supra n. 39) 7. The two possible inscribed fragments have been lost; see Maier (supra n. 89) 18 and n. 77 and *Rantidi* 87 nos. 55 and 67.

[132] *Rantidi* no. 37.

[133] *Rantidi* nos. 37 and 51; for no. 51 see also Maier (supra n. 89) 18 n. 79.

[134] *Rantidi* nos. 4, 26, and 91; Maier (supra n. 89) 18 and n. 79.

[135] In Maier (supra n. 89) 18.

[136] Maier (supra n. 89) 18, Plan I, pl. 6 no. 1.

[137] In Popham (supra n. 39) 7; Masson in *Rantidi* 25, does not include Tomb 4 in his list of sites producing inscriptions.

[138] Maier (supra n. 89) 17, 21.

[139] Popham (supra n. 39) 7 n. 37.

[140] Maier (supra n. 89) 17.

[141] Gjerstad (supra n. 32) 29–47.

[142] Ohnefalsch-Richter (supra n. 47) 10.

[143] Masson in *Rantidi* 25–26.

[144] Maier (supra n. 89) 19.

[145] J.S. Smith, "Preliminary Comments on a Rural Cypro-Archaic Sanctuary in the Polis-Peristeries," *BASOR* 308 (1997) 88–89, and Karageorghis (supra n. 9) 97, 101–102, 110, 113, 140–41. *Favissae* and their distinction from *bothroi* are discussed by M.C. Loulloupis, "A Rural Cult Place in the Soloi Area," in V. Tatton-Brown ed., *Cyprus and the East Mediterranean in the Iron Age* (London 1989) 68–71, and by Smith (supra).

[146] For a good discussion of the history and topography of this site, as well as its oracular attributes, see Młynarczyk (supra n. 16) 76–82.

[147] T.B. Mitford, "Paphian Inscriptions Hoffmann Nos. 98 and 99," *BICS* 7 (1960) 7. Mitford's reading is not accepted by O. Masson, "L'inscription syllabique en Paphien Récent du village de (Paphos)," *RDAC* 1988 pt. 2, 63–68, who offers no interpretation of his own. Masson's objections based on dialectal forms is not persuasive; see the discussion infra n. 171.

[148] Młynarczyk (supra n. 16) 80–81.

[149] Młynarczyk (supra n. 16) 78.

[150] Młynarczyk (supra n. 16) 78–79. To Młynarczyk's example of the worship of Apollo in connection with the Paphian lady at Chytroi (Masson [supra no. 1] nos. 234–250a), can be added their worship at Golgoi. Although Golgoi was renowned in the ancient world for its temple of Aphrodite (Theoc. *Id.* 15.100–103), actual excavation uncovered numerous dedications to Apollo only, see Masson (supra n. 1) nos. 265–300. Inscription no. 262 has been read τὰς Παφίας. This inscription, however, was later seen to consist of mere scratchings and described as "very obscure"; its reading, therefore, is to be regarded as highly suspect; see J.L. Myres, *Handbook of the Cesnola Collection of Antiquities from Cyprus* (New York 1914) 216, 526, no. 1351. For the most complete list currently available of the deities and their epithets given by the syllabic inscriptions, see Masson (supra n. 1) 436.

[151] Młynarczyk (supra n. 16) 78–79; Maier and Karageorghis (supra n. 17) 368–71.

[152] Młynarczyk (supra n. 16) 78–79.

[153] Mitford (supra n. 147) 5.

[154] Mitford (supra n. 147) 6–7.

[155] Młynarczyk (supra n. 16) 85.

[156] Mitford (supra n. 147) 6 and n. 14; Młynarczyk (supra n. 16) 85.

[157] Mitford (supra n. 147) 6 and n. 14; Młynarczyk (supra n. 16) 90–91.

[158] Mitford (supra n. 147) 6; Młynarczyk (supra n. 16) 94 argues, however, that these investigations, described by Mitford as "extensive soundings on the site extending over two seasons," failed to test the area in which she would locate this pre-Hellenistic settlement.

[159] Młynarczyk (supra n. 16) 85–94.

[160] Młynarczyk (supra n. 16) 78.

[161] The numbers of persons initially relocating to Nikoklewes' new foundation is unknown. What population this city had, however, was exponentially increased ca. 312 B.C., when

Ptolemy destroyed the capital of the city-kingdom of Marion and transferred its entire population to Nea Paphos; see Diod. Sicl. 19.79 and Młynarczyk (supra n. 16) 72.

[162] Hdt. 5.104–106.

[163] Tacitus *Hist.* 2.2–3

[164] For the position of the Kinyrad dynasty in Paphos, see F.G. Maier, "Priest Kings in Cyprus," in E. Peltenburg ed., *Early Society in Cyprus* (Edinburgh 1989) 376–91.

[165] Tatian *Gr.* 1; Chariton 8.2.7–9; Clem. *Al. Strom.* 1.21.

[166] Located on the map found in Maier and Karageorghis (supra n. 17) 121.

[167] Masson in *Rantidi* 27; see the commentary for *Rantidi* no. 1.

[168] Mitford (supra n. 17) 12–13, no. 5, pl. 5; *Rantidi* 34–35 no. 1.

[169] Masson in *Rantidi* 35 no. 1.

[170] Masson in *Rantidi* 27.

[171] C.D. Buck, *The Greek Dialects* (Chicago 1955) 146–47, offers only some of the more common dialectal attributes. Among the dialectal attributes not discussed by Buck, the following is an informative example. Cypriot is the only dialect of Greek that interprets the root κρατ- as an *i*-stem noun and the only dialect that places a digamma in *i*-stem endings, where, linguistically speaking, they are not supposed to exist. For a list of *i*-stem words displaying endings with a digamma, see M. Egetmeyer, *Wörterbuch zu den Inschriften in Kyprischen Syllabar* (*Kadmos Suppl.* III, Berlin 1992) 261–262.

[172] M. Sznycer and O. Masson, "A Small Phoenician (?) Inscription," in *Rantidi* 91–93, with references.

[173] Publication of this figurine is in preparation by G.B. Bazemore.

[174] Maier and Karageorghis (supra n. 17) 371–72, with references. For orgiastic rituals in connection with the death and rebirth of Adonis and their comparison with Cypriot rituals, see S. Moscati, *The World of the Phoenicians* (New York 1968) 108.

[175] Justin. *Epit. Hist.* 18.5.

[176] Hdt. 1.199; Justin., quoting Pompeius Trogus, *Epit. Hist.* 18.5.

[177] Tatton-Brown (supra n. 13) 76. Dancing floors and dancing rituals are best documented for the sanctuary of Apollo at Kourion; see S.C. Glover, "The Cult of Apollo *Hylates* at Kourion," in H.W. Swiny ed., *An Archaeological Guide to the Ancient Kourion Area and Akrotiri Peninsula* (Nicosia 1982) 70–74; and B. C. Dietrich, "The Sanctuary of Apollo at Kourion," in D. Buitron-Oliver, *The Sanctuary of Apollo Hylates at Kourion: Excavations in the Archaic Precinct* (*SIMA* 109, Jonsered 1996) 20–21.

[178] Maier and Karageorghis (supra n. 17) 372, with references.

[179] Such is suggested by the odd conflations found in Clem. *Al. Protr.* 2.12, 13.

[180] Sznycer and Masson (supra n. 172) 92, for stone R 103, pl. 24.

[181] Mitford (supra n. 17) 31–37.

[182] Mitford (supra n. 17) 7; Mitford (supra n. 53) 114; *Rantidi* 26.

[183] Masson in *Rantidi* 26.

[184] Mitford (supra n. 17) 31–37 identifies a set of sign variants, which he labels "Middle Paphian," seen in inscriptions dated to the years immediately following the Persian reduction of the city.

[185] The systematic changing of two or more intersecting lines into one long curved stroke,

such as in /re/, /le/, /si/, /o/, /wo/, /ne/, /ka/, etc., and the general rounding of sign forms
are some of the cursive influences seen in Late Paphian. A general study of this development, and its comparison with the few ink inscriptions of the syllabary known, is currently in progress.

[186] The peculiar sign forms of Paphos and Rantidi and their effect outside the Paphian
kingdom are discussed by Mitford (supra n. 17) 1–16; a discussion of regional sign variations is found in Masson (supra n. 1) 57–67 and figs. 1–6. The presence of a Common
form in Paphos is so surprising that the attribution of one inscription to Paphos is rejected
on the grounds that it contains Common forms, see Masson (supra n. 1) no. 335.

[187] Masson and Mitford (supra n. 7) no. 4., line 3, sign 1.

[188] *Rantidi* nos. 1, 8, 45, and 55.

[189] Indeed, the process of the development of Paphian sign forms from the Common can be
reconstructed in detail; this reconstruction is to presented in my article on the origins of
the Cypriot syllabic writing system, currently in preparation.

[190] Masson in *Rantidi* 26.

[191] Maier (supra n. 89) 19–22.

[192] After the Roman period, the next evidence for occupation in this area is in the Middle
Ages; see Maier (supra n. 89) 19–22.

[193] In Popham (supra n. 39) 7.

[194] V. Karageorghis, *Two Cypriote Sanctuaries of the End of the Cypro-Archaic Period* (Rome
1977) 13–14.

[195] In Popham (supra n. 39) 6.

[196] Seneca *Q. Nat.* 6.26.4.

[197] Maier and Karageorghis (supra n. 17) 358 argue that it was similar in fame and veneration as the sanctuary of Apollo at Delphi.

[198] D.T. Steiner, *The Tyrant's Writ: Myths and Images of Writing in Ancient Greece* (Princeton
1994) 61.

[199] Steiner (supra n. 198) 61–64; see also R. Thomas, *Oral Tradition and Written Record in
Classical Athens* (Cambridge 1989) 50–51.

[200] Steiner (supra n. 198) 70–71, 78; Thomas (supra n. 199) 51–53.

[201] Steiner (supra n. 198) 78–79.

[202] Thomas (supra n. 199) 57–59.

[203] Thomas (supra n. 199) 65–68.

[204] R. Thomas, *Literacy and Orality in Ancient Greece* (Cambridge 1992) 62–63.

[205] Thomas (supra n. 204) 56–61, 65–66; Thomas (supra n. 199) 31; K. Robb, *Literacy and
Paideia in Ancient Greece* (Oxford 1994) 84–90.

[206] Thomas (supra n. 204) 65–73.

[207] Masson and Mitford (supra n. 7) no. 1 carries the remains of three lines; nos. 2, 3, and 4
carry patronyms, patronymics, and royal titles.

[208] This important subject has yet to receive the systematic discussion that it deserves. The
maximal formula is expressed in Masson (supra n. 1) no. 154, where the both ritual acts
are observed, the existence of the object and the setting up of the object. Parts of this dedicatory formula are repeated in the great majority of all syllabic inscriptions, both sanc-

tuary dedication and funerary epitaphs, with a simple exchange of proper names. The maximal expression is seldom seen. The dedicatory formulae of the funeral inscriptions of Marion are discussed in G.B. Bazemore, "Gender, Sex, and the Cypriot Syllabic Inscriptions: Females in the Written Record of Ancient Cyprus," in N. Serwint and D. Bolger eds., *Engendering Aphrodite: Women and Society in Ancient Cyprus* (*ASOR Archaeological Reports Series*, Boston in press).

[209] Royal inscriptions in Cyprus include: from Paphos, those of Nikoklewes, Masson (supra n. 1) nos. 1, 6, 7, 91, 92, and Masson and Mitford (supra n. 7) no. 237; of Timocharis, Masson (supra n. 1) no. 16, of Echetimos, Masson (supra n. 1) no. 17, of an unknown king, Masson and Mitford (supra n. 7) no. 1, of Onasicharis the Stasiphilid, Masson and Mitford (supra n. 7) no. 2, of Etewandros, Masson (supra n. 1) no. 176 a and b, of Akestor, *Kourion* no. 217a; from Polis, Timocharis, Masson (supra n. 1) no. 172a; from Kourion, of Diweithemis, *Kourion* no. 3 and a Sta(?), *Kourion*, no. 218, from Soloi, Stasiyas, Masson (supra n. 1) no. 211, and Stasikratis, Masson (supra n. 1) no. 212; from Amathus, King Androcles Masson (supra n. 1) no. 196d; the inscription on the bronze tablet from Idalion by King Stasikypros has been discussed above, Masson (supra n. 1) no. 217; and Evelthon of Salamis, M Yon, "La ville de Salamine," in *Kinyras: L'archéologie française à Chypre* (Travaux de la Maison de l'Orient no. 22, Paris 1993) 144–45. Only in the kingdom of Paphos did royal inscriptions appear before the end of the fourth century B.C., see Tatton-Brown, (supra n. 13) 98–102.

[210] Thomas (supra n. 199) 66.

[211] Masson (supra n. 1) no. 217; acquired by Duke H. de Luynes and published by him in *Numismatique et inscriptions chypriotes* (Paris 1852).

[212] For the most recent discussion of the evidence for the dating of the bronze tablet of Idalion, see L.E. Stager and A.M. Walker eds., *American Expedition to Idalion Cyprus, 1973–1980* (*Oriental Institute Communications* no. 24, Chicago 1989) 464–65.

[213] Stager and Walker (supra n. 212) 464.

[214] Scyl. 103.

[215] Masson (supra n. 1) nos. 194, 195, and 298, for example.

[216] Masson (supra n. 1) nos. 8 and 327, and Masson and Mitford (supra n. 7) no. 237.

[217] Masson (supra n. 1) no. 306 and Mitford (supra n. 17) 38–43.

[218] Masson (supra n. 1) no. 254.

[219] Thomas (supra n. 199) 76; Robb (supra n. 205) 183.

[220] Masson (supra n. 1) no. 143.

[221] This form could represent either a genitive singular, with the addition of -v to the usual Cypriot second-declension ending of $\bar{o}$, as in Buck (supra n. 171) 146 no. 198.1, but it could equally well represent a genitive plural, where the -v is absent from the article; see Egetmeyer (supra n. 171) 195, s.v. "*to*⁴."

[222] Tatton-Brown (supra n. 13) 68–70; Hill (supra n. 13) 104–110.

[223] Tatton-Brown (supra n. 13) 65; Karageorghis (supra n. 9) 19, 109; Hill (supra n. 13) 104–105.

[224] Herodotus's evidence for the literate practices of the Eastern empires is discussed by Steiner (supra n. 198) 127–66.

[225] Steiner (supra n. 198) 127–66, esp. 127–28.

[226] For a discussion of Herodotus's evidence for the use of dispatches by the Eastern kings, see Steiner (supra n. 198) 149–54.

[227] Mitford (supra n. 26) 259–60.

[228] Mitford (supra n. 26) 264–65.

[229] Literacy is to be understood in much different terms than our modern conception and literate practices cannot be isolated from oral ones; see Thomas (supra n. 199) 1–34 and Thomas (supra n. 204) 15–28.

[230] Thomas (supra n. 204) 24.

## 5

The Stamp Seals of Cyprus in
the Late Bronze Age and the Iron Age:
An Introduction*

Andres T. Reyes

When one thinks of Cypriot glyptic, one thinks primarily of the cylinder seals from the island's Late Bronze Age (LBA). That is a tribute to the very fine and perceptive work of the late Professor Edith Porada, whose system for the classification of the different styles cut on the cylinder seals has remained fundamental to the study of Cypriot glyptic for over 50 years.[1] Her groups have been the foundation for all subsequent work on the cylinder seals of Cyprus, and she went on to show the wider significance of this body of material for an understanding of artistic, administrative, religious, and funerary practices in the eastern Mediterranean both in the past and the present.[2]

In contrast, stamp seals from both the Late Bronze and Iron Ages have been neglected as materials for study and dismissed almost as if they were, to borrow the poet Paul Celan's famous phrase, no more than "pebbles and scree."[3] But they too deserve attention for what they reveal about society at the end of the LBA, when they first appear, and during the subsequent Iron Age, when they proliferated and their use became more common on the island. This essay surveys briefly the history of the Cypriot stamp seal, basing the chronology on what can be deduced from those seals recovered from reliable and closely defined archaeological contexts. Within this chronological span, certain seals have been grouped together on the basis of either the

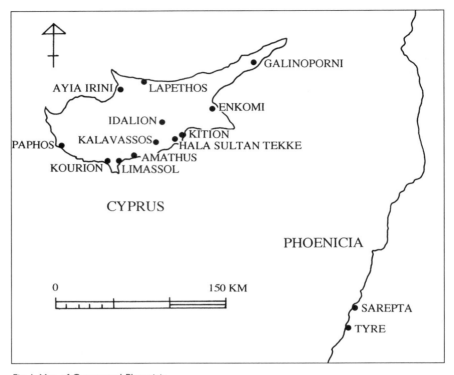

Fig. 1. Map of Cyprus and Phoenicia

styles in which their devices were cut or their shapes, if these are especially distinctive.

It is not possible, of course, to cite every known example of stamps that are diagnostically significant. This essay presents only a few groups as a way of illustrating the history of the stamp seal in Cyprus. From the archaeological contexts in which they were found—their settings, associated finds, and individual locations—the essay proceeds to consider glyptic patterns that pertain to ancient Cypriot society, based on the distinctions to be drawn between seals made of hard stones and those made of serpentines, between devices that are inscribed and those that are uninscribed, and between stamps that were meant for votive and those that were meant for nonvotive uses. A larger work on Cypriot stamp seals provides further argument and additional documentation with more groups, listings, and exegesis.[4] Figure 1 shows the location of all sites mentioned in this essay.

Origins

Despite isolated early finds at sites such as Lemba and Kissonerga in the Paphos district and Alassa in the Limassol district, there was no firmly established glyptic tradition on Cyprus even toward the end of the Middle Bronze Age (ca. the middle of the 17th century B.C.).[5] On the basis of current evidence, Catling's laconic assessment of Cypriot glyptic history at this time, published nearly 30 years ago, still remains accurate: "Seal usage was unknown in Cyprus before the Late Cypriot (LC) period, a revealing symptom of her undeveloped and isolated state."[6] Thus, when ancient Cypriots needed a system of seals and sealing, they adopted in the first instance the Near Eastern cylinder—at least in form, if not in precise function.

This early use of cylinder seals in Cyprus during the LC period coincided with an intensification of interaction between Cyprus and the Near East. The emergence of a local glyptic tradition was linked very likely, then, to the island's increased participation in the trading networks of the LBA, when seals were needed to identify, authorize, and guarantee consignments and transactions. But the absence of sealings and impressions in the Near Eastern manner, either on clay bullae or on clay tablets, strongly suggests that cylinder seals were used in some manner differently on the island than on the mainland, where such material remains are well attested.[7]

The earliest certain examples of local stamp seals with archaeological contexts datable to the LBA are a rectangular stamp of gray serpentine from Apliki in northwest Cyprus, a black serpentine scarab from Yeroskipou near Paphos, and a set of three conoid seals from Kalavasos-*Ayios Dhimitrios* near Limassol.[8] All of these may be assigned on the basis of associated finds to the LC IIC period (13th century B.C.). Their chronological consistency demonstrates that it is at this time that stamp seals first become common on Cyprus. Found as they are in a settlement (Apliki), a necropolis (Yeroskipou), and what appear to be administrative and industrial areas (Kalavasos-*Ayios Dhimitrios*), these seals support the proposition that the adoption of the stamp in preference to the cylinder affected essentially non-religious practices, probably those having more to do with administrative procedure or economic complexity.[9]

Serpentine is probably indicative of local manufacture, with raw materials derived from sources in and around the Troodos Mountains.[10] Colors range from dark, either black or gray, to a light "apple" green. Stamp seals made of hard stones such as rock crystal are much rarer in the LBA.[11] They may well have been carved locally as well, but many of these hard stones would have had to be imported into the island in raw form.

Scarabs with Egyptian or Egyptianizing designs made of glazed materials are contemporary in date and most notably are found at Enkomi and Kition.[12] It is difficult to know which of these were imported and which made locally. As with the cylinder seals, it seems reasonable to suppose that local manufacture of this type of seal was stimulated, at least in part, by the appearance and use of similar objects from the Levant and Egypt.

Of seal shapes attested in Cyprus during the LBA, the conoid is the most prolific and the most enigmatic. Archaeologically, it appears in the time spanning the end of the LC IIC period and the beginning of LC IIIA (ca. 1200 B.C.). Since conoids are not certainly attested in the Aegean, Anatolia, the Near East, or Egypt before their appearance in Cyprus, the shape probably represents local innovation rather than foreign intrusion. If that is the case, then later Near Eastern examples reflect the influence of Cyprus, rather than the reverse.

The fashion for conoids presumably followed as a result of its functional appeal. Stylistic similarities between devices found on cylinder seals and on conoids, as well as the subsequent predominance of the latter over the former, suggest that the conoid took over from the cylinder those functions for which a stamp was more convenient and better suited than a curved shape. The adoption of conoids and other stamp seal shapes, such as the tabloid, in preference to cylinders was a conscious one on the part of the local population.

The stamp seals from Enkomi were found in areas largely given over to residential or industrial use. One example was found in a room that contained copper slag.[13] Another was recovered from a room that may have had a ritual function, positioned as it was adjacent to the room in which the Horned God of Enkomi was found.[14] But this area too seems to have been part of a metallurgical complex.[15] The stamps from the acropolis of Idalion and from the necropolis at Bamboula at Kourion equally suggest nonvotive use.[16]

Two styles shared between cylinders and conoids seem especially important. The first is known as the "Egyptianizing Linear Style," initially identified by Schaeffer.[17] The style on both cylinders and stamps favors as a subject archers or figures in procession wearing long, striated robes (fig. 2). Cylinder seals cut in this style have been found at Enkomi, Kourion, Idalion, Hala

Fig. 2. (a) Impression of black serpentine cylinder with device in the Egyptianizing Linear Style. Once Kenna, now in Geneva, Musée d'Art et d'Histoire 20554. Height: ca. 2.3 cm; diameter: 1.0 cm (after M.-L. Vollenweider, *Catalogue raisonné des sceaux, cylindres, intailles et camées* III [Mainz am Rhein 1983] pl. 143). (b) Impression of black serpentine tabloid seal with device in the Egyptianizing Linear Style. From Idalion acropolis; LCIIIA–B context. In Medelhavsmuseet, Stockholm, Idalion 1323. Length: 1.8 cm. (Photo by A.T. Reyes)

Fig. 3. Device of a conoid seal of olive-brown steatite showing a bull in an Aegeanizing style. Berlin FG 52. Length: 1.9 cm; width: 1.44 cm; height: 1.5 cm. (After E. Zwierlein-Diehl, *Antike Gemmen in Deutschen Sammlungen* II. Staatliche Museen Preussischer Kulturbesitz Antikenabteilung. Berlin [Munich 1969] 40, no. 62, Taf. 16)

Sultan Tekke, as well as the Levant, and comparable stamp seals are known from Enkomi, Kourion, and Idalion.[18] The second of the shared styles is the well known one dependent on Aegean prototypes (fig. 3). Devices cut in this style largely show naturalistic studies of animals, such as may sometimes be found on later Cypriot cylinder seals.[19] Examples are known from Enkomi, Idalion, and the Paphos and Limassol areas.[20]

The small size of a seal means that, as an object, it is readily transported. The seals thus become particularly fine indicators of contact, however defined, between different areas of Cyprus and the Mediterranean. The known provenances of seals in either the Egyptianizing Linear Style or the Aegeanizing one suggest a certain amount of contact between sites extending from Enkomi in the east to areas in the west and south of the island. The northwest of the island especially seems largely isolated, at least in glyptic terms.

The Cypro-Geometric Period

By the end of the second millennium B.C., the stamp seal superseded the cylinder in use on Cyprus. The glyptic history of the island, as with all other areas in the eastern Mediterranean, now becomes particularly difficult to trace. A certain amount of continuity is indicated by the presence of conoids, tabloids, and cylinders in Cypro-Geometric (CG) contexts, but these may well have been manufactured in the LBA.[21] They are all found in tombs, suggesting a use as personal objects. Some LBA cylinders may have been kept as personal possessions, but it is doubtful, on current evidence, that they were ever of significant administrative or perhaps even votive use in the CG period. On the whole, the glyptic remains of the time do not reflect the local prosperity evident elsewhere in the material record of the island, and excavations at CG settlements and cemeteries did not recover seals approaching those of the LBA in quality.

One group of conoids made of blue frit and using Egytianizing motifs may be assigned with confidence to a glyptic center active at this time (fig. 4).[22] Often, a conoid in this group will have a line incised above its base and favor as a device a quadruped confronting a human figure wearing a tall, conical helmet. Roughly half of the known examples were recovered from a necropolis at Amathus, where this group of seals may have been at home. Other examples are known from tombs at Lapethos and Paphos and settle-

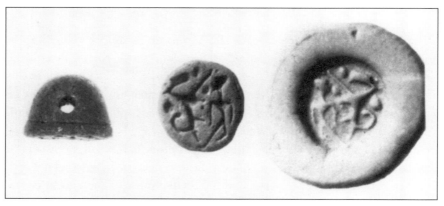

Fig. 4. Device and impression of a blue frit conoid showing a male figure and a quadruped. From Paphos, Skales tomb 57, no. 1; late Cypro-Geometric II context. Height: 1.2 cm; diameter: 1.6 cm. (After V. Karageorghis, *Ausgrabungen in Alt-Paphos auf Cypern* III: *Palaepaphos*-Skales [Konstanz 1983] pl. 74)

ments in Sarepta and Tyre on the Phoenician coast, suggesting a certain amount of contact between kingdoms in the western half of the island and Phoenicia.[23] These contexts suggest personal and private use. Although made of blue frit, often associated archaeologically with luxury goods and a material not without a certain value in the ancient world, it is not likely that these seals were a significant part in the workings of the local economy, in the way that stamps may have been in the LBA.[24]

Ceramic evidence from the Phoenician sites suggests that this particular type of conoid had already begun to be produced in the CG I period (ca. 1050–950 B.C.). The example from Sarepta dates to early in that time. The example from Tyre has been assigned to the late 10th or early 9th century.[25]

The Cypro-Archaic Period

The necropolis at Amathus and the Iron Age sanctuary at Ayia Irini are the two sites that provide significant archaeological and chronological data for the glyptics of the Cypro-Archaic (CA) period. For the latter site, the dates that follow use Lewe's revision of Gjerstad's chronological scheme, now supported to an extent by recent excavations on Samos.[26] Lewe's dates for the different periods of the sanctuary at Ayia Irini are as follows:

Period 4: 650/640–600/590 B.C.
Period 5: 600/590–550/540 B.C.
Period 6: second half of the sixth century B.C.

The chronology for the tombs at the necropolis of Amathus follows dates summarized by Tytgat.[27]

The stamp seals of the CA period constitute a bewildering array of shapes made out of both hard stones and serpentines and cut in different styles. The majority of seals (roughly 70%) are scarabs or scaraboids, and it is apparent that, whatever the reasons for the sudden proliferation of stamp seals at this time, there is much glyptic experimentation, particularly in the seventh century B.C.

It is not possible, within the scope of this essay, to present all possible groups of related seals. The impracticality of this exercise is additionally compounded by the possibility that particular seals may legitimately be assigned to several different groups. Thus, for example, cubical seals, with

Fig. 5. Green jasper scarab showing a warrior with a sword fighting a lion. From Ayia Irini; context uncertain. In Medelhavsmuseet, Stockholm, A. I. 2445. Length: 1.6 cm; width: 1.2 cm; height: 1.8 cm. (Photo by A.T. Reyes)

devices cut on each of six sides, may embody several different styles, aside from the more straightforward classification in terms of shape. A comprehensive treatment of the Iron Age stamp seals is currently in preparation, and suggested classifications and cross-classifications for the various seals will appear there. For present purposes, as a way of illustrating what the stamp seals may teach or at least hint at regarding the ancient world, only one group is presented below.

This is a group whose devices show a figure cut in what has been called a Sub-Geometric style (fig. 5).[28] The devices all show males with pointed chins and spiked helmets, with limbs, joints, bodies, and extremities articulated by gouges and blobs. The figures cut in this way are seen in a variety of activities: fighting lions, riding horses, driving chariots.[29] Serpentine seals from Amathus, Kourion, and Ayia Irini demonstrate that the sequence had begun by the middle of the CA I period (ca. mid eighth century B.C.), and the type persisted through the CA II period, as the example from Amathus shows.[30]

The type is, in a way, reminiscent of CA terracottas, also with pointed chins and tall helmets. Terracotta sculpture represents ancient art at its most popular level, a medium of mass production distinguished from limestone or marble or metalwork in its relative cheapness. The warriors on the seals may be taken as glyptic analogues to these figures, and since over 300 seals were recovered from the sanctuary at Ayia Irini, better known for the life-size and half-life-size anthropomorphic terracottas discovered set up around the altar, these devices may, like those statues and statuettes, be described as typically Cypriot—a material record of life at a general, rather than an exclusive, level.[31]

This generality is equally suggested by the widespread appearance of the

Sub-Geometric type throughout the island. Aside from Ayia Irini and Amathus, examples are known from Kourion and the Karpass region.[32] The majority are made of serpentines (roughly 65% of the total), but hard stone examples are known, suggesting that the use of these seals spanned different levels of society, since it seems likely that the hard stone seals, made of materials difficult to procure and not necessarily indigenous to the island, are the more valuable stamp seals.

As ever among the Archaic gems of Cyprus, only the hard stone seals have, in addition to their devices, inscriptions in the Cypriot Syllabic script. These are in the Greek, rather than Near Eastern, manner, with the name of the owner in the genitive, carved retrograde on the seal itself, in order that the name is read properly once impressed.[33] An example of an inscribed hard stone seal made of jasper is known with a figure cut in this style. It is from Galinoporni in the Karpass but otherwise has no precise context. Since none of the examples from the sanctuary at Ayia Irini are inscribed, it may well be that the seals of this group were largely talismanic or votive, with some hard stone examples being used, in addition, for other purposes. The stringholes on the seals themselves certainly indicate that they could be threaded and suspended, and the excavators reasonably suggested that they had been "hung up on the hurdle-fence of the temenos enclosure and on the wooden posts of the shelter along the temenos wall."[34] Seals from Kition must have originated from within the precincts of the sanctuary as well, though the excavators discovered them in *bothroi*.[35] More valuable hard stone seals are sometimes found with metal settings and were clearly used not only as charms, but also as jewelry that could eventually be dedicated. A rock crystal example from Kourion, still with its metal setting, was found near the semi-circular altar of the precinct.[36]

Stamp seals are represented on limestone and terracotta votive sculptures of the Archaic and Classical periods, worn singly or with a pair or more suspended around the neck. They were also worn diagonally across the chest like a bandolier.[37] Cypriot "temple boy" statues of the Classical and Hellenistic periods also represent seals in relief along their chests or around their necks.[38]

The Sub-Geometric type is found on a wide variety of stamp seal shapes, in addition to the scarabs and scaraboids attested at the Ayia Irini sanctuary. This variety in shape helps substantiate the notion that the Sub-Geometric device represents a sort of koine within the island. Examples are known on cubical seals, a seal in the shape of a lion, and a seal in the shape of two conjoined heads.[39] These are seals that are larger than scarabs and scaraboids, and their dimensions suggest use by important individuals. But it goes beyond the evidence to say that these are royal seals or even official seals.

Overarching Patterns and Social Implications

So large a body of material as the stamp seals of Cyprus initially brings with it a corresponding sense of confusion in its train. But immediate distinctions may still be drawn to produce some order: between seals of the LBA and seals of the Iron Age, between seals made of hard stones and those made of serpentines, between inscribed and uninscribed seals, between seals in votive and nonvotive contexts. These larger distinctions may be further elaborated and refined on the basis of evidence touched on above.

To begin with, the stamp seals of the LBA and those of the Iron Age may be distinguished in terms of primary use. The former seem to have been used more for administrative or industrial activities, whereas the bulk of the evidence for the latter suggests more personal uses: as votives, talismans, charms, or amulets, at least for the serpentine stamp seals. The hard stone examples, the inscribed ones in particular, hint at other administrative or commercial uses.

In both the LBA and the Iron Age, it is reasonable to infer that hard stone stamp seals are associated with a higher station of society. They are made of more valuable materials, and fewer hard stone stamps are known from Cyprus than serpentine ones, suggesting, if not rarity or exclusivity, at least some degree of speciality. In addition, in the CA period hard stone seals alone have been found with metal settings. They, rather than the serpentines, tend to be inscribed.

Although both hard stone and the serpentine stamp seals were used as votives in the Archaic period, they are not, in general, found in the same findspot. This indicates as well that their spheres of use are to some extent distinct. Parenthetically, it should also be noted that there is a third sphere of use occupied by those Cypriot seals made of glazed materials with devices that copy Egyptian motifs. These are the Cypriot seals that traveled most widely throughout the Mediterranean in quantity, in contrast to the local serpentine and hard stone stamps, which are, on present evidence, more confined in their appearances outside the island.[40]

In the Archaic period, serpentine seals are generally found in votive contexts, whether these are tombs or sanctuaries. Inscribed stones suggest the common use of safeguarding property or authenticating particular transactions. A number of late fourth- or early third-century B.C. clay sealings recovered from the palace site at Amathus were very likely part of an archive comprising documents made of papyrus or parchment. A published example showing an impression probably made by a hard stone seal and depicting a kore-figure does suggest that this method of sealing documents was a local practice. There seems no reason not to extrapolate the evidence for such use backward chronologically into the CA II period at least.[41]

Equally important as evidence for Cypriot seal usage is a set of clay loomweights, perhaps Cypro-Classical in date, from Paphos, from the remains of what appeared to be a weavers' quarter and metal area. Each has a gem impression. These may have been intended to signify ownership or manufacture in some sense.[42]

Sealings from Kition, probably impressed with hard stone rather than serpentine seals, may indicate some local commercial use, but only two are known so far.[43] These two sealings show typically Phoenician devices, but, since they were unearthed in a Phoenician city, they cannot be taken as primary evidence for Cypriot usage. Nevertheless, the proliferation of hard stone seals in Cyprus during the Archaic period may represent a by-product of Phoenician activity within the island, since the styles on many of the early hard stone seals of the seventh century B.C. imitate Phoenician devices. Devices in Greek styles began to appear around the middle of the sixth century B.C., but the Phoenician style never entirely vanished. In general, however, the majority of Cypriot stamp seals, the serpentine examples in particular, tell of life on a less international plane. They "pertain not to an epoch of mysterious greatness or of 'giants that were in those days,' but to the infinitely little in which our autobiography begins."[44]

NOTES

* I am grateful to Joanna S. Smith and Ellen Herscher, the organizers of the colloquium "The Archaeology of Script and Seal Use on Cyprus in the Second and First Millennium B. C." for the invitation to present this essay. I am especially grateful to Dr. Smith for her criticisms of earlier versions. For continued help on this material, I am grateful to Sir John Boardman, V. Karageorghis, and P.R.S. Moorey.

[1] E. Porada, "The Cylinder Seals of the Late Cypriote Bronze Age," *AJA* 52 (1948) 178–98.

[2] As a recent editorialist for the *New York Times* put it, commenting on the still prevalent significance of Professor Porada's work on the understanding of ancient—and, therefore, modern—society: "To awaken the past by one's commitment to it, to become the matrix where past and present converge, that was Porada's culture" (V. Klinkenborg, "One Scholar and the Matrix of the Past," *New York Times*, 1 March 1998, 14).

[3] *Night* (1959).

[4] A.T. Reyes, *The Stamp Seals of Ancient Cyprus* (Oxford 2001).

[5] E.J. Peltenburg, "Lemba Archaeological Project, Cyprus, 1976–77: Preliminary Report," *Levant* 11 (1979) 29–30; E.J. Peltenburg, "Lemba Archaeological Project, Cyprus, 1985," *Levant* 19 (1987) 221; P. Flourentzos, *Excavations in the Kouris Valley* I: *The Tombs* (Nicosia 1991) 15, pl. 14, no. 1.

[6] H.W. Catling in *CAH* [3] II.1, 173.

[7] See J.S. Smith, *Seals for Sealing in the Late Cypriot Period* (Diss. Bryn Mawr College 1994), on the function of cylinder seals in LBA Cyprus.

[8] J. du Plat Taylor, "A Late Bronze Age Settlement at Apliki, Cyprus," *AntJ* 32 (1952) 163, pl. XXVI.b; O. Masson, "Cylindres et cachets chypriotes portant des caractères chypro-minoens," *BCH* 81 (1957) 19–20, fig. 14; K. Nicolaou, "A Late Cypriote Necropolis at Yeroskipou, Paphos," *RDAC* 1983, 144, pl. XX.5; E. Porada, "Cylinder and Stamp Seals," in A.K. South, P.J. Russell, and P.S. Keswani, *Vasilikos Valley Project 3: Kalavasos-Ayios Dhimitrios*, volume II: *Ceramics, Objects, Tombs, Specialist Studies* (*SIMA* 71:3, Göteborg 1989), 35–37.

[9] On Apliki and Yeroskipou see supra n. 8. Kalavasos: see, e.g., D. Christou, "Chronique des fouilles et découvertes archéologiques à Chypre en 1995," *BCH* 120 (1996) 1076–77. On the function of these seals see Smith (supra n. 7) 51–52.

[10] C. Xenophontos, "Picrolite: Its Nature, Provenance, and Possible Distribution Patterns in the Chalcolithic Period of Cyprus," *BASOR* 282/283 (1991) 127–38.

[11] E.g., see E. Porada, "Glyptics," in J.L. Benson, *Bamboula at Kourion* (Philadelphia 1972) 146–47 on B1635 (rock crystal).

[12] J. Leclant, "Appendix III: Les scarabées de la tombe 9," in V. Karageorghis, *Excavations at Kition* I: *The Tombs* (Nicosia 1974) 148–50; R.-P. Charles, "Appendix II: Les scarabées Égyptiens d'Enkomi," in P. Dikaios, Enkomi: *Excavations 1948–58* II. *Chronology, Summary and Conclusions, Catalogue, Appendices* (Mainz am Rhein 1971) 819–23.

[13] E. Porada, "Appendix I: Seals," in Dikaios (supra n. 12) 806, no. 23.

[14] Porada (supra n. 13) 801, no. 19.

[15] See, e.g., A.B. Knapp, "The Bronze Age Economy of Cyprus: Ritual, Ideology, and the Sacred Landscape," in V. Karageorghis and D. Michaelides eds., *The Development of the Cypriot Economy: From the Prehistoric Period to the Present Day* (Nicosia 1996) 78.

[16] Idalion: *SwCyprusExp* II, 591–92.

[17] C. F.-A. Schaeffer, *Enkomi-Alasia* I (Paris 1952) 87–89; J.M. Webb, "The Cylinder Seals," in J.-C. Courtois and J.M. Webb, *Les cylindres-sceaux d'Enkomi (Fouilles françaises 1957–1970)* (Nicosia 1987) 74–84.

[18] Webb (supra n. 17) 74–75; W.M.F. Petrie, *Ancient Gaza* IV: *Tell el Ajjūl* (London 1934)

5, pl. XII.4; Porada (supra n. 13) 809, no. 31a, pls. 183–84; *SwCyprusExp* II, 556, no. 95, pp. 564–65, no. 1323, pl. CLXXV.19; Porada (supra n. 11) 145, no. B1631, pl. 38; A.P. di Cesnola, *Salaminia (Cyprus): The History, Treasures, and Antiquities of Salamis in the Island of Cyprus²* (London 1884) 131, fig. 144.

[19] D. Collon, *First Impressions* (London 1987) 73; B. Buchanan and P.R.S. Moorey, *Catalogue of Ancient Near Eastern Seals in the Ashmolean Museum* III. *The Iron-Age Stamp Seals* (Oxford 1988) 78.

[20] *SwCyprusExp* II, 550, no. 643, pl. CLXXXVI.2, 555, no. 891; V.E.G. Kenna, *Corpus of Cypriote Antiquities 3: Catalogue of the Cypriote Seals of the Bronze Age in the British Museum* (*SIMA* 20:3, Göteborg 1971) 19–20, no. 19, pl. V.19, p. 26, no. 56, pl. XIII.56; Porada (supra n. 11) 146–47, pl. 38.

[21] E.g., V. Karageorghis, *Palaepaphos-Skales: An Iron Age Cemetery in Cyprus* (Konstanz 1983) 165–66, no. 115, pl. CXV.115, 301, no. 92, pl. CLXXIX.92; *SwCyprusExp* II, 129, no. 78, pl. CCL.32; M.-J. Chavane, *Salamine de Chypre* VI: *Les petits objets* (Paris 1975) 151–52, nos. 436–47, pl. 44.

[22] A.T. Reyes, "A Group of Cypro-Geometric Stamp Seals," *Levant* 25 (1993) 197–205.

[23] W.P. Anderson, *Sarepta* I (Beirut 1988) 393, 641. P.M. Bikai, *The Pottery of Tyre* (Warminster 1978) pl. 26, no. 14; pl. 85, no. 14.

[24] P.R.S. Moorey, *Ancient Mesopotamian Materials and Industries* (Oxford 1994) 186–89. On this material, see also F.L. Vergès, *Bleus égyptiens* (Louvain and Paris 1992).

[25] Anderson (supra n. 23); Bikai (supra n. 23).

[26] B. Lewe, *Studien zur archaischen kyprischen Plastik* (Diss. Johann Wolfgang Goethe-Universität zu Frankfurt am Main 1975) 84–92; H. Kyrieleis, "New Cypriot Finds from the Heraion of Samos" in V. Tatton-Brown, *Cyprus and the East Mediterranean in the Iron Age* (London 1989) 52–67.

[27] C. Tytgat, *Les nécropoles sud-ouest et sud-est d'Amathonte: 1. Les Tombes 110–385* (Nicosia, 1989).

[28] J. Boardman, "Cypriot, Phoenician, and Greek Seals and Amulets," in V. Karageorghis et al., *La nécropole d'Amathonte, Tombes 110–385* (Nicosia 1991) 161–62 on 237/272.

[29] E.g., *SwCyprusExp* II, 764–65, no. 2445, p. 767, no. 2526; M. Maaskant-Kleibrink, *Catalogue of the Engraved Gems in the Royal Coin Cabinet, The Hague* (The Hague 1978) 74, no. 6.

[30] Amathus: Boardman (supra n. 28) with Tytgat (supra n. 27) 181–84. Ayia Irini: *SwCyprusExp* II, 770, no. 2626; 773, no. 2749. Kourion: E. Gubel, "The Seals," in D. Buitron-Oliver ed., *The Sanctuary of Apollo Hylates at Kourion: Excavations in the Archaic Precinct* (Jonsered 1996) 165–67 on no. 4 (side C).

[31] *SwCyprusExp* II, 797–810.

[32] Kourion: Gubel (supra n. 30); Karpass region (Galinoporni): O. Masson, *Les inscriptions chypriotes syllabiques* (Paris 1983) 328, no. 328; H.W. Catling, "The Seal of Pasitimos," *Kadmos* 11 (1972) 63, no. 7, fig. 2.

[33] For examples, see Catling (supra n. 32).

[34] *SwCyprusExp* II, 809.

[35] G. Clerc, "I. Scarabées, amulettes et figurines," in G. Clerc, V. Karageorghis, E. Lagarce,

and J. Leclant, *Fouilles de Kition* II. *Objets égyptiens et égyptisants: Scarabées, amulettes et figurines en pâte de verre et en faïence, vase plastique en faïence. Sites I et II, 1959–1975* (Nicosia 1976) 15–16, 114–16, nos. 516 and 1072.

[36] Gubel (supra n. 30) 163.

[37] E. Lagarce, "Remarques sur l'utilisation des scarabées, scaraboïdes, amulettes et figurines de type égyptien à Chypre" in Clerc et al. (supra n. 34) 167–82.

[38] C. Beer, *Temple-Boys* I (Jonsered 1994) pls. 48–49.

[39] Cubical seal: Gubel (supra n. 30). Lion shape: J. Boardman, *Intaglios and Rings* (London 1975) 112, no. 211. Conjoined heads: J. Boardman, *Archaic Greek Gems* (London, 1968) 162, no. 591.

[40] A.F. Gorton, *Egyptian and Egyptianizing Scarabs* (Oxford 1996) 175–77.

[41] T. Petit, "Syllabaire et alphabet au 'palais' d'Amathonte de Chypre vers 300 avant notre ère" in C. Baurain, C. Bonnet, and V. Krings eds., *Phoinikeia Grammata: Lire et écrire en Méditerranée* (Namur 1991) 485, no. 11, fig. 12; P. Aupert and P. Leriche, "La muraille médiane de l'acropole" in P. Aupert ed., *Guide d'Amathonte* (Paris 1996) 103.

[42] F.G. Maier, *Alt-Paphos auf Cypern: Ausgrabungen zur Geschichte von Stadt und Heiligtum 1966–1984* (Mainz am Rhein 1985) 19, pl. 8.6a–b.

[43] Clerc (supra n. 35) 114–16, nos. 516 and 1072.

[44] D.G. Hogarth, *The Wandering Scholar* (London 1925) 1–2.

— 6 —

Seals and Writing in the Ancient Near East and Cyprus: Observations from Context*

◈

Barry B. Powell

Κύρνε, σοφιζομένῳ μὲν ἐμοὶ σφρηγὶς ἐπικείσθω
τοῖσδ' ἔπεσιν, λήσει δ' οὔποτε κλεπτόμενα,
οὐδέ τις ἀλλάξει κάκιον τοὐσθλοῦ παρεόντος,
ὧδε δὲ πᾶς τις ἐρεῖ· 'Θεύγνιδός ἐστιν ἔπη
τοῦ Μεγαρέως πάντας δὲ κατ'ἀνθρώπους ὀνομαστοῦ'...

O Kyrnos, as I speak with poetic wisdom, let a *sphragis* lie
upon my words, so that if stolen, they will be detected, and
no one will substitute a worse line for the good ones that
are there, but everyone will say, "These are the words of
Theognis of Megara famous throughout the world."

—*Theognidea* 19–23

So does Theognis, who may have lived in the sixth century B.C., give us a refined, self-conscious metaphor in which the *sphragis*, the seal to his collection of poems inscribed on a roll of papyrus, is not a lump of clay impressed with designs but, evidently, his name embedded in the verse itself. Theognis's sophisticated conceit does not deviate far from an association of seals and writing so old that the elegiac poet could never have fathomed it: by a seal to ensure against the falsification, injury, theft, and chicanery that a sophisticated economic life, conducted in writing, encourages. Hearing Joanna Smith's call

227

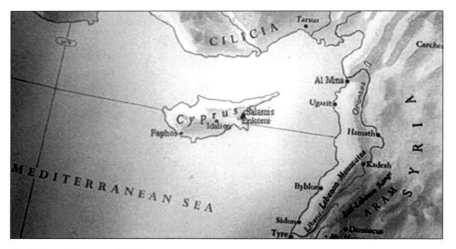

Fig. 1. Map of Cyprus and the Levant

for context in our approach to seals and writing on Cyprus,[1] I want in my brief discussion to offer my own version of this context, for without context we will never plumb the mysteries of seals and writing in Cyprus or anywhere else. First I will make some general remarks about seals and writing, then attempt to see how Cyprus fits within this picture.

A quick look at a map of the eastern Mediterranean reveals how rich, famous, oddly-shaped Cyprus points with its curious finger to the eastern littoral, to where the Orontes debouches into the Mediterranean north of the polyglot, multiracial, culturally-seminal, commercial community of Ugarit (fig. 1). In the Late Bronze Age (LBA), Ugarit was the principal locus for the exchange of cultural information between Greece and the East; in the Iron Age, the commercial north Syrian port of Al Mina at the mouth of the Orontes served a similar function. Small wonder that half of all Cypriot seals have been found in ruins near the modern village of Enkomi, which looks toward Ugarit and Al Mina. The ruins near Enkomi may be of Bronze Age Alashiya, whose king corresponded with the Egyptian court in the 18th Dynasty about the exchange of copper.[2] The seal was an invention of the ancient Near East, not native to Egypt, Anatolia, or the Mediterranean, and closely tied to the invention of writing itself around 3400 B.C. in southern Iraq.

As writing spread, evidently appearing in Egypt by 3300 B.C., and forms of writing changed, the seal spread too, and the technology of manufacturing seals.[3] They seem to have been made in two ways: actually engraved by means of sharpened copper tools, or by means of a bow-driven drill or wheel.[4] Engraved seals are more valuable, the so-called Elaborate and Derivative Cypriot styles first described by Edith Porada, while Porada's so-called Common Seals appear to have been cut on the wheel.[5]

With the art of writing spread not just the technology of making seals, and the social need to do so, but the actual seals, which could have very great intrinsic value and were often capped in gold. They turn up in odd places, for example, a seal found in a tholos tomb in the Messara in Crete but manufactured in Babylon in the reign of Hammurabi (early second millennium B.C.), or a scarab stamp seal with the name of Ramses II (13th century B.C.) found in Mycenae, and other eastern seals from Perati in Attica.[6] An antique Syrian seal was found in the Bronze Age wreck off Cape Gelidonya; the ship seems to have been traveling west.[7] A gold scarab, bearing the name of Akhenaten's queen, Nefertiti, was found, along with Aegean, Kassite, and Assyrian seals, on board an earlier ship wrecked at Ulu Burun.[8]

In Mesopotamia itself, designs from 2,000-year old seals influenced contemporary production.[9] The hard stone, lapis lazuli, found in Afghanistan, was especially prized for making seals. Fully 34 of the astounding collection of 39 cylinder seals found in the burned remains of the Mycenaean palace at Thebes in 1963 were made of lapis lazuli.[10] Truly that collection was a king's ransom; no similar single nonfunerary deposit of lapis seals has ever been found anywhere. The Theban collection included Early Dynastic, Old Babylonian, Mitannian, Hittite, Kassite, and Cypriot seals. Someone (Theban or no) must have sought far and wide to assemble it.

The collocation into one place of seals manufactured over 1,000 years apart reminds us of the enormous length of time in which these objects could be in circulation; because of their high value, ease of transportation, and rugged nature, seals are therefore of limited value in providing chronological conclusions, even when found in stratified contexts. Some seals in the Theban collection appear to have been reworked in Cyprus,[11] so the collection may well have come into the palace of Mycenaean Thebes through the very workshops in Enkomi where, as Jennifer Webb has shown,[12] much Cypriot seal production was concentrated.

In spite of an extraordinary diversity of styles and a sometimes bewildering array of applications, many design motifs on seals remain strikingly conservative across cultural boundaries and through time. The tree of life,

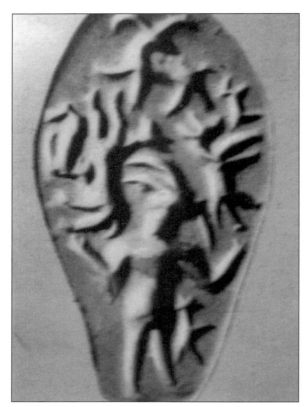

Fig. 2. Stamp seal of serpentine with design of caprid-headed Master of the Beasts from Luristan ca. 3300 B.C. (The Louvre, Cabinet des Médailles; after P. Amiet, *Art of the Ancient Near East* [New York 1977] fig. 738)

Fig. 3. Persian cylinder seal showing "hero" taming lions. (Pierpont Morgan Library, Corpus no. 824, courtesy of Pierpont Morgan Library, New York)

Fig. 4. Hittite royal seal impressed on tablet sent to king of Ugarit, 13th century B.C. (The Louvre, Cabinet des Médailles; after P. Amiet, *Art of the Ancient Near East* [New York 1977] fig. 737)

for example, appears in the Uruk period at the end of the fourth millennium, and is still prominent in the late Assyrian period.[13] The master of animals is one of the most persistent iconographic themes, appearing in figure 2 on a seal from Luristan ca. 3300 B.C. and on the Persian seal in figure 3 nearly 3,000 years later.[14]

We guess that the social functions associated with the use of seals were conservative too, although here we are on shaky ground. Certainly, the seal remained closely associated with writing, its partner in social control. Writing will appear, for example, where we might expect a sealing, as on a Cretan jar-label inscribed with Cretan hieroglyphic signs from around 1700 B.C.;[15] and sealings often have writing on them (although rarely in the Aegean), as in figure 4, an impression from a Hittite royal seal sent to Ugarit in the 13th century, or on countless Mesopotamian seals.

Scholars used to think that writing began when primitive peoples drew pictures to express their thoughts, but Denise Schmandt-Besserat has explained how Western traditions of writing—there are but two others, Chinese and Mesoamerican—go back to around 8000 B.C., when mostly nomadic dwellers in Iraq and Iran kept track of commodities by means of geometric clay tokens.[16] Earlier, simple shapes were replaced around 4000 B.C. by incised, complex ones to correspond with the increased economic complexity of urban life. Different shapes designated such different commodities as pigs and sheep and bushels of grain. A transaction was apparently confirmed by threading tokens on a string, then sealing the knot in the string with a lump of clay impressed by a stamp seal, as in figure 5, where above the hypothetical reconstruction are pictured actual examples of such stamped bullae.

Stamp seals, used in this way, are the earliest seals. Sealings made with

Fig. 5. Two bullae from Susa (Louvre, Sb 6298 and 9279, courtesy Louvre, Paris) and reconstruction of string of tokens held by impressed bulla. (After D. Schmandt-Besserat, *Before Writing* I [Austin 1992] 109, figs. 53, 54)

Fig. 6. Neolithic "seals" from Greece. (Volos Museum, M 2850; Larisa Museum, M 5020; Volos Museum, M2444, M 5095, M 5094; after D.R. Theocharis, *Neolithic Greece* [Athens 1973] fig. 273)

them come from the early fourth millennium B.C., made by impressing an engraved object into mud or clay. I do not believe that such Neolithic objects as the so-called seals from Sesklo in Greece from the middle Neolithic, perhaps 5000 B.C. (fig. 6), are really seals. We do not understand their use, but they do not seem connected with economic activity and do not belong to the historical development that we trace in Mesopotamia. Interestingly, seals and sealings are never found in the New World—they are a uniquely Near Eastern development.

By around 4000 B.C., when the first seals appear, the Mesopotamians had been inscribing clay tokens that designate commodities for 4,000 years, so the technique of engraving was natural for them, as was the practice of impressing an engraved object in clay (or mud), a ubiquitous substance of which commodity tokens had been made for thousands of years. As a type, the original stamp seals never disappear, and in various periods became the predominant form. On Cyprus, Andres Reyes has shown how in the Iron Age the stamp seal replaced the cylinder seal;[17] for some reason in Mesopotamia a similar pattern emerged at the same time, for the stamp seal became more common than the age-old cylinder seal.[18]

Fig. 7. Scene from the side of a chlorite bowl, ca. 2600 B.C., showing a man in a net skirt holding a serpent in either hand, standing between two leopards lying back to back with heads turned toward him. On the right, a lion and eagle attack a bull; to the left is a zebu. Probably Iranian, but found at Khafajeh northeast of Baghdad. (British Museum, WA 128887; after P. Amiet, *Art of the Ancient Near East* [New York 1977] fig. 269)

A more secure way of preserving a transaction than stringing tokens on a line was to enclose the tokens in a hollow bulla, a device also discovered in the fourth millennium B.C., although it is later than the seal. Some bullae are plain, but others have the shapes of the tokens impressed on the outside of the clay so you can tell what is inside the hollow ball without breaking it. Such impressions of tokens are not sealings, which authenticate a transaction conducted by a specific individual or by the office he represents; seals seem always to be tied to persons. Rather, such impressions are a public inventory.

On other bullae we detect the earliest evidence for cylinder seals, an invention that may depend on the availability of stone cores that were a byproduct of drilling out hollow stone bowls,[19] which appear at about the same time as the earliest cylinder seals and have external designs easily paralleled on the seals themselves. Figure 7, for example, shows once again the master of the animals. The advantage of a cylinder seal, once you have stumbled on the idea of it, is that you can produce a continuous scene across a broad expanse of clay, on a stopper or other bulla. The greater range of design, when compared to the stamp seal, allowed the users of seals to make finer bureaucratic and social distinctions, which also appear toward the end of the fourth millennium;[20] Jennifer Webb has suggested how different styles of seals might have worked in this way on Bronze Age Cyprus.[21]

Around 3200 B.C. someone noticed that the system for accounting by

Fig. 8. Middle Babylonian (ca. 1550–1155 B.C.) tablet from Alalah. (BM 131449, courtesy of the British Museum, London)

means of hollow bullae and tokens could be simplified by using a solid tablet that bore impressed signs, which mimicked the shapes of tokens.[22] Freed from the limited repertory of token shapes, scribes now applied the same principle of logographic representation implicit in the use of solid tokens to new often pictographic signs. The phonetic principle was found, no doubt in an effort to record personal names, and the formalized linear cuneiform logosyllabic script came into being, truly the international script of the Bronze Age, with an astonishing geographical range and flexibility, and still used in the early centuries of the Christian era.

Sealings on the new solid tablets are, however, at first extremely rare, probably because the tablets were contained in something else which was sealed; sometimes we can detect the fibers of baskets on the back of solid bullae. Later, but still in the third millennium, the clay envelopes that enclosed tablets often bear seals (fig. 8), or the seal is rolled across the tablet itself.

We need to state very strongly the importance of mud and its refined counterpart, clay, to this whole tradition of sealing and writing, because the technology of writing and the medium of writing are closely tied. Just because you can write does not mean that you will write on anything. For example, the classical Greeks never wrote on clay tablets, whereas their Mycenaean forebears were happy to do so (we are glad that they did!). The classical Greeks' preference for papyrus derives from Phoenician practice, whence the classical Greeks received their tradition of writing. The Egyptians, too, might well have written on clay—there was plenty of it on the banks of the Nile—but they preferred instead this wonderful and abundant substance of their own invention. Nonetheless, whoever invented Egyptian hieroglyphic writing was familiar with the earlier Mesopotamian cuneiform, and with this knowledge came the cylinder seal. The Egyptians even incorporated the picture of the cylinder seal in their signary as a determinative for the word *treasurer*. Here the seal seems held by a pin within a frame and suspended from a string; presumably Egyptian officials must have worn them around their necks. Such seals were used in the same way as in Mesopotamia, to impress mud or clay stoppers on jars, but the seal designs always consist of hieroglyphic writing, another instance of intimate relations between writing and the seal. Figure 9 shows a sealing of Hor-Aha, "Horus the Fighter," from the First Dynasty, about 3000 B.C. The Egyptian scribe always had this advantage over his Mesopotamian counterpart—that he could write and draw pictures at the same time.

Fig. 9. Jar-sealing from the First Dynasty, ca. 3000 B.C., of King Hor-Aha, "Horus the Fighter," per-haps the founder of Memphis. The hawk signifies "Horus," the arm with shield "fighter," enclosed within a palace facade design designating royalty. The meanings of the hieroglyphic signs of the goose (? = *gb*, the earth god) and the step (logogram for terraced hill) are not clear. (After W.B. Emery, *Archaic Egypt* [Baltimore 1961] 58, fig. 18.b)

Later in Egypt, during the Middle Kingdom (ca. 2055–1650 B.C.), the cylinder seal dropped away (as it was to drop away in Iron Age Cyprus and Mesopotamia), replaced by the stamp seal, mostly in the form of the famous scarab;[23] uninscribed scarabs appear as amulets as early as the Sixth Dynasty (ca. 2300 B.C.), symbolic in Egyptian religion of the newborn sun and the resurrected soul. Threaded on wire, scarabs became finger rings by the New Kingdom (ca. 1550–1069 B.C.), evidently the origin of modern finger rings. In Egypt, seals, whether cylindrical or in the form of stamps, were never impressed directly on papyrus documents, as Mesopotamians used their seals on mud and clay tablets. Ordinarily the Egyptians impressed their seals into globs of mud or clay set over knots in rope or string, which could tie a roll of papyrus or seal a box or door or tomb. Such sealings are common finds in Egypt.

The intimacy between a technology of writing and the medium on which it is customarily imposed is well illustrated on Assyrian reliefs from the eighth and seventh centuries B.C. In figure 10 the scribe on the left holds a stylus aloft with which to impress characters on a wax-filled tablet, probably a hinged *deltos*;[24] the scribe on the right grips a brush between thumb and forefinger in order to write on a flexible substance, probably papyrus.[25] Here

Fig. 10. Two scribes before an official, from the palace of the Assyrian king Tiglath-Pileser III
(744–727 B.C.). (British Museum 118882, courtesy of the British Museum, London)

is parallel accounting, the man on the left presumably writing Assyrian in
cuneiform logosyllabic script, while the other makes a duplicate record in
Aramaic written in West Semitic syllabic script. Assyrian and Aramaic are
closely related languages, probably mutually intelligible to some extent, but
logosyllabic cuneiform and West Semitic syllabic have no evident historical
relation to each other and do not function in similar ways. One technology
shuts out the other.

Presumably the left-hand scribe is Assyrian, the right-hand scribe
Aramaean, each providing a check on the other's honesty. Someplace in the
hierarchy will stand someone—perhaps the man on the far left with a staff
of authority, supervising the scribes—who can read both scripts and languages. Beardless, all three men are probably eunuchs, who could devote
themselves properly to the life of the scribal elite, as did the eunuchs of the
Chinese imperial court. Bilingualism, then, is a fundamental feature to
Mesopotamian writing traditions. By the middle of the third millennium, all
men learned in cuneiform could write at least in Sumerian and in a Semitic
dialect usually called Akkadian. Later, some could read West Semitic dialects
in West Semitic syllabic script, as well as cuneiform. Bilingualism in the

Fig. 11. Folding tablet from Bronze Age shipwreck at Ulu Burun. (KW 737; after G.F. Bass et al., "The Bronze Age Shipwreck at Ulu Burun: 1986 Campaign," *AJA* 93 [1989] fig. 19)

Greek alphabetic tradition, by contrast, is never found at any time, a fact that deserves explanation.

The *deltos*, too, is an eastern device; a famous actual example survives from the Bronze Age shipwreck at Ulu Burun (fig. 11).[26] Holding a *deltos*, the scribe impressed the hard-edged stylus into the wax coating of the wood in the same way as he would into moist clay; functionally, *deltoi* are temporary, reusable tablets, although sometimes they were used to store texts permanently.[27] The Egyptians, whose hieroglyphics required a brush, never used the *deltos* at any time. The Levantine Western Semites, who lived constrained between greater worlds, took papyrus from the Egyptians, no doubt when they adapted their own script from Egyptian, but also borrowed the *deltos* from the clay-loving Babylonians. The use of both *deltos* and papyrus as writing media at the same time appears to be a Western Semitic innovation, carried east by West Semitic scribes (as in fig. 10) and passed to the Greeks some time around 800 B.C., when a Euboean invented the Greek alphabet on the basis of the Phoenician syllabary; the adapter may well have received his model on a *deltos*. Figure 12 shows a student writing in his *deltos*, probably a memorized poem. For permanent storage the Greeks, like the

Fig. 12. Seated boy writing in a *deltos*. Red-figured kylix by the Eucharides Painter, 500–480 B.C., from Orvieto. (*ARV*² 231.82; University of Pennsylvania Museum MS 4842, courtesy of the University of Pennsylvania Museum)

Egyptians and Levantines, used papyrus, as in figure 13, where a woman labeled ΣΑΠΠΩΣ reads a literary text from a papyrus roll.[28] What, we would like to know, were the Cypriots writing on?

Surviving examples of the undeciphered Cypro-Minoan writing (fig. 14), which most agree derives from the undeciphered Cretan Linear A, are dated from between 1600 and 1100 B.C.; they are Late Bronze Age in date. T.G. Palaima gives the following summary of the entire meager corpus of extant Cypro-Minoan texts:[29] 8 clay tablets, 83 clay balls, 6 clay cylinders, and numerous inscribed artifacts, such as cylinder seals, gold rings, ivory objects, and pottery. This sounds like a Near Eastern inventory, and surely the practice of writing on clay in Cyprus depends on Mesopotamian models, even if modulated by Crete, as does their use of cylinder seals. The great mystery is whence comes the purely phonetic system of writing that Cretans and Cypriots are impressing on clay. The Phoenician syllabary seems to derive from Egyptian logosyllabic (although the evidence is thin[30]),

Fig. 13. A seated woman, labeled Sappho, reads from a roll. The words ΕΠΕΑ ΠΤΕΡΟΕΤΑ can be read on the edge of the roll, and ΘΕΟΙ ΗΕΡΙѠΝ ΕΠΑѠΝ ΑΡΧΟΜΑΙ and some other letters, difficult to make out, are inscribed on the roll. Red-figured hydria by the Group of Polygnotos, ca. 440–430 B.C., from Vari. (*ARV*² 1060.145; Athens 1260, courtesy of the National Archaeological Museum, Athens)

Fig. 14. One of the longest Cypro-Minoan inscriptions, inscribed on both sides of a cushion-shaped tablet from Enkomi, ca. 1200 B.C. (Enkomi [Dikaios]1687, Cyprus Museum Nicosia; Photo by J.S. Smith)

but the Aegean syllabary has no plausible Near Eastern antecedents. Cretan clay tablets, Cretan seals, and the practice of writing on clay tablets may depend on Mesopotamian models, but the Aegean syllabary, to speak of a collective entity, must be a purely Cretan invention. On Cyprus, Cypriots reshaped the Cretan writing to suit their own purpose, and so did the Mycenaeans in Greece or Crete, but the basic principles behind the writing remained the same.

It is important to emphasize how very few Cypro-Minoan inscriptions we have, a total of 2,500 individual *signs* as against 7,000 for Linear A and over 30,000 for Linear B.[31] When we remember the close association between seals and writing, Jennifer Webb's distribution maps showing the overwhelming concentration of Late Bronze Age local and imported seals at Enkomi[32] lend support to the further suggestion that Cypro-Minoan also was used mainly at Enkomi. Cypro-Minoan was probably a local invention there, employed locally. Outlying examples may derive from some association with Enkomi where Cypriot (presumably) entrepreneurs governed some of the production and international transshipment of copper.

In the Late Bronze Age, in this northeast corner of the Mediterranean, bold experiments with writing were taking place with an unprecedented and unparalleled intensity. Enkomi lay only 76 miles across the sea from Ugarit, well within that unique community's economic and social sphere, where at this same time was used Mesopotamian cuneiform, Hittite hieroglyphic, Egyptian hieroglyphic, Cypro-Minoan, and the formally unique West Semitic abecedarium consisting of wedges impressed into clay (shapes unrelated to those of Mesopotamian cuneiform).[33] Tablets bearing more than one script seem to come from the same findspots.[34] Surprisingly, the so-called Ugaritic alphabet, from the 14th century B.C., is the earliest attestation anywhere of the famous West Semitic system that will include Phoenician, Aramaic, and Hebrew writing, whence Greek alphabetic writing spun off in its eccentric course. *Exceptio probat regulam*: someone who wished to write on clay the ordinarily linear West Semitic, of which our earliest monumental examples are 300 years later than the Ugaritic examples, invented new graphic forms that could easily be impressed in clay. An enemy's destruction of Ugarit in the early 12th century B.C. preserved for us the anomalous clay-inscribed versions of the syllabary, while the ordinary linear examples on papyrus, which must precede in time the idiosyncratic Ugaritic, have been completely lost. We need a good fire, in

Fig. 15. Cypriot bilingual inscription from Idalion, perhaps early fourth century B.C. (British Museum WAA 125.320, courtesy of the British Museum, London)

the way Linear B tablets were preserved, to produce good finds when scribes are writing on moist earth in a rainy winter climate.

In eastern Cyprus, too, such traditions of bilingual multiculturalism were of long standing. Nicolle Hirschfeld has pointed to at least multiple systems of marking, if not actual languages, at Enkomi during the Late Bronze Age.[35] Later, the bilingual in figure 15 from the fourth century B.C. presents similar texts in West Semitic on the top and Cypriot Syllabic on the bottom.[36] The inscription records a dedication by the Semitic prince Baalrom, son of Abdimilk, in the fourth year of the reign of Milkyaton, King of Semitic Kition and Hellenic Idalion, to Reshef-Mikal in the Phoenician text, to Apollo Amyklos in Cypriot Syllabic; this inscription was instrumental in the decipherment of Cypriot Syllabic in the 1870s. Administration under the reign of King Milkyaton must have been bilingual and bicultural; even the names of the gods have been syncretized.[37]

The possible reasons we have so few Cypro-Minoan documents, then, are, first, that the script probably had an extremely limited use and range and, second, that the last settlement at Enkomi was not burned to the ground and left to the winds, like Ugarit in the early 12th century B.C., where we have found so many tablets in modern times, but was simply abandoned near the end of the 11th century B.C., when its inhabitants moved to nearby Salamis. According to an old story, Salamis was founded by the Trojan fighter Teucer, son of Telamon, king of the island of Salamis in the bay of Athens.[38] An early Greek settlement does seem likely, and it may be in Salamis on Cyprus that a Greek adapted Cypro-Minoan to Greek, taking his model from a former inhabitant of Enkomi. Our earliest example of Cypriot Syllabic comes from just this time, around 1025 B.C.[39]

Although Cypriot Syllabic spread fairly widely in the island, traditions remained parochial enough that a different variety of Cypriot Syllabic evolved at Paphos in the southwest of the island. Cypriot Syllabic, too, must have been written on clay—if we had better fires at Enkomi, we would have better evidence—and it must have continued principally to record economic accounts. Bonny Bazemore has reminded us that nearly all examples of Cypriot Syllabic come from such sanctuaries as that at Rantidi,[40] where dedications are clumsily, even ineptly scrawled on stones, an unnatural medium legible only by the gods. Still, the famous and unique tablet of Idalion,[41] which records a contract between a physician (and his sons) and the king and city of Idalion, reminds us how complex such documents might sometimes

Fig. 16. Bronze tablet from Idalion (21.4 × 14 cm), ca. 478–470 B.C. (Cabinet des Médailles, Bibliotheque Nationale, Paris, inv. 2297; after O. Masson, *Les inscriptions chypriotes syllabiques. Recueil critique et commenté*[2] [Paris 1983] no. 217)

Fig. 17. Miniature (8.8 × 5.1 cm) ivory tablet from Marsiliana d'Albegna in northern Etruria. (Florence, Museo Archeologico; after M. Guarducci, *Epigrafia Greca* I [Rome 1967] fig. 89)

have been. Figure 16 is a skeuoform, really, made in imitation of a flat wax tablet, not a *deltos*. We possess an amuletic imitation of this kind of wax tablet in figure 17 from an eighth-century grave in Italy, which interestingly bears one of the very oldest Greek abecedaria on the upper rim. The bronze Idalion tablet, with its special contents, intends to make them imperishable, truly graven in bronze, unlike ephemeral marks in the familiar wax.

Many unbaked clay tablets survive buried from deep tells in Mesopotamia, where rainfall is sparse and the water table low, but the wetter climate of Cyprus may have dissolved the clay or mud on which users of Cypro-Minoan and the Cypriot syllabary kept their records. Hence the exiguous finds. The important tradition of seal carving, nonetheless, and the generous finds of seals over long periods of time, reveal that invisible tradition.[42] As in so many other ways, the Cypriots, in writing, recast imported forms to fashion things unique to their exceptional island.

NOTES

* My thanks to John Bennet, Emmett L. Bennett Jr., and Joanna S. Smith for reading drafts of this paper and kindly making many suggestions.

[1] Smith, this volume.

[2] *CAH*[3] II.2, 201–205; W.L. Moran, *The Amarna Letters* (Baltimore 1987) 388; also see A.B. Knapp ed., *Near Eastern and Aegean Texts from the Third to the First Millennia B.C.*

(*Sources for the History of Cyprus* II, Altamont, NY, 1996); for an additional reference to Alasia from Ugarit, see M. Yon, "La maison d'Ourtenou dans le Quartier Sud d'Ougarit (Fouilles 1994)," and P. Bordreuil and F. Malbran-Labat, "Les archives de la maison d'Ourtenou," *CRAI* (1995) 427–56.

[3] See a discussion of Gunter Dryer's 1977 and 1988 discoveries of early writing at Abydos in V. Davies and R. Friedman, *Egypt Uncovered* (New York 1998) 35–38.

[4] H.J. Nissen, "Aspects of the Development of Early Cylinder Seals," in M. Gibson and R.D. Biggs eds., *Seals and Sealing in the Ancient Near East* (Malibu 1977) 16–18.

[5] See Webb, this volume.

[6] Illustrations in G.A. Christopoulos ed., *History of the Hellenic World: Prehistory and Protohistory* (Athens 1974) 150, 296. On cylinder seals in the Aegean see H.-G. Buchholz, "XII. The Cylinder Seal," in G.F. Bass, *Cape Gelidonya: A Bronze Age Shipwreck* (*TAPS* 57.8, Philadelphia 1967) 148–59; J.S. Smith assembled all cylinders in the Aegean to 1989 in *Cylinder Seals in the Aegean: Contextual and Spatial Analyses of Exchange* (M.A. thesis Bryn Mawr College 1989).

[7] G.F. Bass, *Cape Gelidonya: A Bronze Age Shipwreck* (*TAPS* 57.8, Philadelphia 1967) 163–64; G.F. Bass, "Evidence of Trade from Bronze Age Shipwrecks," in N.H. Gale ed., *Bronze Age Trade in the Mediterranean* (*SIMA* 90, Jonsered 1991) 69.

[8] G.F. Bass, C. Pulak, D. Collon, and J. Weinstein, "The Bronze Age Shipwreck at Ulu Burun: 1986 Campaign," *AJA* 93 (1989) 12–29.

[9] H.A. Frankfort, *Cylinder Seals* (London 1939) 220.

[10] E. Porada, "The Cylinder Seals Found at Thebes in Boeotia," *AfO* 28 (1981) 1–78.

[11] K. Demakopoulou and D. Konsola, *The Archaeological Museum of Thebes* (Athens 1981) 53; Porada (supra n. 10) 9.

[12] Webb, this volume.

[13] Cf. Webb, this volume, pl. I.6, pl. II.3, pl. III.3, 4, 5, 7, 8. For discussion, Frankfort (supra n. 9) 204–205.

[14] Cf. Webb, this volume, pl. I.1,3,7.

[15] G.A. Christopoulos (supra n. 6) 159.

[16] D. Schmandt-Besserat, *Before Writing* I (Austin 1992); summary in D. Schmandt-Besserat, *How Writing Came About* (Austin 1996). But cf. P.E. Zimansky's review of Schmandt-Besserat in *JFA* 20 (1993) 513–17.

[17] Reyes, this volume.

[18] Frankfort (supra n. 9) 223.

[19] E. Porada, "Of Professional Seal Cutters and Nonprofessionally Made Seals," in Gibson and Biggs eds. (supra n. 4) 7.

[20] W.L. Rathje, "New Tricks for Old Seals: A Progress Report," in Gibson and Biggs eds. (supra n. 4) 25–32.

[21] Webb, this volume.

[22] Schmandt-Besserat (supra n. 16).

[23] E.g., P.E. Newberry, *Egyptian Antiquities: Scarabs: An Introduction to the Study of Egyptian Seals and Signet Rings* (London 1906) 61–85.

[24] Certainly the scribe holds a deltos in a relief of Sennacherib at Nineveh: cf. B. André-

Salvini, "Les Tablettes du monde cunéiforme," in É. Lalou ed., *Les tablettes à écrire de l'an-tiquité & l'époque moderne* (*Bibliologia* 12, Turnhout 1992) 15–33, fig. 14.

[25] C.B.F. Walker thinks the scroll is made of leather in "Cuneiform," in J.T. Hooker ed., *Reading the Past: Ancient Writing from Cuneiform to the Alphabet* (Berkeley 1990) 46. Similar representations are found in reliefs from the palaces of Tiglath-Pileser, Sennacherib, and Assurbanipal at Kalhu and Nineveh (seventh century B.C.).

[26] Bass et al. (supra n. 8) 10; R. Payton, "The Ulu Burun Writing Board Set," *AnatSt* 41 (1991) 99–106; P. Warnock and M. Pendleton, "The Wood of the Ulu Burun Diptych," *AnatSt* 41 (1991) 107–110; D. Symington, "Late Bronze Age Writing-Boards and Their Uses," *AnatSt* 41 (1991) 111–23. Other folding tablets have been recovered from a well in Nimrud from the eighth century B.C., see D.J. Wiseman, "Assyrian Writing Boards," *Iraq* 17 (1955) 3–13. Cf. J.E. Curtis and J.E. Reade eds., *Art and Empire: Treasures from Assyria in the British Museum* (New York 1995) 190–91.

[27] One of the Nimrud tablets recorded the astronomical omen series Enuma Anu Enlil and was intended for the palace of Sargon II at Khorsabad. Curtis and Reade (supra n. 26) fig. 198.

[28] H. Immerwahr, "Book Rolls on Attic Vases," in C. Henderson Jr. ed., *Classical, Mediaeval, and Renaissance Studies in Honor of Berthold Louis Ullman* I (*Storia e letturatura* 93, Rome 1964) 26.

[29] T.G. Palaima, "Cypro-Minoan Scripts: Problems of Historical Context," in Y. Duhoux, T.G. Palaima, and J. Bennet eds., *Problems in Decipherment* (Louvain–La-Neuve 1989) 123–24.

[30] Recent epigraphic finds in upper Egypt of what appears to be a writing related to west semitic, about which general comments were made in the *New York Times*, 14 December 1999, may lend support this long-held view.

[31] Palaima (supra n. 29) 124.

[32] Webb, this volume, figure 2.

[33] C. F.-A. Schaeffer, "Matériaux pour l'étude des relations entre Ugarit et Chypre," *Ugaritica* III (Paris 1956) 227–28.

[34] For findspots see P. Bordreuil and D. Pardee, *La trouvaille epigraphique de l'Ougarit 1, Concordance* (*Ras Shamra–Ougarit* V, Paris 1989).

[35] Hirschfeld, this volume.

[36] O. Masson, *Les inscriptions chypriotes syllabiques: Recueil critique et commenté*[2] (Paris 1983) 246–48, no. 220, pl. XXXVII.2.

[37] For their possible identity, cf. M.L. West, *The East Face of Helicon* (Oxford 1997) 55.

[38] *CAH*[3] II.2, 215–16.

[39] Evidently a Greek name O-PE-LE-TA-U (Opheltas?). See E. Masson and O. Masson, "Appendix IV: Les objets inscrits de Palaepaphos-Skales," in V. Karageorghis, *Palaepaphos-Skales: An Iron Age Cemetery in Cyprus* (Konstanz 1983) 411–15. For uncertainties about this inscription, see B.B. Powell, *Homer and the Origin of the Greek Alphabet* (Cambridge 1991) 90, n. 42.

[40] Bazemore, this volume.

[41] Masson (supra n. 36) 235–44, no. 217.

[42] Cf. J.S. Smith, *Seals for Sealing in the Late Cypriot Period* (Diss. Bryn Mawr College 1994).